# Developmentality

# Developmentality

## An Ethnography of the World Bank–Uganda Partnership

Jon Harald Sande Lie

Published by
Berghahn Books
www.berghahnbooks.com



**Library of Congress Cataloging-in-Publication Data**

Developmentality : an ethnography of the World Bank-Uganda partnership / Jon Harald Sande Lie.
pages cm
Originally presented as the author's thesis (doctoral)—University of Bergen, 2011, under the title: Developmentality : an ethnography of the new aid architecture and the formation of the World Bank-Uganda partnership.
Includes bibliographical references and index.
ISBN 978-1-78238-840-1 (hardback : alk. paper) —
ISBN 978-1-78238-841-8 (ebook)
1. Economic assistance—Uganda. 2. World Bank—Uganda. 3. Uganda—Economic policy. 4. Economic development—Uganda—International cooperation. 5. Economic development—International cooperation. 6. International economic relations—Political aspects. I. Title.
HC870.L54 2015
332.1'532096761—dc23

2015003126

**British Library Cataloguing in Publication Data**

A catalogue record for this book is available from the British Library

Printed on acid-free paper.

ISBN: 978-1-78238-840-1 (hardback)
ISBN: 978-1-78238-841-8 (ebook)

# Contents

# Acknowledgements

This book is the result of research conducted as part of a larger research programme at the Department of Social Anthropology, University of Bergen (Norway), headed by Professor Bruce Kapferer. This research programme – 'Challenging the State: Transmutation of Power in Contemporary Global Realities' – provided for an inspiring environment where alternative and critical ideas were welcomed, contested and refined. The research group's many critical interventions and stimulating discussions are cherished and missed. I am indebted to the whole group for their academic generosity and inspiration. Professor Leif Manger deserves an extra appreciation for his critical comments and help in turning my ethnography and ideas into anthropology and a written text.

I also wish to thank the Norwegian Institute of International Affairs (NUPI), my current employers, who provided enough academic space to finalize this book project. Several colleagues have provided important, critical and inspiring comments on earlier chapter versions, and my thanks go to Axel Borchgrevink, Benjamin de Carvalho, Francesca Jensenius, Iver B. Neumann, John Karlsrud, Knut G. Nustad, Niels Nagelhus Schia, Ole Jacob Sending, Randi Solhjell, Stein Sundstøl Eriksen and Øyvind Eggen. Additionally, Maia Green and Jeremy Gould both provided invaluable comments on an earlier version of this book. I would also like to extend my appreciations to Susan Høyvik and Nigel Smith for their help in proof reading and copy editing the manuscript. Needless to say, but notwithstanding: all remaining shortcomings are mine alone.

This book is dedicated to Jenny, Julia and Elisabeth.

# Introducing Developmentality

International development is inextricably linked to the practice and institutions of development aid. Despite the inherent asymmetries, it is founded on a relationship between donor and recipient institutions, today expressed as one of partnership based on mutuality, trust, recipient ownership and participation. In practice, however, few would deny the inherently lopsided nature of aid relations. This book deals with how and why these asymmetries persist despite the many bold and sincere attempts to revamp and dismantle them, some even put forward by those considered to be the privileged part of the donor–recipient relationship. Why does this proactive and radical rhetoric lag so much behind the reality it purports to address, and what are the mechanisms that reproduce the paternalism of development? How do development donors reassert their control even after they have formally granted their recipients greater freedom and responsibility in managing processes formerly controlled chiefly by the donors? Drawing upon multi-sited ethnographic fieldwork within the World Bank in Washington DC and a Ugandan ministry, this book offers an ethnography of their partnership relation, arguing that this lopsided aid relation is continuously reproduced but through a more indirect, subtle and tacit kind of power than the previous direct coercion. Moreover, the conditions for such tacit governance are produced by precisely the same policies and practices that the Bank has put in place in seeking to dismantle its own trusteeship while granting recipients greater freedom to manage their own development process. I call this power 'developmentality' (Lie 2015).

I coined and first employed the 'developmentality' concept in 2004 (see Lie 2004; also available as Lie 2009). At that time, the only scholarly use of the term was in relation to child psychology (see e.g. Fendler 2001) and no references to the field of development existed. Applications of the governmentality perspective to the neoliberal turn of development have since then proliferated, including some instances of 'developmentality' (see Ilcan and Phillips 2006, 2010; Legg 2006; Mawuko-Yevugah 2010). Of these, Ilcan and Phillips (2010) provide the most interesting and thorough conceptualization of developmentality, although in its plural form. There are many common denominators with regard to applying a governmentality approach to the organization of development aid, but Ilcan and Phillips' 'developmentalities' pertains exclusively to the UN Millennium Development Goals, whereas I employ the developmentality concept to the new aid architecture and the partnership formation within the aid sector in general, and World Bank–Uganda relations in particular. Hence, whereas they focus on programmes, I focus on distinct institutions with a general argument on the formation of partnership, and while much of the governmentality-inspired literature takes an excessively top-down view of development, this book – and indeed the developmentality concept – is empirically driven and founded on practices.

Developmentality emerges from the new formation of development partnership formed in the nexus of the new rhetoric of participation and established practices of conditionality (Lie 2006b, 2010). The conventional aid relationship has changed. A fundamental shift came with donor withdrawal from direct operational activities and running their own projects to a more distanced role focused more on funding the activities of their local partner institutions and organizations now granted the overall responsibility for policy making and implementation. This transition – also referred to as a move from first-generation to second-generation reform (Harrison 2004) – represents the centrepiece of what has become known as the new aid architecture. It is characterized by a new form of partnership based on the morally charged ideas of ownership and participation (Nelson and Wright 1995; Cleaver 2001). This transition, driven largely by ambitions of making aid more effective, has been based on the idea that more ownership and greater participation of aid recipients in processes previously controlled by donors would translate into improved sensitization and enhanced recipient commitment – which, in turn, would yield better results and more development per dollar invested.[1] This new partnership formation has served other objectives as well. By being more inclusive and bottom–up oriented, it could respond to the criticisms levelled against donor–recipient relations for their trusteeship, donor imposition of one-size-fits-all policies and top–down conditionality approaches. With the new partnership formation, development assistance now promised to be more contextual, sensitized and inclusive – based more on the needs of the recipient than those of the donor.

There is, however, a sizable discrepancy between the formal order and rhetoric of development and its practice. This disjuncture should not be understood solely as resulting from bad planning, flawed policies, weak implementation or lack of commitment by the involved actors. Instead, it should be recognized as logically connected: when donors lose control in one way, they seek to reassert it in others. Another way of seeing this disjuncture is by inverting the conventional relationship between policy and practice (see Mosse 2004a). Aid practitioners' obsession with policy making rests on the assumption of altering and directing future practices by establishing causality between development design and input and expected output. But what if, as Mosse asks, 'instead of policy producing practice, practices produce policy, in the sense that actors in development devote their energies to maintaining coherent representations regardless of events?' (ibid.: 640); and what if 'development practice is not driven by policy? … What if the practices of development are in fact concealed rather than produced by policy' (Mosse 2005b: 2; Mosse 2006). Seen this way, the new policies and rhetoric of partnership, participation and ownership are the result of – and, indeed, serve to legitimize – existing dynamics, lopsided relations and practices. This is not because of bad intentions or some well-orchestrated conspiracy: it simply shows the potential formative power that established development discourses and structures might have.

This book redirects the analytical attention from the formative power of development discourses to a focus on actors and practices. That makes it possible to see how development practice is driven not by policy but by a multi-layered complex of relationships and epistemic knowledge battles within and between donor and recipient institutions regarding the partnership formation, with development practitioners striving to maintain coherent representations of their actions as instances of the established policy.

It should thus come as no surprise that aid donors still try to direct, guide and govern their recipients even after formally handing over responsibility for the development process to their partners and counterparts (Borchgrevink 2008). These governance mechanisms have, however, taken on a new form. Instead of being direct and coercive, they are now more subtle, tacit and indirect – and they are based on the donor's framing, restricting the freedom granted to the recipient institutions by the 'liberal' new aid architecture and its notion of partnership. In practice – as this book shows – development cooperation is characterized by two conflicting logics: on the one hand the liberal agenda of empowering aid recipients to make their own decisions; on the other hand, the donors' need to exert control and promote their own policies. Through processes of responsibilization, aid recipients are expected to govern and develop themselves – all the while remaining accountable to the donor for implementing what are formally their own policies but in reality bear a heavy donor imprint. This reproduction of asymmetrical donor–recipient relationships should not be seen as a failure to implement the new aid architecture and the partnership ideals: it is more of an active process through which the donor institution works to get its own policies acknowledged as those of the recipient. This nexus of control and freedom, conditionality and participation, amounting to a governance strategy, is succinctly phrased by a donor informant: 'ownership exists when they do what we want them to do but they do so voluntarily' (Randel, German and Ewing 2002: 8). This draws attention to a form of indirect governance based on the framing of liberalism and freedom, and contingent on crafting the conditions where questions of *who rules* and *how* are never asked – in a word, *developmentality* (Lie 2010; 2015). Drawing on Foucault's concept of governmentality (1991), developmentality describes and analyses various governance instruments and techniques within the aid sector that are contingent on liberal ideas and promises of freedom enabling the aid recipient to develop itself – but only within and in accordance with the donor's established development discourse. Thus, developmentality is rendered possible by the liberal partnership formation, which at the same time undermines its underlying tenets and credentials. This book addresses this paradox by exploring the new aid architecture and its conceptions of partnership in principle as well as in practice, introducing the developmentality concept to grasp what is unique about this way of managing partnership relations between donor and recipient institutions in the development sectors. The developmentality concept is outlined in detail in the next chapter. The remaining part of this chapter provides the empirical context and background for the developmentality concept, as well as my study of it.

## Introducing and Approaching the New Aid Architecture

International aid has been intentionally transformed over the last two decades, leading to what is now described as a new architecture of aid. The advent of the new aid architecture has involved a change from first- to second-generation reform (Harrison 2004).[2] First-generation reform came in the late 1970s, with economic liberalization, privatization, state deregulation and market fundamentalism, as epitomized in the World Bank's infamous structural adjustment programmes and the Washington consensus (Williamson 1990, 2000).[3] Second-generation reform emerged from the mid-1990s, when donors and the Bank became increasingly concerned with systemic and political reform of their aid recipients, seeking to alter and improve state structures as part of the evolving agenda for good governance (Abrahamsen 2004b; Weaver 2010). Whereas the first-generation reform focused on 'a reduction in the scope of state action, [second-generation reform] is concerned with the *nature* of state action ... The ethos is that "process" is as important as "policy"' (Harrison 2004: 18). This should be seen as interlinked with the emerging partnership discourse; as the donor confers on the recipient greater responsibility and freedom to manage the overall development process – from planning to implementation – the recipient's governance structures and practices become increasingly important to the donor. Revamping both the structural and ideational levels of aid, this process has involved moving from 'uneasy modes of bondage based on harshly imposed borrowing conditions' (Gould 2005a: 1) to a partnership formation packaged in the jargon of more liberal and morally charged concepts of participation and ownership. Yet, despite the move from first- to second-generation reform and the recasting of aid relations in terms of partnership (Abrahamsen 2004a), '[i]t is clear that neither structural adjustment nor conditionality have gone away and, to some, it might seem politically dangerous to suggest otherwise' (Harrison 2001a: 658). The new form of conditionality serves to promote specific processes and not policies. It involves a new focus on the state as second-generation reform aims 'to construct an appropriate system of government to allow governance states to absorb and operationalise funds and technical assistance' (Harrison 2004: 21).

The 'new aid architecture' refers to three broad transformations of international aid (Mosse 2005a). First, there is a focus on neoliberal policy reforms rather than conventional investment projects. Donors no longer run projects independently, but collaborate to make concessional lending available for governments and assist them in implementing their own development policies. Second is the international commitment to poverty reduction – moving beyond the conventional policy agenda of economic growth to include more 'soft' and less-quantifiable dimensions, like environmental and social issues.[4] Thirdly, donors' reform agendas focus on institutional and general governance issues, transcending the traditional emphasis on economic and financial management.

The new aid architecture is not limited to cases involving the World Bank. Organizing aid around the concept of partnership and broadening the former economic growth agenda are ideas that permeate the international development apparatus, ranging from civil society organizations and NGOs to bilateral aid cooperation and the multilateral system of which the Bank is part. Today, all seem to have embraced the idea that better partnership modalities based on recipient participation and ownership in the making and implementation of policies are not only an ethically better way of organizing development assistance but also vital to greater aid effectiveness. Needless to say, it was the latter rationale that prompted the Bank to embrace the new aid architecture (see Burnside and Dollar 2000; Mallabye 2004; chapter 3, this volume). Promoting local perspectives and sensitivity through participation, and greater commitment among local, implementing partners through ownership, have been assumed to translate into more development per dollar, although the official reasoning drew on moral assertions of emancipatory politics, empowerment and redressing established aid asymmetries.

The new aid architecture drew inspiration from the NGO sector's experience with partnership and participation during the NGO decade of the 1980s (Chambers 1983; Rahnema 1992). However, it was not until the late 1990s, when the Bank came into the picture, that the ideas gained momentum and proliferated among bi- and multilateral actors. In 1997, World Bank president James Wolfensohn – two years after assuming office, having come from the investment banking sector – embarked on a 30-month reform initiative called the Strategic Compact – 'a self-described "renewal" plan aimed at re-establishing the Bank's pre-eminent position as the world's leading development agency' (Weaver and Leiteritz 2005: 369). Driven by external and internal factors,[5] the Strategic Compact involved four key elements. First, a move away from one-size-fits-all standard approaches to more country-specific programmes, involving decentralization of project and staff, where the Bank's country managers would head their specific country portfolios. The second element involved moving beyond the growth paradigm to invest in neglected sectors such as social, environmental and governance-related projects, a process that facilitated the establishment of new thematic networks within the Bank. The third concerned the Bank as a 'knowledge bank' producing development expertise, reflecting the analytical work done in the thematic networks and how this knowledge is to be shared actively within and outside the Bank. Fourth was the Bank's internal reorganization along a matrix system, whereby the Bank's 'networks' were separated from its 'operations', as a way of strengthening implementation of the three first elements (ibid.; Pincus and Winters 2002). Chapter 4 in this volume examines the knowledge bank from within, arguing that the matrix system serves to institutionalize a 'battlefield of knowledge' (Long and Long 1992) in which different knowledge systems and competing thematic networks vie for influence over the operational side of the Bank – and, in the process, the networks pay more heed to operational demands than to their own thematic profile. Chapter 3 focuses on the operationalization of the first two elements, known as the Comprehensive Development Framework (CDF; Wolfensohn 1999), which outlines the Poverty Reduction Strategy Paper (PRSP) as the Bank's interpretation of the new aid architecture outlining its new partnership model and the broadened development scope. Through the Rome Declaration on Harmonization (2003) and the Paris Declaration on Aid Effectiveness (2005), signed by almost all authoritative bi- and multilateral development agencies, the new aid architecture, with its gatekeeping notions of partnership, participation and ownership, has become a ubiquitous part of managing global development. In aid-speak, this meant 'putting the last first' (Chambers 1983; Baaz 2005; Cornwall and Scoones 2011) – which in Bank parlance is known as putting developing countries 'in the driver's seat' (Wolfensohn 1999).

The partnership discourse emerged from recognition of the shortcomings of top–down approaches and the ineffectiveness of externally imposed expert knowledge (Cooke and Kothari 2001). To mitigate external trusteeship, the aid relation has been recast as one of partnership (Abrahamsen 2004a). 'Authentic partnership implies, inter alia, a joint commitment to long-term interaction, shared responsibility for achievement, reciprocal obligation, equality, mutuality and a balance of power' (Fowler 2000: 3). The equal relationship of partners is seen as a value in itself, as well as an instrumental way of strengthening the impact of aid by creating local commitment, or ownership, while fostering and enabling recipient participation (see Pouligny 2009). Whether partnership is seen as a reality or as an ideal to strive for, most analysts agree that practice has generally fallen so far short of the ideal requirements of partnership that the main function of the term seems to be to mask existing asymmetries in the relationship (Crewe and Harrison 1998; Baaz 2005). Donor representatives, however, are more prone to take the 'partnership' label at face value (Wallace, Bornstein and Chapman 2006; Chapman and Wendoh 2007). Chambers notes three usages of the term 'participation': first, as a cosmetic label to make whatever is proposed appear good due to the formal requirements of a participatory approach, even though practice tends to remain top–down; second, as a co-opting strategy for mobilizing local labour in order to reduce project costs, meaning 'they' (the recipients) participate in 'our' (the donors') projects; third, as a process of empowerment that enables local people to make their own analyses, to take command, to gain in confidence and to implement their own choices and decisions so that 'we' participate in 'their' project (Chambers 1995). The developmentality concept proposes an alternative understanding, viewing the partnership discourse as a 'new governance mechanism'.

The new aid architecture should be understood against what makes it novel – that it is meant to replace top–down conditionality approaches. Conditionality represents the antithesis of the bottom–up thinking integral to participation and partnership. The top–down conditionality approach involves most of the ideas that the partnership discourse intends to overcome, such as donor trusteeship and one-size-fits-all policy prescriptions without sensitivity to context, local knowledge or borrowers' domestic political constraints and needs (Stone 2008). Conditionality does not automatically ignore recipient knowledge and needs, but when these do not fit with those of the donor, the donor-devised policy conditions trump local concerns. Compared to participation, conditionality is a less theorized term. This is due to its paternalistic connotations and because there is no normative programme behind the concept (apart from pushing one's will through) as with participation; moreover, it represents ideas and practices that development practitioners generally frown on. Conditionality is more of a descriptive term employed by scholars and practitioners to denote a particular policy package or means for enforcing certain policies. These two meanings are interlinked. As policy, conditionality is highly associated with the Washington Consensus and the Bank's structural adjustment programmes of privatization, liberalization, state deregulation and market fundamentalism. As this policy package has not been generally abandoned, conditionality is associated more with the *means* employed by the donors to enforce their policies and get recipient institutions to subscribe to these – meaning that donors make their aid conditional on the pursuit of particular policies among recipient institutions. Aid-tying set by the donor is an integral part of everyday life in aid relations. Conditionality 'is not an aim in itself but an instrument by which other objectives are pursued' (Stokke 1995: 3); thus conditionality represents an exercise of coercion aimed at pursuing the donor's stipulated goals. However, concerns have been voiced as to what conditionality may achieve, as donors have been insufficiently motivated to punish recipients for non-compliance (Collier 1997), reflecting the general donor dilemma: the need to 'choose between underspending their budget (and thus losing influence both within their development-country partners and within their own governments) and giving aid to bad-policy countries' (Mosley, Hudson and Verschoor 2004: 218).

'He who pays the piper calls the tune' expresses the common understanding or donor–recipient relationships, despite the advent of the new aid architecture and the rhetorical dismissal of conditionality. The donor still controls the vital resource in the relation – funds – and thus holds the power to decide what to fund and when to stop funding, thereby retaining effective control, regardless of by whom and how the policies are devised or implemented.

Classic anthropological theory points to more complex relations between giver and receiver. In *The Gift,* Mauss (1954) asserts that exchanges of goods and resources are driven by other incentives than merely economic profit. Gifts serve to maintain social relationships and reproduce social systems. In gift economies it is not only the benefactor who is expected to give. Equally important are the expectations placed on the recipient; that is, the obligations to receive *and return* the gift. This reciprocal aspect, or the gift's 'total prestation', is thus a matter of respect and acknowledgement, involving the honour of both giver and receiver. While it is by no means certain that a gift relation between bureaucratic institutions is best understood as a system of 'total prestations',[6] Mauss's work does alert us to the fact that there are flows in both directions between donor and recipient. Stirrat and Henkel (1997) use Mauss's insight to analyse 'the development gift', and to show that through 'partnership' the donor achieves legitimacy, mission validation and a symbolically important link to the poor and marginalized. Thus, while the recipient's dependence on funding is concrete and evident, there are less obvious forms of symbolic capital flowing the other way. While this is still an asymmetrical relation, there is dependence in both directions, and power does not rest unambiguously with one party alone. In aid relations, not only does an aid recipient need a donor, but a donor also needs a recipient. And with greater responsibilities and freedom conveyed the recipient institution — as per the new aid architecture — it becomes paramount to have good partners as well as forge a good partnership. For the donor this becomes a balancing act, and upholding the partnership necessitates continuous negotiations and compromises. For instance, as Harrison (2001a: 673) argues, the World Bank's dependence on Uganda as an example of success meant turning a blind eye to corrupt practices and mismanagement in the state apparatus.

The formation of partnership takes place in the pragmatic interplay and interdependence of the rhetoric or participation and the practices of conditionality. The notion of developmentality draws attention to this apparent paradox inherent in development aid: the nexus between the contradictory approaches of conditionality and participation. Both participation and conditionality are girding ideas of the new aid architecture, where the former seeks to overcome the latter. This signals a profound shift from top–down approaches to bottom–up ones, where donor institutions withdraw from direct operational activities to a remote role of monitoring and funding – producing and produced by an *audit culture* (see Strathern 2000b). The shift on the donor side from direct to indirect engagement in the development process is thus paralleled by a shift from a passive to an active client on the receiving end. This means – at least on the rhetorical level – a transfer of power and influence from donor to recipient institution, with 'a strategic shift in the management of North–South relations away from the carrot and the stick of credits and conditionalities to a subtler dynamics of alleged mutual complicity' (Gould 2005c: 63). Such mutual complicity is arguably concealed and produced by the partnership discourse formed in the nexus of participation and conditionality. It provides the setting for the developmentality concept and this book's analysis of the World Bank–Uganda partnership.

Exploring the effects of the new aid architecture and the Bank–Uganda partnership formation, the concept of developmentality attends to the disjunctures between the donor and recipient institutions, as well as between the official order and rhetoric of participation on the one side, and the practices of control, governance and conditionality on the other. Using the concept of developmentality for analysis, this book shows how the Bank can speak the language of participation and ownership, all the while tightening its conditionality criteria for loan disbursement. Although Bank staff may not see these mechanisms as based on conditionality, Uganda is still compelled to undertake reforms and engage in lengthy, repetitive performance rituals as part of the new partnership model in order to get funding. These rituals might appear as a charade, since representatives from both sides know that the Bank will ultimately provide lending regardless of events, but they have at least two important features that amount to developmentality. First, they serve the purpose of making the Bank's policies those of the recipient. Second, they serve to make the recipients accountable primarily to the Bank for implementing their 'own' policies.

## Multi-sited Ethnography: Approaching the Bank and the Ministry

The concept of 'developmentality' has been developed from an extended case study of the partnership relation between the World Bank and its Ugandan counterpart. Recognizing the *relational* aspect of power – that power is not something that someone has, but is activated, formed and accentuated in the practical encounter between different actors, as the partnership relation – this study explores and analyses how the World Bank–Uganda partnership is articulated at various levels – in structure and practice, in discourse and agency, formal and informal – on the donor and recipient sides as well as in their encounter. Multi-sited fieldwork was required for this ethnography, or aidnography (Gould 2004), of the adventurous aidland (Mosse 2011; Lie 2006a), to unpack policy and capture the relational aspect of power and, indeed, the partnership relation itself (McGee 2004; Green 2012). The ethnographic approach provides a way to give 'voice for the underrepresented, a vehicle for revealing the local practices that expert discourses conceal' (Kelly 2012: 79–80). In 2005 and 2006 I spent two months of participatory observation and data collection at the World Bank headquarters in Washington DC, and ten months in Uganda, mostly within the government ministry responsible for managing Uganda's relations with external donor agencies, but also collecting data among other donors and local stakeholders implicitly involved or affected by the formation of partnership between the Bank and its Ugandan counterpart.

To an anthropologist, walking into a village to conduct fieldwork is probably easier than entering a ministry or a multilateral institution. However, gaining access to the Bank and the Ugandan ministry proved to be less long-consuming and bureaucratic than I had expected – at least initially – and in practice it did not differ so much from my previous fieldwork in Ethiopia's north-eastern Afar region in terms of 'following the loops', as the anthropological credo goes, and having to gain acceptance from authoritative informants who served as gatekeepers.

My first inquiry about fieldwork for the present study went to a few Bank staffers whose contact details I had acquired from colleagues and friends. Via email, I introduced my project of studying the partnership relation between the World Bank and Ethiopia in the context of good governance. My original interest in Ethiopia before shifting focus to Uganda drew on my previous work where I had studied a small agro-pastoral development project (US$ 150,000) and the partnership relation between a Norwegian NGO and its two Ethiopian partner institutions, which initially led me to the concept of developmentality (Lie 2004). The small project was celebrated as a participatory, bottom–up project based on equal partnership throughout the aid chain, with all informants emphasizing how the project had attended to the wishes and concerns of the beneficiaries.

However, I found that this was at best only partially true. Yes, the project, which aimed to enhance the livelihoods of agro-pastoralists, included a good governance component – incongruous in an area where there were hardly any formal governance structures. The good governance component had been brought in because of external expectations – not in connection with any participatory approaches. Two years prior to the fieldwork I had worked as an assistant for the Norwegian NGO involved in this project. I was to survey all its partners, asking them what they were doing regarding good governance, as the Norwegian Agency for Development Cooperation (NORAD),[7] the back-donor, had recently added 'good governance' to its checkpoint laundry list of standardized reporting and application forms, thus signalling new topical areas of importance. This had come as a requirement from the Development Assistance Committee (DAC) of OECD, to enable them to monitor and, in effect, direct the diverse aid activities of all DAC member countries in faraway places. Although the project workers in Afar could not explain how the good governance component had been made part of the project, it was nevertheless formally framed as drawing on participatory planning, as was the rest of the project – and that was what kindled my first interest in developmentality.

Passing through Addis Ababa on my way home from six months of fieldwork, I met some diplomats from the Norwegian embassy. They mentioned the ongoing drafting of the new Ethiopian poverty reduction strategy, where the donors' push for good governance policies was proving contentious for the government. The recurrence of good governance and donor involvement in the domestic strategy process provided the momentum for my approach to the Bank.

Within a few days I had received a positive response to my email request about fieldwork: there was a team within the Bank that found my work relevant, and they would help to facilitate my study. However, they advised against studying the Bank's partnership model in Ethiopia, on the grounds that relations were politically tense, which, coupled with a rather closed governmental bureaucracy, would not allow the necessary access on the recipient side of the partnership. Amongst various alternatives they suggested Uganda, which they described as politically open, and as having a successful development story with cordial relations with the Bank, and thus research access should be easier – adding, of course, that studying what they regarded as a development success story would also be more conducive to their own work than yet another critical study of an aid failure. Shifting my empirical focus to the Bank's partnership in Uganda, I began with two months of fieldwork at the Bank in early 2005 – by which time the positive portrayals of Uganda had started to deteriorate, due to President Museveni's announcement that he would amend the constitution and lift the term limits on the presidency to allow him to run for a third term in office. Referred to as the 'political transition', this gave rise to critical concerns about democracy and good governance issues among the Bank's Uganda team and the overall donor community in Uganda (see chapter

6). The political transition politicized the partnership relation, causing friction between the Bank and its Ugandan counterpart and challenging donor harmonization in Uganda. Inevitably, the political transition and the demotion of Uganda from being a donor darling came to serve as a prominent political backdrop to the partnership formation, and my study of it.

The re-envisioning of Uganda also affected my research. My preparatory contacts with the Bank had led me to expect unrestricted access to staff, processes and meetings in both Washington DC and Kampala – but now the growing tensions in the Bank–Uganda partnership meant restricted access, curtailing the possibilities of participatory observation. Instead of being part of the processes, I now had to seek out data and informants, from the offices I was allotted in the Bank (see chapter 4) and from a branch within the Ugandan Office of the Prime Minister (OPM) designated for coordinating the various government agencies' approaches to and dialogues with foreign donor institutions (see chapter 5).[8] The entry point for attaining these privileged vantage points for conducting research was that I placed myself at their disposal as a self-financed, voluntary intern. I offered to contribute wherever they deemed relevant, in exchange for being allowed to collect data. This deal proved more rewarding for me than them – neither in the Bank nor at the OPM was I ever given any significant duties, even though I would have welcomed them. I must assume that there were no tasks for me. Perhaps they found my qualifications inappropriate to their needs, or the rising tensions between the two may have made them reluctant to include me. Or it might just be another example of the challenges associated with 'studying up' (Nader 1972; Gusterson 1997): that the powerful ones on the top may simply refuse to be studied ethnographically from the bottom (Lie 2013). In any case, I do not blame them and can understand that it is problematic to include an outsider in their ongoing work. Instead of working there, I used these offices as bases from which to conduct research. Being physically on the inside and associated with the host, I was not only introduced to various people and occasionally invited to meetings and seminars, but it was also easer to establish contact and touch base with informants. Although my methodology involved a mix of approaches, including participatory observation, much of the research took the form of meeting people for discussions, conversations and interviews. In general, the regular routine involved going every day to one of the offices I had been allotted (in the Bank and the OPM), and then taking things from there.

Both these fieldwork contexts were highly bureaucratic settings involving strict formal codes. Following the loops and drifting with my informants was possible, but only up to a point. The bureaucratic character of the field often meant that I was excluded from certain settings, especially those now deemed to be of a 'too political' character. The sudden rise in political tensions between the Bank and Uganda was not only detrimental to their partnership, but also affected my research by curtaining its empirical sphere. Once, at a meeting in Uganda between government and donor officials, having introduced myself in the usual presentation round, I was asked to leave. That was the only time I was actually expelled, but I was refused access to other meetings on grounds of 'politics' and tension between the parties – all the while the Bank had an apolitical mandate and both sides kept insisting on the apolitical nature of their partnership. Although this challenged my research, such events told me something about the partnership and the empirical field, while also serving as a good entry point for meeting and discussing with informants; it demonstrated that processes of exclusion and the challenges involved in living up to the ideals of ethnographic fieldwork may prove just as interesting and rewarding for data collection as actual processes of inclusion.

Take, for instance, the following arrival story: early in my Uganda fieldwork and on the request of a ministerial senior official, I had to present a letter stating who I was and that I was an independent researcher – meaning independent of the Ugandan government, the Norwegian embassy and the World Bank. The official wanted the letter to be signed by either the embassy or the Bank's country office, but neither of them wished to do so. Both referred to my 'independence', but it was clear that they now considered my research to be too political, and they had no wish to be formally associated with it, for fear of liability – even though what they were being asked to sign stated precisely the opposite. Finally, and after about a month of transcontinental 'micro-diplomacy', the ministry official signed the letter himself, after delivering a tirade about development bureaucracy and how donors say aid is apolitical while refusing to sign the letter, due to political concerns. In effect, this yielded greater understanding and sympathy towards my project from an important gatekeeper to the Ugandan bureaucracy, and good ethnography to my partnership analysis. As the official added laughingly, 'this story will provide you with information for at least one chapter!' Well, it did not come out as a full chapter, but made more than a footnote in demonstrating how a lack of practical access to data might in itself be a good source of information and could say something about the field.

The World Bank is by far the most influential development agency, not only in Uganda but also worldwide (Harrison 2004, 2006; Moore

2007). It holds both a gatekeeping and a formative role vis-à-vis global development discourses: what the Bank does, and how it does it, matters not only for its aid-receiving partners but also for other donor agencies. The Bank surpasses any other development organization in financial muscle and staff size; moreover, the extensive economic research undertaken by its staff has made the Bank a self-proclaimed knowledge bank with a tremendous databank available to development practitioners and researchers. Coupled with the means and methods available for disseminating and applying this knowledge (its loan and credit schemes accompanied by certain policies), the Bank enjoys a tremendous outreach and holds a prominent position in framing the policies and practices of the international development apparatus (Pincus and Winters 2002; Einhorn 2006; Marshall 2008). What happens within the Bank also has a bearing on its external activities and the discourses it disseminates (Einhorn 2001; Wade 2001, 2002b; Weaver 2008). Chapter 3 in this book outlines the official Bank discourse and partnership modality, while chapter 4 moves beyond the official discourse and focuses on the Bank's internal practices. We will see a less coherent and monolithic institution, where external representations and formal order – later conveyed to client countries like Uganda – are the result of internal knowledge battles and competing interests.

Uganda has been a net importer of development aid and policies ever since independence in 1962. Over the last decade and a half, foreign aid has made up about half of Uganda's annual national budget, usually fluctuating between 47 and 52 per cent (Fisher 2014).[9] This dependence on aid has largely sustained its asymmetrical relations with the outside world, causing patterns of paternalism and neocolonialism (Hansen and Stepputat 2001; Harrison 2004). However, due to the post-independence political ruptures and frequent coups d'état,[10] it was not until 1986, when President Yoweri Museveni came to power through an armed rebellion with his non-partisan National Resistance Movement system, that Uganda experienced sufficient political stability for domestic and external development efforts to take root.

Interestingly, soon after assuming office, the erstwhile revolutionary Marxist Museveni embraced the neoliberal structural adjustments advocated by the World Bank and other international donors (Museveni 1997; Rubongoya 2007). This created fertile ground for a largely frictionless aid relation, with donors turning a blind eye to the dictatorship in favour of the impressive economic growth experienced by a newly stable Uganda. Museveni's domestic and international standing was further enhanced when, in 1995, he reintroduced democracy and put a two-term limit on the presidency. Now an elected president, Museveni was hailed as a representative of the new breed of African freedom fighters who voluntarily introduce democracy after ascending to power by the gun. Uganda was celebrated as a success story and Museveni soon became a donor darling, receiving ever-increasing amounts of development assistance despite his criticisms and mockery of international donors, which were taken as an expression of an empowered, emancipated leader (Mwenda 2010). The influx of development assistance was further intensified by donor needs for a success story: developmental criticisms had been mounting after international development lost momentum, rationale and funding when the end of the Cold War brought a stop to development as a geopolitical ideological instrument. Because of its cordial donor relations and good performance, in 1999 Uganda became a pilot country for the World Bank's new aid architecture and partnership formation (Dijkstra and van Donge 2001; Cargill 2004).

In a nutshell, being a pilot country of the new aid architecture formally meant that Ugandan authorities would devise their own national development plan while the Bank would retreat from direct operational work to a remote position as mere financier of the government's own activities. In development speak, it meant moving away from the infamous Structural Adjustment Programmes (SAPs) where disbursement of loans and credits was made conditional on abiding by the Bank's market fundamentalism and neoliberal policies. The new Poverty Reduction Strategy Paper model – officially launched in 1999 and subsequently put to use and disseminated as the Bank's primus modus operandi when establishing new or renegotiating old partnership agreements[11] – was meant to be less patronizing, by pivoting on the government's own development strategy as formulated in the PRSP (Wolfensohn 1999). However, while the content of the PRSP is to be devised by the receiving government, its structure and function are defined solely by the Bank. Moreover, the government-produced PRSP requires Bank approval in order to become effective, cement the partnership relation and release funds – which means that the freedom vested in this model is framed and thus restricted. The PRSP model saw good possibilities in Uganda, where the government had already made its own comprehensive development plan a few years earlier and, enjoying cordial relations with the donors, had asked them to support it. Indeed, some have argued that Uganda was not only a PRSP pilot country but also its model (Mallaby 2004; Mugambe 2010). From the beginning, the new aid architecture, as epitomized by the PRSP model and its partnership formation, found conducive grounds in Uganda. The ethnographic account in this book shows how the Ugandan PRSP gradually came to resemble any other Bank-supported development strategy as the developmentality regime took form in the nexus of participatory and conditionality approaches, leading to diminishing government ownership of Bank-supported policies as well as growing frictions in the once- cordial partnership relation.

## Combining Post-development and Actor-oriented Approaches

Developmentality is not only a feature at the structural and formal levels of aid. As a form of power it is even more compelling in development practice, when and where donor and recipient institutions encounter each other (Crush 1995; Ziai 2007; Da Costa 2010). This has implications beyond the empirical scope and the analytical approaches: just as it is necessary to engage both the donor and recipient sides in order to explore the partnership formation, it is also essential to explore partnership at its structural and practical levels. Hence, this book draws on multifaceted empirical and analytical approaches, not only by examining the concept of partnership in donor as well as recipient institutions, but also by analytically engaging the concept of partnership at its formal and practical levels. That said, it is important not to compartmentalize these entities (Rossi 2006) but rather to explore how they impinge on each other and are mutually constitutive to and of each other. This is crucial, and not only for analytical reasons. It also reflects the perspectives of development actors by conforming to the very partnership idea that connects donor and recipient institutions, and aid practitioners' rationale of putting the partnership policy and other development discourses into practice. Interestingly, while these practices and encounters are enabled by the new aid architecture and its partnership formation, they might also undermine the very same order that instigated these practices in the first place.

This book provides an ethnographic exploration and analysis of this seeming paradox and how the new aid architecture unfolds in practice at different levels of the partnership that links benefactor and beneficiary institutions together. The paradox points to a disjuncture between policy and practice that cannot be grasped at the level of discourse or practice alone, but that necessitates combining a post-structural approach to development with an actor-oriented analysis (Lie 2007, 2008a; Friedman 2012). Combining different analytical approaches is necessary due to the character of the empirical field and the multi-sited ethnographic approaches for cutting across the dichotomies between donor and recipient, the global and the local, and the formal and the informal, to enable us to track the new aid architecture in the multiple contexts that are shaping and shaped by it (see Lewis et al. 2003; Mosse and Lewis 2005). The intention behind the new aid architecture and its partnership formation is to merge otherwise polar entities: donor and recipient. Studying how this logic is articulated on one side of the aid chain only would be reductionist, both analytically and empirically, and would undermine the social forces that affect and are affected by the new aid architecture. A multi-faceted analytic approach makes it possible to grasp these cultural logics, recognizing that they are always multiplying and are contextually produced (Marcus 1995; Falzon 2009). Viewing the development partnership from only one side (donor or recipient) or one level (structure or practice) obstructs us from analysing its relational aspects and how actors and ideas, and structures and practices, impinge on each other and shape practice.

Analytically, and in order to approach the different levels of aid in their contextual and multiple settings, I combine two different perspectives – post-development theory, and an actor-oriented approach. Post-development theory offers a post-structural critique of institutional development, drawing on and extending Foucault's reconceptualization of power–knowledge formations as discourse (Escobar 1984; Gardner and Lewis 1996). Post-development theory seeks to clarify how the development discourse articulates and imposes First World knowledge onto the Third World. The institutional donor apparatuses infuse this discourse with significant power, making post-development scholars focus on 'the way in which discourses of development help shape the reality they pertain to address, and how alternative conceptions of the problem have been marked off as irrelevant' (Pieterse 2000; Schuurman 2000; Nustad 2004: 13). Applying Foucault's work on the appropriation of mind in modern societies to North–South relations, post-development scholars argue that development produces postcolonial subjects and permeates the South as a category defined purely in relation to the North (Brigg 2002; Escobar 2007). Such a colonialization of the mind arguably draws on institutional development's disciplinary and normalizing processes understood as an intentional project to expand modern, Western reason – leading some to argue that 'development colonised the world by ordering it into "us" and "them", the "developed" and the "underdeveloped"' (Nustad 1998: 42; see also Manzo 1991; Brigg 2002). Such a view gives rise to fundamental social theoretical concerns regarding the discourse–agency relation and the power that one imbues discourses with. More profoundly, it puts into question our conceptions of subjectivity and individual freedom. In *The Anti-Politics Machine,* part of the post-development canon, Ferguson writes, of the discursive power over the individual found in the development sector, that 'whatever interests may be at work and whatever they may think they are doing, they can only operate through a complex set of social and cultural structures so deeply embedded and so ill-perceived that the outcome may be only a baroque and unrecognizable transformation of the original intention' (Ferguson 1994: 17; Jensen and Winthereik 2012). Such a version of post-development runs the risk of social reductionism and totalitarianism, since everything becomes (subject to) discourse, rendering the concepts of agency and individual freedom meaningless. As such, post-development becomes counterproductive to its seminal post-modern rationale of waging a war on totality (see Sachs 1992; Calhoun 1995; Escobar 1997): while post-development criticized institutional development for neglecting the variety and complexity among aid recipients, post-development fails to address the same variety within institutional development as a result of its neglect of agency, caused by too strict a discursive focus. 'By believing too much in the powers of discourse, one is disabled from tracing all those minor infrastructural and interactional transformations that partnership brings about in multiple settings' (Jensen and Winthereik 2012: 98). Post-development is therefore criticized for substituting the dead hand of determinism: when there is no freedom in discourse and no possibility to resist discursive power, there can be no autonomous subject that prevents any meaningful concept of freedom and, consequently, the possibility of emancipatory politics. The neglect of agency, it is argued, makes an empirical travesty of post-development (see Fraser 1989; Peet 1997; Kiely 1999; Oksala 2005).

Empirical complexity, actor perspectives and practice are notable by their absence from the analysis, even though many post-development scholars are social anthropologists. This might be due to at least two factors. Firstly, post-development perspectives emerged in the heyday of post-modernism and deconstruction, and everything seemed to be interpreted as or within discourse. Indicative was the gradual retreat of the social from much social science, due to what Kapferer (2005) called 'the rise and rise of social reductionism', where structural explanations and analysis seemed to prevail over actor approaches (see Grønhaug 2001). This has caused forced oppositions – between structure and agency, determinism and freedom, objectivism and subjectivism – in which the idea of the social is bypassed, creating dichotomies that distort our understanding of the interplay of different social forces (Kapferer 2004a). Secondly, the lack of agency and the over-reliance on discursive approaches are also due to a misinterpretation of Foucault's very notion of discourse (Venketesan and Yarrow 2012). As Gledhill (2000: 150) argues, Foucault sees power as relational and 'present in *all* social relationships, permeating society in a capillary way'. The first point of resistance to discursive power 'must thus be individual strategies [that] counter specific forms of domination, even in minute, everyday ways' (ibid.). Here we see an ambiguity in Foucault's work: his insistence on power being relational and enabling individual resistance is not reflected in his analysis or empirical material. As noted by Gledhill, Foucault's 'talk about power inevitably provoking "resistance" has little real substance. His capillary model of power privileges the "micro-politics" of resistance, yet his analyses remain "top–down"' (ibid.: 152).

Post-development, I hold, has inherited this ambiguity: by analysing institutional development solely from a discursive perspective, agency is not only neglected, it is also equated with discourse, as discourse becomes the only analytical approach to account for the level of actors. The development discourse becomes 'a machine in which everyone is caught' (Foucault 1980), where the discourse overrides individual agency and, consequently, subjects are deprived of their ability to choose and resist.

Too strict a conception of discourse and its formative power has implications for how one treats actors, practice and complexity: it becomes an ethnographic blind alley where the rationality of instrumental policy is replaced with the anonymous automaticity of the machine (Mosse 2013). I found that such a strict notion of the post-development discourse and its formative power did not resonate with my empirical experience. Informants on the donor and recipient sides were perfectly aware of what they were doing and trying to achieve, and of the limitations and obstacles they were facing (Lie 2007). Rather than being on a discursive dope and unintentionally reproducing the development discourse, actors involved in the development apparatus can be manipulative or strategic, and can reject or reproduce whatever they are subject to. This relates to the classic problem of ideological consciousness: whereas Marx saw subjects as deriving from a commanding ideology ('they do it because they do not know what they are doing'), Zizek (1989) argues for individual reflexivity where people act consciously in relation to ideology ('they know they are subject to an ideology, and yet they do it'). Actually, this is not just an either/or question, as it can also be both – but at different times. The point here is that the level of ideological consciousness and the result of structure–actor or discourse–agency interfaces must be determined empirically (Long 2001). On top of theory concerns, experiencing this empirically – that people are involved in the aid partnership sometimes knowingly, sometimes unconsciously, sometimes reluctantly and sometimes indifferently –

made me realize I would have to complement post-development with an actor-oriented approach.

Why then should we bother at all with post-development theory, given its determinism and serious shortcomings in accounting for agency? In brief, the answer is that development takes place at different levels, and post-development provides a privileged vantage point for grasping the structural and discursive levels of aid. However, this macro-level should not be confused or equated with agency and practice, as some post-development scholars seem to do. Combining post-development and actor-oriented approaches rests on a critique of the former and its shortcomings. It also nuances the post-development approach, making it less totalitarian while demonstrating its relevance as *one* approach to *one* level of institutional development. Most importantly, combining different approaches enables us to reinstate the social as part of the analysis – to see how individual and collective actors affect, and are affected by, what post-developers describe as 'development discourses'. The analytical point of departure becomes the intersection of what are otherwise seen as polar entities: discourse and agency, structure and actor, donor and recipient, the formal and the informal.

Combining a discursive and actor-oriented approach is premised on seeing the data these approaches cast off at the same analytical level: as different knowledge systems. This allows us to analyse what happens in the encounter between discourses and actors – how, why and when they intersect and influence each other. These encounters are expressions of what Long has described as a 'social interface': the 'critical point of intersection between different social systems, fields or levels of social order where structural discontinuities, based upon differences of normative value and social interest, are most likely to be found' (Long 2004: 35; Long 1989). The idea of interface implies a shift in analytical focus, from the various discourses and systems of knowledge towards the various situations where these meet and become articulated. It requires an actor perspective, making the theoretical conception of a priori formative discourses obsolete, and advances an empirically grounded analysis of knowledge and social power. Interface studies focus on the discontinuities in social life (e.g. values, knowledge and power) that typically arise when different and often conflicting lifeworlds or social fields intersect, creating 'battlefields of knowledge' (Long and Long 1992). By manifesting issues of friction and contestation, these battlefields reveal both the inner workings of development and what might be worth focusing on analytically. However, the outcome of these knowledge battles must be determined empirically.

Those operating in such interfaces often act as brokers (Bierschenk, Chauveau and Olivier de Sardan 2002; Lewis and Mosse 2006b). In encountering and working within the development discourse, project staff on the donor as well as the recipient sides, locally and at headquarters level, can be manipulative and strategic with regard to imposed discourses and expert knowledge systems. Translating between different knowledge realms – formal and informal, donor and recipient – and converting ambiguous meaning and conflicting interests into seemingly coherent policy comprises a large portion of what development agents do. By applying techniques of brokerage they can have a tremendous impact on the local articulation and reception of global ideas and externally funded projects. As the intersecting point of local knowledge and external discourse, these actors, or brokers, can apply techniques to ensure that external ideas and projects gain relevance, influence and legitimacy at the local implementing level. The very point of brokerage itself underpins the importance of directing analytical attention to actors and of seeing discourses of development as articulated through actors. Actor-oriented perspectives, interface and brokerage permit analytical distance from the self-representations of the actors involved; this can help to avoid normative confusion regarding actor intentions – since brokerage does not necessarily imply intentions of manipulation on the sly. Brokerage is a concept that exists exclusively for the sake of analysing what happens in a situation of interface. Brokers are social actors implanted in a local arena who serve as intermediaries and thus represent the social carriers and discursive bearers of donor–recipient relations. They operate in social interfaces and 'translate the discourse and actions of given actors in terms [that] make sense to partners situated far away at the other end of the brokerage chain' (Bierschenk, Chauveau and Olivier de Sardan 2002: 17). As such, brokerage and interfaces, as articulated by actors at various levels of the aid chain connecting donor and recipient organizations, represent privileged entry points for studying local expressions and effects of global ideas and discursive power, like the power found in developmentality and the new aid architecture.

Combining the post-development and actor-oriented approaches in multiple settings makes it possible to grasp the situated complexity and variety of the new aid architecture and its partnership formation. This enables us to study how different systems of knowledge – at the formal or informal level, at the actor or discourse level, or among donor or recipient institutions – intersect and interrelate. And that in turn prevents compartmentalization of the lifeworlds of donors and recipients – as so happens with interface studies (Rossi 2006). An empirical actor-oriented approach helps to open up the black boxes of institutional development discourse by addressing the contextual interchange between policy and practice. It offers the possibility of understanding how meanings associated with development are produced, disputed and consumed in practice, illuminating the multiple connotations and denotations the term holds for those involved in institutional development.

For empirical and theoretical reasons, the multi-sited, mixed-methods approach thus became a necessity when making this ethnography of the new aid architecture, its partnership formation and, by implication, developmentality. Using multiple approaches is also a precondition for escaping the kind of analytical and empirical reductionism associated with both post-structuralism and actor-oriented approaches in their purest form. The very notion of partnership serves as the node from which this extended case study of the World Bank–Uganda partnership unfolds so that we may grasp institutional development at its various empirical and analytical levels, including the many contexts where these intersect. Moreover, unpacking the new notion and reformation of partnership as part of the new aid architecture requires connecting micro and macro in the present and the past to study the impacts of world systems and globalization in particular situations and localities (Evens and Handelman 2005, 2006; Sahlins 2004) – as will be shown in this book's developmentality analysis of the situated articulation of the World Bank–Uganda partnership.

## Notes

1. These ideas were operationalized and ratified by international donor agencies (multi- and bilateral) through the declarations of Rome (2003) and Paris (2005) on issues of aid effectiveness, ownership, harmonization, alignment, results and mutual accountability.
2. Stokke (1995) makes a similar distinction between first- and second-generation conditionality.
3. Williamson originally coined the term 'Washington consensus' to denote the least common denominator of policies pursued by Washington-based institutions such as the World Bank, the IMF and the U.S. Treasury Department to Latin America during the 1980s. The term covered a set of ten specific policy prescriptions constituting the 'standard' reform package; since then, the term has been used in a different and broader sense, as synonymous with market fundamentalism, privatization, liberalization, neoliberal policies, deregulation of state institutions and the intentionally expanding role of the free market.
4. Important here is the emergence of the 'sustainable development' concept, which has managed to merge the predominant rationale of economic

growth with those of social and environmental issues (Wade 2004; Bøås and Vevatne 2004).

5. Among the external factors were: changes in the Bank's environments, postwar geopolitics and the demise of the role of development's soft power to contain communism; altered interests among the Bank's major donor member-states; waning public support and budget constraints; the increase in private capital flows to developing countries; and developing countries graduating to become donor countries. Internal factors included: a recognized lack of efficiency; low compliance rate among borrowers to established conditions and legal covenants attached to loans; and weak organizational culture within the Bank, with rewards and promotions distributed based on quantity, causing the project management to wane after project approval – in turn, derailing project implementation (Weaver and Leiteritz 2005).
6. Mauss's work has a wide geographical and historical scope. In the introduction he quotes *Håvamål* from *Edda,* and asserts that in Scandinavia, amongst others, exchange and *contracts* are implemented as gifts, which in theory are voluntary but in practice and reality represent an obligation (Mauss 1954) – a perspective with parallels in the disconnect between donor partnership rhetoric and the actual practices of such partnership.
7. NORAD is a government directorate under the Ministry of Foreign Affairs, and provides funding and policy guidance to Norwegian NGOs.
8. I was based at OPM's Section for Policy Coordination, Monitoring and Evaluation.
9. This percentage has declined somewhat in recent years due to the discovery of oil in western Uganda and increased Chinese activities in the country. It was said that, in 2005, donor contributions made up about 48 to 52 per cent of the national budget. A representative of the Bank of Uganda writes that 'Uganda is a country that is heavily dependent on budget support to finance nearly 50% of its total expenditures' (Atingi-Ego 2005: ii). On top of this comes aid not given as budget support. In 2005, net official development assistance to Uganda was US$ 1,191 million, up from US$ 604 million in 1999 which was the level (although fluctuating) during the 1990s. In 1985 it was US$ 179 million and in 1989 US$ 446 million. In 2007 it was US$ 1,736 million (source: World Development Indicators, see http://data.worldbank.org/indicator/DT.ODA.ODAT.CD?page=1).
10. Between 1962 and 1986 Uganda experienced six violent changes of government: Idi Amin's 1971 coup and subsequent eight-year reign, when between 100,000 and 500,000 civilians were killed, is the most infamous. The Museveni-led Bush War (1981–86; also known as the Ugandan Civil War or Resistance War) brought a similar number of casualties and losses.
11. The PRSP model was rapidly rolled out by the Bank. By September 2003, it had already been implemented in fifty-four countries, with more to follow suit (Gould 2005a: 3).

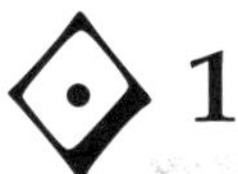

# Developmentality

The ideological content and structural set-up of the new aid architecture depart significantly from previous grand approaches to development – like the modernization and dependency theories that, since the mid 1960s, have provided and reflected the main inputs to development thinking.[1] Although different – notably in seeing (under)development as a technocratic, apolitical endeavour or as an active political process respectively – these approaches share some common features: donor-driven, top–down and paternalistic, presenting themselves as all-knowing and criticized for not being context-sensitive in offering a one-size-fits-all solution to the challenges of underdevelopment. The new aid architecture is different: its ideas of partnership, ownership and participation all seek to establish a more inclusive development regime that is sensitive to contextual matters, through a bottom–up approach to planning and implementation. As such, it emphasizes and supports local initiatives and national actors over externally imposed ideas, strategies and approaches. In development jargon, this means that conditionality has been abandoned in favour of partnership and participation. As this book will show, however, practice has not followed the rhetorical representations. The confluence of participatory and conditionality approaches draws on the inherent ambition among donors to retain control, producing the tacit governance mechanism of developmentality.

## From Post-Conditionality to Developmentality

Harrison (2001a, 2004) analyses the new partnership formation that is emerging with the new aid architecture, akin to his idea of second-generation reform, in terms of post-conditionality – a concept that is related to but somewhat different from developmentality. Drawing on an analysis of the World Bank–Uganda relation, he holds that the government's adoption of and shared interest in the Bank's prevailing policy discourses made it redundant for the Bank to apply conditionality. Experiencing the conducive grounds for its policy, the Bank made Uganda a pilot country under the new PRSP regime and partnership model. Thus, under certain conditions, Harrison claims, the external–national distinction becomes less useful for understanding the dynamics of partnership. Some states, among them Uganda, 'embody a politics of donor intervention which cannot adequately be encapsulated by the general notion of conditionality' (Harrison 2001a: 658). That is, when donor ideological hegemony means that the donor policy prescriptions become accepted as orthodoxy within key state institutions managing the relations with external actors, there is no longer any need for donors to apply explicit conditionality. The post-conditionality concept thus serves as a 'useful characterization of a set of significant developments within donor–state relations ... and forms of donor intervention which are not merely based on the threat of sanction which is at the heart of the conditionality mechanism' (ibid.). Like developmentality, post-conditionality is contingent on how aid recipients have internalized the donors' way of thinking, and whether there is a political environment conducive and receptive to donor policies. Post-conditionality thus signifies a move away from the direct coercive measures of conditionality to a situation where donors apply their productive capacities to use funds to promote change – and that 'requires more carrots that sticks' (ibid.: 659).

In these respects, the concepts of post-conditionality and developmentality harmonize. But there is one important distinction to be made between them. Harrison posits the post-conditionality concept as being based on donor selectivity, meaning that donors (the Bank in particular) choose to operate only in those countries where there already exists a conducive policy environment, where the client has adopted the donor prescriptions, and thus where coercive measures of conditionality are not needed – or where carrots work better than sticks. Post-conditionality is thus a denotation of client states where such conducive environments already exist, but it does not say anything about how such conducive environments are produced. Developmentality attends to the production of such conducive environments. The distinction, then, is that post-conditionality is dependent on that which is also produced by developmentality: docile counterparts, credible partners, a conducive policy environment, and 'ownership' by rendering the donor's policies as those of the recipient. Altering people's mentalities to influence their actions is thus integral to the new partnership formation, and should be recognized as a form of indirect rule.

## Governmentality – A Passage to Developmentality

The changes implied with the new aid architecture draw attention to Foucault's conception of power as governmentality, or the 'conduct of conduct' (Foucault 1991, 2010), reflecting a transition from direct to indirect rule aimed at shaping, guiding and directing the behaviour and actions of individuals and groups in particular directions. There is thus a distinction to be made between Foucault's early and later works, which also somewhat parallels the changes implied with the new aid architecture and the formation of partnership, as well as how scholars address institutional development. The early Foucault saw power–knowledge formations in terms of discourse, which came to appear as a rather totalizing modality of power operating over individuals – particularly as interpreted and applied by those writing from a post-development perspective (see e.g. Ferguson 1994; Escobar 1995; Gledhill 2000). To counter the critique of a totalizing discourse and as a way to enhance actor perspectives, the later Foucault introduced the power modality of governmentality (Lemke 2000; Arce and Long 2000a).

As a form of power, governmentality means a withdrawal on the part of the ruler from active interference in the daily life of the ruled, under the pretext of greater freedom and self-governance. Governmentality signifies a new form of liberal power, whereby the ruled are granted the freedom to govern themselves – but only as long as this is in accordance with the mentality of the ruler, who now holds a more remote position akin to that of an auditor who provides and monitors the realm, within which the ruled can operate. With 'governmentality' Foucault introduced a new conception of productive power as an alternative to the traditional understanding of power as repressive and coercive, drawing on the sociological literature and its ideas of collective and historical mentalities as used by Emile Durkheim and Marcel Mauss, among others.[2]

'Governmentality' represents a merger of the terms 'government' and 'mentality', indicating that governance is related to the mentality of the governing and the governed. Governmentality is seen as a form of power that deals with the practical tasks of government, as a feature pertaining to the rationality or 'art of government' (Foucault 1991: 92) comprising a distinct way of thinking about the nature of government and practices of political rule amounting to the conduct of conduct: 'a form of activity aiming to shape, guide or affect the conduct of some person or persons' (Gordon 1991: 2). Governmentality is a productive and relational power concerned with subjects' self-governance.[3] It emerged as an effect of modern state formation from the eighteenth century,[4] and in the wake of challenges to direct rule to overcome the contradictory movements of the expanding territorial and administrative states and the greater centralization of state systems (Dean 1999; Foucault 1991, 2007; Neumann and Sending 2010).

Governmentality involves processes and techniques for making the discourse or mentality of the ruler that of the ruled – as indicated by the semantic linkage of 'government' and 'mentality' in the term 'governmentality', implying that the technologies of power are interlinked with the political rationality underpinning them. This paved the way for an intentional political economy based on technologies involving 'mechanisms of calculation, surveillance, control and regulation that set the terms and are constitutive of a domain of social existence' (Ong 2002: 236). A governmentality perspective, then, allows us to investigate the specific practices and techniques of governance as empirical phenomena and thus bypasses the formalistic view on institutions, power and their nominal organization by addressing the 'mentality' of the systematic knowledge that gradually gains status as normal. A governmentality analysis implies exploring the techniques that make self-governance possible, and how a social field is structured to shape the conditions for consensus and the prerequisites of acceptance: '[G]overning people is not to force people to do what the governor wants; it is always a versatile equilibrium, with complementarity and conflicts between techniques which assure coercion and processes through which the self is constructed or modified by himself' (Foucault 1993: 203–4). The evolution of governmentality has thus depended on its apparently liberal nature.[5] As a mode of power, governmentality does not deprive individuals of responsibility for their own lives and self-governance: 'As the choice of options for action is … the expression of free will on the basis of a self-determined decision, the consequences of the action are borne by the subject alone, who is also solely responsible for them' (Foucault 1988; Lemke 2001: 201).

This dual process of being granted freedom and responsibility for self-governance while still being accountable to the institution that grants this freedom encapsulates the girding propositions of the new aid architecture: the aid recipient is granted greater freedom to develop itself, but this freedom is curtailed, since it cannot be executed outside the confines defined by the donor's partnership model. In order to receive support, the recipient's self-development and its 'own' development strategy must keep to the donor's realm. And this means that the recipient is made accountable to the donor for implementing their 'own' policies. As Gould notes:

> The new aid architecture draws on a set of thinking around partnership and participation pertaining to an ideology of mutual interest [that] has achieved hegemonic status in the rhetoric of aid across the board – from the megalithic multinational financial institutions (like the IMF and the World Bank) through transnational private aid agencies (like CARE and Oxfam) to bilateral donors (like SIDA and USAID) and national NGOs (non-governmental organizations) in dozens of northern and southern countries. This suggests that the new modalities of managing inequality are infused with some sort of 'governmentality'. (Gould 2005c: 64–65)

This reference to Foucault's (1991) concept of governmentality draws attention to a line of political theory that attends to the exercise of authority by the governing over the governed through internalized disciplines of power (see Burchell, Gordon and Miller 1991; Dean 1999; Rose 1999; Rottenburg 2009) – or the orchestration of power that Foucault termed the 'conduct of conduct' (Cruikshank 1999). According to this line of thought, 'a "partnership mentality" might be seen as a mode of governing key actors populating the aid domain, [and] of ensuring their complicity in a policy regime that reflects the aims of external creditors' (Gould 2005c: 65).

The governmentality perspective has a seductive fit with the contours of the aid architecture and its seemingly liberal notions and practices of partnership, ownership and participation that make it possible to rule, not through coercion or policy imposition, but through complicity – by installing concepts of self-discipline among subjects and aid recipients that serve the interests of the donor institution. In development aid, this entails processes that make the donor's discourse and policy those of the recipient, in order to enable self-governance on the part of the latter. Exploring aid relations through the optics of governmentality can help us to understand how aid recipients assume responsibility for policies and practices engineered and imposed by external players. We find that donor–recipient relations constitute an indirect exercise of power that involves altering people's mentalities in profound ways – in other words, 'developmentality'.

## Developmentality

The concept of developmentality attends to the effects and intentions of the new aid architecture and how the institutional set-up and content of aid partnerships constitute means for governance, despite the liberal rhetoric. Developmentality points to the liberal yet calculated and rationalized practices, established by authoritative actors within the global development apparatus, that have supplied the new aid architecture with a range of techniques and a particular knowledge formation, both designed to shape the conduct of involved actors through reciprocal partnership instead of trusteeship and conditionality. The liberal rationality of the new aid architecture is reflected in both the current policy regime (with good governance and capacity building) and the institutional set-up of aid relations (partnership and participation). Developmentality draws attention to the proposition that, despite indications of a transfer of power from donor to recipient, donor institutions are applying new forms of governance that enable them to retain control by orchestrating the 'conduct of conduct' of aid recipients.

The new aid architecture includes a normative set of ideas pertaining to the underpinnings of the descriptive governmentality analysis. Recipients are granted greater liberty to take control of their own development strategy under the labels of 'partnership' and 'participation'. Good governance among recipients has become the prerequisite for being granted this freedom, as well as being the goal for donor support, since good governance is expected to enable recipient self-governance without donor interference. Weaker governance means more donor control; thus, better governance equals less donor involvement. In practice, the assessment of governance and the objective of good governance policies are defined largely by the donor institutions. However, both the process and objective of the new aid architecture hinge on participatory actors being given responsibility for their own development. Instead of punishing non-discursive practice, the new aid apparatus centres on risk management – as in liberal-democratic societies – where subjects/recipients are made responsible for dealing with their own problems through various governance techniques. Although donors bear the responsibility for financing development efforts, an explicit part of the new aid architecture is that responsibility for poverty reduction resides with the developing countries themselves (see Ilcan and Phillips 2010). The donors may have renounced their dominant position, but they retain control, albeit indirectly, by: instigating the processes and objectives; framing and thereby limiting the degree of freedom and room for manoeuvre by upholding their means to sanction deviant or non-discursive practice; and administering and monitoring the partnership arrangement. When recipients are made responsible through empowerment and partnership, they become active agents – but they are still restricted in their choices, since their active engagement is contingent on accepting the assumptions of the donors' prevailing development discourse.

Although aid conditionality is denounced by donors as a policy package and as a way to enforce certain policies, it is still there – in a more tacit and indirect form that allows for continued donor control over the development process. The ideas of participation and partnership, coupled with more subtle routines of conditionality for maintaining indirect control, illustrate the centrifugal and centripetal aspects of donor power. This form of individualizing-cum-totalizing is central to developmentality – while donors give up control, they also retain it through other means, like new liberal techniques of (self-)discipline and (self-) management, various calculative practices and contractualism.

Developmentality captures how the asymmetrical power relation inherent in donor–recipient relationships is reproduced in profound ways, although the rhetorical claims integral to the new aid architecture may suggest the opposite. It draws attention to the disconnect between donors' rhetorical claim of having handed over power to the clients, and the practical effect of the new aid modality, managerial routines and governance mechanisms that enable donors to maintain control, but now in a more subtle manner. The core of developmentality as a means of governing at a distance depends on the Bank's ability to make its policies and objectives those of the recipients. This enables the 'conduct of conduct', and is premised on construing those on the receiving end as free, active agents. However, this freedom is limited as they have to abide by the donors' discursive frames: freedom is contingent on their internalization of donors' concepts and idioms. It could thus be argued that the aid architecture forces freedom onto clients, since their participation is a condition for support: consequently, freedom becomes a means to rule. Involvement in the new aid architecture necessitates and produces self-disciplined clients by enlisting and moulding them as agents responsible for own development.

The new aid architecture has certain characteristics that amount to developmentality. First and foremost, the new aid architecture holds that clients are responsible for their own development, including planning, implementation and monitoring. The donor has retreated from operational activity and allegedly assumed the role of merely a supervisory funding agency enabled by partnership and the responsibilization of recipients. However, clients know that they cannot propose whatever they might wish, because funding requires plans endorsed by the donor. The free and active engagement of clients has its limitations, as they must adhere to the dominant development tenets of the day. Second, donors uphold participation and self-governance on the receiving end as central means and objectives of development – as shown by the widespread popularity of the good governance agenda, which holds issues such as anti-corruption measures, democracy, accountability and the like as important to an acceptable development process. This brings us to the third element – the ideas of empowerment, emancipation and capacity building, all explicitly aimed at shaping those on the receiving end in accordance with principles of good governance. We find a fourth element of developmentality in the numerous instruments and formats for planning, monitoring and reporting to which client states are subjected: these structure interventions and policies according to certain logics, and enable donors to monitor, and thus govern, from a distance. Fifth, aid disbursement is not only a result of the donor giving their approval to the client's policy choices – it is just as much subject to the donor's assessment of the performance of their client. Finally, the Foucauldian notion of a subject-less power alerts us to the possibility that developmentality is just as important for structuring the actions of donor institutions and people as it is for recipients.

Developmentality, as governmentality, denotes 'forms of action and relations of power that aim to guide and shape (rather than force, control or dominate) the action of others … [and] includes any program, discourse or strategy that attempts to alter or shape the actions of others or oneself' (Cruikshank 1999: 4). Instead of being restrictive and the antithesis of freedom, the power of governmentality is liberal and productive. Through the use of freedom as a formula for rule, the individual – or aid recipient – becomes responsible for self-government. In this context Abrahamsen asserts that 'the modern self is both the object of improvement and the subject that does the improving' (Abrahamsen 2004a: 1459). Swap 'the modern self' with 'aid recipient', and this quote captures an essential part of the developmentality perspective to the new aid architecture: donors withdraw from operational activities by empowering recipients and entrusting them with increasing responsibility for the development portfolio through greater participation and improved partnership. Under the aegis of liberalism, increased freedom in the hands of recipients could be seen as both a means and an objective for governance by the donors. The autonomy, self-governance and freedom conveyed to the recipient institution have their limitations – whatever the recipient undertakes in the name of partnership must be in accordance with the donor's stipulated and acceptable realm. A frictionless partnership exists when the recipient has internalized the donor's rationale and acts as the donor wishes, without further ado. The partnership formation implies a process of gradually making the donor's idioms and mentality those of the recipient. Altering people's mentalities and practices in profound ways is thus integral to aid partnerships, and constitutes a form of power, or developmentality, vital for managing North–South relations. As long as recipients operate within the discursive frames orchestrated by the donor, they can enjoy a sense of freedom previously unknown. The donor institutions not only provide their recipients with this freedom (or even force it upon them): they also demarcate the framework within which this freedom is to be exercised. This form of neoliberal governance, integral to the new aid architecture, then uses 'freedom as a formula for rule' (Abrahamsen 2004a: 1459). The freedom entails greater decentralization of power and decision making, away from any central node and towards various quasi-autonomous organizations and institutions. The concept of developmentality points to how such liberal decentralization is accompanied by various calculated and rationalized control mechanisms, in turn enabling the donor institutions to 'govern at a distance' (Dean 1999). The move towards freedom and decentralization is frequently described as a new managerialism that accords actors on the receiving end a degree of autonomy and the responsibility for their own decisions and actions (see Strathern 2000b). The freedom is, however, restricted as it is accompanied by various governance techniques – for example, auditing, accounting, monitoring and evaluation – restricting the freedom by putting the aid recipient under continuous scrutiny and thereby linking the plethora of disparate practices and units to a centralized strategy at the state or multilateral levels. The new aid architecture and the power of developmentality thus involve techniques and practices similar to what Rose called 'the instrumentalization of a regulated autonomy' (Rose 1996: 57).

The notion of developmentality points to donor institutions' calculated ability to regulate the autonomy of aid recipients. Control is maintained parallel to donor withdrawal from direct operational involvement. Developmentality is made possible by, and works through, promises of greater freedom, simultaneously framing and thus restricting this freedom on the receiving end of the partnership relation. The liberal but confined modalities of partnership, participation and ownership serve to 'conduct the conduct' of aid recipients – recipients become responsible for their own development, but remain accountable to their donors for their success or failure. There is autonomy – and hence responsibility – on the side of the recipients, which at least nominally is among the intentions of the new aid apparatus. But this autonomy is controlled and restricted, and the degree of autonomy experienced by aid recipients is contingent on their internalizing the donor's policies and procedures: its discourse – or mentality. Friction in this relationship reduces the recipient's freedom and autonomy, entailing the possibility of greater direct control by the donor – and showing that developmentality is a productive power that requires docile recipients. The power of developmentality is relational. It obtains and resides in different sites, distant from any central governing body. Empirically, it is found in the encounter between the governing and the governed, or in the interface between donor and recipient institutions. That explains the need for multi-sited fieldwork in order to explore the idea of developmentality on both sides of the aid chain as well as in the partnership relation itself.

## Challenging Developmentality

It should be stressed that I do not propose developmentality as a hegemonic, totalizing or monolithic power. Doing so would mean reproducing the fallacy of the early post-development approaches that, in neglecting agency and analysing development as a powerful discourse, portrayed development as a hegemonic ideological construct (Ferguson 1997; Green 2003; Lie 2008a). The potential for resistance to institutional development and indeed developmentality exist at both the empirical and theoretical levels. Identifying resistance is, as argued above, premised on actor-oriented perspectives (Scott 1985, 2009; Long 2001, 2004). The developmentality concept itself is empirically grounded but serves more general purposes: as a framework to understand and analyse other, contemporary configurations of aid relations, and the disjuncture between official order and practice more generally.

Developmentality builds on a relational notion of power, meaning that power is not something that someone has or does not have. Rather, it is a property accrued, shaped and articulated in the practical encounter between different actors – be they individual or collective actors, within or between donor and recipient institutions. To grasp the relational aspect of power empirically involves moving analytical attention from the level of discourse to that of actors. The concept of interface (Long 1989, 2004) facilitates both an actor orientation and a focus on knowledge encounters, holding that the effect and outcome of such encounters are not a priori given but need to be studied in their particular, situated contexts. Interface conveys an advantageous analytical entry point to grasp how different situated social knowledge intersects, and how discontinuities between different knowledge systems yield struggle between or over knowledge in attending to how 'actors' goals, perceptions, values, interests and relationships are reinforced or reshaped' (Arce and Long 1992: 214; Arce and Long 2000b). Interface is a constituent part of any battlefield of knowledge (Long and Long 1992) in pointing to the 'notion of multiple realties and arenas of struggle where different lifeworlds and discourses meet' (Long 1992b: 271). Herein lays the potential for identifying resistance to, or deviations from, the formal order of development and the power of developmentality. Attending to such critical points of intersections between different actors and social systems brings to the fore the extent to which actors shape or are shaped by each other or external knowledge systems. Here, actors can employ various strategies, coping mechanisms and counterworks (Arce and Long 1993; Fardon 1995) to manage donor power and developmentality, thus assuming the roles described as translators and brokers (Bierschenk, Chauveau and Olivier de Sardan 2002; Lewis and Mosse 2006b; Hendry and Watson 2001). The concept of interface requires exploring the effect of donor–recipient relationships empirically, preventing pre-empirical assumptions about prevailing will and interests (Mosse and Lewis 2006).

The analytical orientation of interface and seeing power as an attribute of relations are reflected in the research design and empirical material of the present book. The renderings and practices of aid relations, the new aid architecture and the formation of developmentality are explored at both the donor and recipient sides of the aid chain as well as in their practical encounter, at the formal and structural level as well as the informal level and in practice.

Importantly, one should refrain from applying developmentality as a well-oiled machine of disciplinary power, as tends to be the case with other governmentality-inspired studies of development (cf. Watts 2003), precisely because this glosses over practices and resistance deviating from the formal order. Instead it is important to be attentive to and recognize such disjunctures when they appear – and this is made possible by the developmentality concept in attending the micro-physics of power and in seeing power as relational and shaped in situations of interface, thereby making the individual or collective actor the locus of analysis. We should refrain from accepting potentially totalizing models emerging from the development practitioners' side, and from our analysis of them. In attending to power empirically and as relational, anthropologists tend to cherish the empirical fuzz that distorts such models and analysis by putting disjuncture first, thus refusing to concede to development its own claim of order and logic, knowing that such claims are always fragile, contested and built on compromise (van den Berg and Quarles van Ufford 2005). Developmentality, formed and analysed in situations of interface, allows us to set aside the models and self-representations of aid bureaucrats and practitioners, and to uncover the inner workings of the development sector, its agencies and their practices.

What does the developmentality concept bring to the table that is not already captured by governmentality? Why should we think in terms of developmentality and not governmentality when analysing aid relations? The reasons are at least fourfold. First, Foucault wrote about governmentality emerging as an *effect* of modern European state formation. However, the revamping of institutional development along the liberal lines of ownership and participation where the aid recipient is granted the freedom and responsibility to develop itself has been highly intentional, initiated by authoritative development actors at different levels on both sides of the partnership dyad. Secondly, developmentality removes the focus from the vested state power and state centrism of governmentality, while applying the same governance mechanisms and processes to non-state actors, thus showing that the power modality of governmentality transcends its seminal state-bound origin. Thirdly, developmentality points to the particularities of the development sector and the close fit between the indirect governance of governmentality and the evolving partnership idea and practices. The notion of partnership that draws on recipient ownership and participation now seems an obvious way of managing aid relations. With the developmentality concept, we can go behind the formal order and liberal appearance to unmask how the current partnership formation actually provides for new governance mechanisms that not only undermine the nominal partnership idea but also reproduce asymmetrical aid relations and donor trusteeship.

## Developmentality and the Sovereign Frontier

Developmentality is not irrelevant to our understanding of the state, although the concept seeks to disengage the connotations to state power associated with governmentality. In fact, developmentality put the spotlight on profound concerns over externally driven processes of state formation – and sovereignty. There has been a resurgence of the state on the structural and policy levels of bi- and multilateral aid following the new aid architecture and the Bank's partnership formation, pivoting around the PRPS model. Aid-recipient states have assumed a more prominent position: instead of being subjected to externally imposed policy conditions, as under the first-generation reform era of externally imposed structural adjustment programmes (Harrison 2004), developing states are now granted the responsibility – some say freedom – to devise their own development strategies. With this transition from a passive to an active state, donors have become increasingly concerned with the nature of the state: it should preferably produce conducive policy environments able and willing to devise and implement correct, fundable policies – as shown by the prominent role accorded to good governance policies.

With the developmentality concept, the boundaries between the external donor and internal recipient institutions become blurred. Developmentality puts a focus on the Bank's ability to shape the policies and practices of its Ugandan counterpart, thereby undermining the liberal tenets of the partnership itself, as well as profoundly transgressing the sovereign boundary that demarcates the state's supremacy over its domestic political realm (Ferguson and Gupta 2002; Harrison 2004; Hansen and Stepputat 2005). However, it is not only practices of partnership that challenge the state and its sovereignty: the donor discourses of good governance, democracy and democratization connect firmly to the dynamics of state formation and sovereignty (Kapferer 2004c; Ferguson 2006).

In its classic meaning, sovereignty authorizes the state to have the final word, by having supreme and independent authority of and within its physical and conceptual domain (Friedrich 1946; Montgomery 2002) – with the sovereign being 'he who decides on the state of exception' (Schmitt 2006). Krasner (1999, 2004) distinguishes four usages of 'sovereignty', understood as ideal types to which practice aspires or against which practice is assessed. These are *domestic* sovereignty, which refers to the state's internal organization and the maintenance of public authority; *interdependence* sovereignty, which concerns the ability to control transborder movement; *international legal* sovereignty, referring to the reciprocal recognition of states as sovereign; and finally *Westphalian* sovereignty, which concerns the ability and right to exclude external actors from domestic authority structures. These four can in turn be grouped into an internal and an external dimension of sovereignty (Krasner 2004). The domestic and interdependent types of sovereignty refer to an internal dimension: matters pertaining to the state–citizen relationship, to the internal organization of the state apparatus, and to features generally considered as being within the supreme realm and designated scope of the state apparatus. The external dimension comprises the international legal and Westphalian notions of sovereignty. It refers to factors exogenous to the state – such as whether it is perceived as legally equal and sovereign by other states and thus entitled to engage in international organizations and ratify international treaties; and whether it is rightfully entitled to exclude external actors from interfering in its domestic realm by invoking the principle of non-intervention which, if violated, extends the legitimate use of force outside its borders.

The problem with these nominal versions of sovereignty as constitutive of statehood (Mitchell 1991; Bartelson 1995) is that they are biased towards the European experience, where sovereignty emerged as part and parcel of the early modern period of European state formation (Harrison 2004; Hansen and Stepputat 2005; Manger 2011). The nominal idea of sovereignty is fairly static, as well as being too provisional for grasping the practices of today's external–internal relations and challenges to post-colonial state formation (Bayart 1993; Mamdani 2002). Given the specificities of state formation in Africa, Krasner's typologies appear less suited as a template and point of reference for assessing the formation of sovereignty in, for example, Uganda.

In studying the World Bank–Uganda partnership and the workings of developmentality, issues pertaining to sovereignty become relevant for at least two reasons that together constitute a paradox. First, among the Bank's primary objectives is to build sovereign states with the credentials and properties for qualifying as legitimate partners able to govern and develop themselves in accordance with the discourses of good governance. Second, however, partnerships with the Bank are restricted to sovereign states and their legitimate, supreme governments as the sole allowed legal counterparts and signatories to partnership and lending arrangements. Being in partnership with the Bank can then be seen as a token of that state's sovereignty and international recognition. Herein lies the potential paradox. While Bank partnerships formally require sovereignty, the practices and effects that these same partnerships convey and imply may well undermine it. This paradox points to the ambiguous relation between the internal and external dimension of sovereignty. Erosion of and challenges to the internal dimension do not necessarily undermine the external dimension. A state may fail to deliver services to the citizenry from which it gains its internal sovereignty as well as be unable to control transborder movement, and yet still be considered legally equal by other states. The Bank–Uganda partnership is precisely a result of the government's inability or unwillingness to deliver according the internal dimension. The formal arrangement of this partnership is premised on Uganda being recognized as sovereign, and the aim is to support and empower the government to fulfil the internal dimension of sovereignty. However, the process and power mechanisms involved in this partnership not only bypass the external dimension but also undermine the internal one as the Bank increasingly involves itself in the state's internal political affairs on the levels of policy as well as procedure (as will be shown in chapters 5 and 6). And while both parties informally recognize that their partnership formation challenges the state's authority and puts its sovereignty into question, this element is muted; the Bank needs a sovereign counterpart and attends to the participation and ownership rhetoric, whereas on the recipient side it would be domestic political suicide for the government to admit to having come under the sway of external donors.

Harrison's work (2004) on governance states in Africa helps us to make sense of this sovereignty paradox, empirically and analytically. He proposes an analytical framework that moves beyond the static, juridical concept where sovereignty is an either/or matter: his approach is more open and sensitive to practice, by distinguishing between *boundaries* and *frontiers*. Boundaries are clearly demarcated lines, frontiers are zones: 'A sovereignty "zone" is not linear; it defines a space within which different actors can work to define sovereignty in different ways' (ibid.: 25). This produces a less severe delimitation between sovereign and non-sovereign, offering a perspective more sensitive to the empirical realities of post-colonial state formation, where sovereign frontiers are constantly (re-)worked by the forces and actors working therein. 'The conceptual expansion from a "line" to a "zone" allows us to consider the "content" of sovereignty – its construction, discourse, the interplay between actors – more fully than would be possible if we were merely concerned with the extent to which an imagined boundary has been defended or violated' (ibid.: 26).

Thinking in terms of sovereign frontiers allows us to move beyond the static nominal idea of sovereignty to engage sovereignty more empirically, as will be shown in chapter 7 of this volume. This is in line with Agamben (2005) who, in calling for the inclusion of practice and effects of political crisis to our study of sovereignty, argues that sovereignty should be understood on political and not juridico-constitutional grounds. This entails going beyond the legal character and debate of sovereignty, and viewing sovereignty 'not as an attribute but rather an ongoing and variable project of states which is more or less realised in practice' (Alonso 2005). Rather than trying to find an overarching definition of sovereignty, we should recognize it as connected to and emerging from a set of historically contingent practices in the juncture of both international and intra-national processes through which a state, over time, gains sovereignty (Kapferer 2004b; Howland and White 2009; Whitfield 2009). Such a focus on practices accommodates 'the need for more embedded and "emic" understandings of what sovereign power actually means' (Hansen and Stepputat 2005: 5). By providing an ethnography of the World Bank–Uganda partnership and exploring the power of developmentality, this book offers such an empirically grounded analysis of state formation and the role of external actors in state-building processes.

With its focus on practice, the concept of developmentality challenges not only the formal rendering of the new aid architecture but also, in effect, the state and how we think about sovereignty. It helps us to understand the sovereignty paradox by shifting attention away from the limiting concerns of seeing the external donor–internal recipient relation solely as a matter of external imposition, national independence or self-determination, and showing how these concerns interact and work together. The sovereign frontier thus represents a field of both contestation and mediation where African states shape and are shaped by global forces that transcend the state. Analysing the sovereign frontier empirically can reveal new and emerging types of powers that affect processes of state formation and challenge state legitimacy and sovereignty, thereby causing a crisis of the state (Kapferer and Bertelsen 2009b). The crisis of the state brings into focus how sovereign borders on the margins of and within the state get redrawn. In the Bank–Uganda partnership these challenges generally emerge with and from features that can be captured by the developmentality analysis of the new partnership formation – and that is what this book is all about.

## Notes

1. In a nutshell, modernization theory was reflected in practice, and dependency theory illustrated the prevailing ideology. While aid practitioners embraced the former – perhaps due to its instrumental value in operationalizing a development programme – dependency theory never managed to alter practice, although it came to be the dominant ideology among academics, NGOs and leftish policymakers (see Grillo and Rew 1985; Eriksen 1989; Porter 1995). Recall the post-development argument about discursive formation and reproduction, asserting that aid practice is still a reflection of its seminal mindset, i.e. modernization theory.
2. Durkheim ([1893] 1997) linked forms of social solidarity to the ethos of the welfare state, making possible a political doctrine of governing society through *solidarisme,* which concerns the 'drawing of human beings into a common identification or bonds' (Dean 2007: 41).
3. The later Foucault operated with three notions, or modalities, of power – dominance, strategy and governmentality – all of which are contingent on separate historical trajectories. *Dominance* is a direct type of power that leaves no doubt as to who governs whom, akin to Weber's notion of power (Weber 1970), and where subordinate persons enjoy only marginal liberty. It does, however – and in contrast to Weber – recognize that power is rela-

tional and thus cannot exist without the contingency of opposition which ultimately resides in the individual himself. *Strategy* is a game between different wills in which the question of who will prevail is determined empirically – in contrast to dominance, where it is always clear who the master is. Strategy is thus a ubiquitous feature of human interaction where ideological manipulation, rational arguments and moral advice constitute a form of power by structuring the fields of action for others. *Governmentality* lies in between dominance and strategy. It refers to a fairly systemized and regulated mode of power that goes beyond the explicit rule over others, and follows a specific form of reasoning, akin to a liberal, economic rationality. Governmentality is connected to technologies of the self – that is to say, self-reflexive practices and strategies of self-governance. Whereas dominance rests on discipline, and strategy is a contest of wills, governmentality draws on the ability to frame situations by providing means, opportunities, choices and ways of acting and thinking about these (Foucault 1991, 1994; Lemke 2000, 2001; Dean 2007).

4. Foucault asserts that the thinking about the art of government emerged in late sixteenth-century Europe, and provided the starting point for modern governmentality by triggering a transformative process that gradually 'governmentalized' the increasingly administrative state: '[I]n the late sixteenth century and early seventeenth century, the art of government finds its first form of crystallization, organized around the theme of reason of state … But … right until the early eighteenth century, this form of "reason of state" acted as a sort of obstacle to the development of the art of government' (Foucault 1991: 96–97).
5. To Foucault, liberalism is not simply a political doctrine of political or economic theory, but a style of thinking concerned with the art of governing (Gordon 1991: 14) that indicates a decentralization and dispersal of power away from a central node to decentralized individuals. At the same time, governmentality is about the orchestration of power. Hence, governmentality implies the double movement of centralization and dispersion of power (Foucault 1991: 88), or ruling in the nexus of totalizing and individualizing (see Gordon 1991). This has implications for individuals, for whom it becomes imperative to be individualized so that they can be free to fulfil their societal obligations: individuals are to govern themselves, but are simultaneously forced into this freedom.

# 2

# The World Bank and the New Aid Architecture

## The Official Discourse

The World Bank is a vast and complex entity, and which part you see is largely determined by how you choose to engage it. This chapter offers a view from the top in engaging the Bank's official discourse, while the next one will provide a more bottom-grounded view in presenting different rank-and-file perspectives. Adding a diachronic dimension to the official discourse reveals a similar dynamic as the synchronic ethnography outlined in the next chapter, which is that the official version and external representation of the Bank are the result of contestation and resistance in which some ideas finally prevail in what is best described as battlefields of knowledge (Long and Long 1992). The outcome of such knowledge battlefields is not given, regardless from where the ideas emerge, and hence these next two chapters devoted to the Bank speak to each other in bringing history and structure into ethnography, and agency and culture into our understanding of history and structural change (Sahlins 2004). This approach – playing on the interface between structure and actor, the formal and informal, and how they impinge on each other – helps to avoid losing the analysis in structure or ideology (as the post-development approach often does) without resorting to the radical individualism that often comes with a purely actor-oriented approach.

This chapter provides the empirical framework and conditions for developmentality by outlining and putting into context the emergence of the new aid architecture within the Bank, and its novel ideas about how to reconfigure the partnership relation. Despite being promoted by and seen as the brainchild of the then incumbent Bank's president, these ideas were critically contested because they were seen to deviate too far from the Bank's established practices and discourse. The following two chapters will together help to 'embed our analysis of official discourses in an understanding of the contending ideas and interests within the institutions that generate and propagate them' (Fox 2003: 523), as such demonstrating that although policies and discourses serve to anchor practices (Swidler 2001), they should not be equated with each other.

## New Policies and Procedures in the Making within the Bank

Since the mid-1990s, processes internal to the World Bank have explicitly sought to alter the ways and means by which it engages client governments. These aspirations for change have been driven by various rationales, including ideational change within and outside the Bank, the ongoing search for enhanced operational efficiency and effectiveness, revitalization of relevance after the end of the Cold War when institutional development lost its geopolitical dimension, and not least as a response to critical voices demanding change in how the Bank conducts its business (see Pincus and Winters 2002; Einhorn 2006; Woods 2006). Continuous change has taken place within a sturdy but supple framework driven by an expansionist mission creep (Einhorn 2001; Andrews 2008; Chwieroth 2008). The Bank has assumed new methods and objectives beyond its original goal of reconstruction and development to speed economic progress everywhere – as stipulated when the Bank was created at the Bretton Woods Conference in 1944 to aid in the postwar reconstruction of Europe. The Bank's mission creep has led to an ever-growing pervasive gap between the talk, decisions, actions and results of the organization – that is, a hypocrisy trap (Weaver 2008). Although the change from previous structures of aid modalities and policies to the new aid architecture indicates a dramatic shift in the Bank's political culture of governing and orchestrating relations with client countries, the question remains: has there been a parallel change in practice?

The evolution of the new aid architecture illustrates the Bank's paramount role in shaping the international aid system, while also reflecting its interplay with dominant development ideas. When the Bank started to think in terms of a new aid architecture, the concepts of participation and partnership were already commonplace within the international development discourse. The way in which the Bank institutionalized and operationalized these ideas, however, shows its leverage for radically changing the way of organizing international aid in terms not only of Bank–client relationships but also of how client states relate to other bilateral donors. The emergence of the new aid architecture within the Bank largely coincides with the 1995–2005 Bank presidency of James Wolfensohn, who announced his resignation in the course of my fieldwork. Without being reductionist in ascribing too much institutional influence to one person, much of this chapter centres on Wolfensohn's achievements – not only because he was a key protagonist in the formative period of the aid architecture within the Bank, but also because his resignation spurred widespread discussion about his legacy, the current state of the Bank and its future among my informants. This thus provided a particularly well-suited vantage point to grasp the organization, or at least parts of it, regarding recent internal and external reforms (i.e. the Strategic Compact [Weaver and Leiteritz 2005]) pertaining to the new aid architecture and its partnership formation. Although widely discussed and articulated among Bank staff – at least when they are new and before they either become internalized in Bank operations or lose momentum and evaporate into oblivion – many of these ideas and their present outline draw on the official discourse as articulated in formal Bank documents and policies.[1] Such policy-guidance documents have formal authority, as they emanate either from presidential speeches or from documents and strategies approved by the Bank's board, giving them a clear articulation and mandate. Because of this formal authority they are widely read, referred to and heeded by people internal and external to the Bank, and thus provide a good approach to the discourse of the Bank and its gatekeeping ideas: that development depends upon non-economic factors, that the Bank should empower and involve recipient institutions; and that the Bank should have a leading role in global development initiatives.

## Leading the Way

In the main entrance hall of the World Bank there is a small but highly symbolic statue. The bronze sculpture, *Sightless among Miracles,* portrays a young boy leading an old, blind man with a stick, to which both of them cling. The man has been blinded by a parasitic disease – onchocerciasis, or river blindness. The sculpture is meant to symbolize partnership, collaboration, leadership and interconnectedness – the stick, being the young boy's means to direct and lead the way for the elder, links the two together. At the same time, the boy knows that one day he might be at the other end of the stick, that their fates are interconnected, and that partnership is thus necessary. The statue celebrates the Bank's Onchoceriasis Control Programme (OCP), which was initiated in 1973 to reduce the extent and effects of river blindness in Western Africa – a curable illness that got its name because of its geographical locus around rivers and the blindness it causes. Today, OCP is celebrated as one of the most successful programmes in the history of development assistance. Robert Calderisi, a former World Bank senior official and international spokesperson on Africa, writes that the OCP programme is the only clear success of the Bank; it 'took 25 years and a concerted partnership between donor governments and international pharmaceutical companies' (Calderisi 2006: 163). The statue, however, celebrates not only the OCP's positive effects in combating river blindness, but also the concept of partnership due to the many actors it managed to bring together to work on a mutual objective and common cause. OCP and the statue are symbols of the symbiotic and synergetic effects perceived to derive from partnership – an idea central to today's development architecture.

Under the heading 'Defeating river blindness in Africa: successful human development through global partnership participation', the plaque on the statue reads that it:

> represents a once typical scene in many African nations. The adult has been blinded by a parasitic disease called Onchocerciasis, or river blindness ... Close collaboration between a wide range of development partners listed on the statue base ... has led to highly effective control of this devastating disease. Hence, this once commonplace image of blind adults being led from place to place by children is progressively becoming a scene from the past.[2]

Two hallmarks are seen as the reason for the success of the programme. First is the comprehensive regional approach, and second is the programme's success in congregating various actors to work together with the mutual goal of eliminating the disease. The OCP brought together the World Bank, the World Health Organization (WHO), the United Nations Development Programme (UNDP), and the Food and Agriculture Organization (FAO) on the implementing side. These organizations engaged in a partnership with Merck Pharmaceutical Company, a private company, who did not charge for the medicines, in return for a production subsidy. Jimmy Carter, who through his Carter Center was already engaged in the river-blindness campaign, brought together the medical company, various governments and the World Bank at a WHO conference at which it was decided that the medical company should develop and produce a medicine to counter river blindness to be distributed by the various governments, whereas the World Bank was to manage the financial side and thus be non-operational. The success of the programme is largely ascribed to its design.

From 1996 the programme was expanded into the African Programme for Onchocerciasis Control (APOC), which includes the nineteen remaining African nations where onchocerciasis is endemic. This expansion retained the programme's hallmarks – partnership and comprehensiveness among actors and sectors – with a particular increase in NGOs and private companies. The OCP initiative and its gradual expansion both reflect and inform the new aid architecture as it evolved from the mid-1990s onwards, particularly in terms of comprehensiveness, participation, partnership and private sector engagement, but also of the need for one, strong coordinating body in such comprehensive approaches: that is, the World Bank, as a facilitator and knowledge bank, leading the way from a backstage position withdrawn from direct operational engagement, and now acting as coordinator, knowledge provider and financier. Subsequently, the statue and the river-blindness programme have become highlighted for symbolizing partnership, co-operation and strong leadership (see Mallaby 2005) – all vital elements of the new aid architecture as it evolved within the Bank from the late 1990s.[3]

## Background for Initiating on a New Aid Architecture

The novelty of the 'new' aid architecture is best illustrated by comparing it with what it replaces. Institutional development, ever since its initiation in the wake of the Second World War, has passed through various discursive phases, and the new aid architecture emerged from the mid-1990s. Within the Bank these changes largely coincide with the 1995–2005 tenure of James Wolfensohn as Bank president during which radical changes were made that challenged the ideational and structural legacy of the 1980s (Gilbert and Vines 2000).

The 1995 appointment of Wolfensohn was somewhat controversial due to his background as an investment banker with no previous experience in the field of development. Wolfensohn was selected because of his expertise in and eagerness for institutional reforms, with a mandate to revitalize the institution so that it could regain the position as the world's leading development agency, to overcome the post-Cold War development impasse, allegations of trusteeship and challenges from the rapid increase of private development lending and investments (Mallaby 2005; cf. Bull and McNeill 2007).[4] Although his tenure provides a good vantage point for understanding Bank reforms, most of the changes should not be ascribed to Wolfensohn alone. What he did was to give momentum to processes already ongoing within the Bank and to changes that were underway in international development discourse. Nevertheless, his resignation in 2005 'represents an ideal opportunity to reflect on the legacy of the initiatives and reforms undertaken in the previous decade that continue to direct many existing trajectories in development policy' (Stone and Wright 2007: 1).

Ritzen, a former vice-president of the Bank's Development Economics Department, gives a schematic overview of the Bank's sixty-year history in terms of the major objectives, instruments and discipline it pursued and applied (Ritzen 2005: 72). From its inception and throughout the 1950s the Bank focused on reconstruction through technical assistance and engineering. In the 1960s the focus was on economic growth, delivered through projects and finance. In this period international development activities proliferated, driven by a belief in intentional development and external intervention, producing and produced by modernization theory and Rostow's influential *The Stages of Economic Growth: A Non-Communist Manifesto* (Rostow 1961). In the 1970s the 'basic needs' approach prevailed, with sector investments and the work of development planners. The basic needs approach was intended to eradicate poverty in the shortest amount of time, so it sought to provide poor people with the essentials for achieving the minimum required levels for subsistence. By the 1980s, and as a result of the oil crisis of the late 1970s which had devastating macroeconomic effects through depression and global stagflation, it had become accepted that macroeconomic discipline, enforced through structural adjustment of national economics such as deregulation and privatization, was the way to go. This was enforced via structural adjustment loans under the dominance of macroeconomists. In the late 1990s came a shift that emphasized policy reform and institutional development through holistic approaches, including social and pro-poor aspects – in contrast to the previous decade's narrow focus on economic growth and fiscal reforms. According to Ritzen (2005), the current era is characterized by a focus on poverty reduction from the Bank's side, enhanced through a multidisciplinary approach rooted in the Poverty Reduction Strategy Papers (PRSPs), as the central mechanism for the arrangement of partnerships between the Bank and client governments. The PRSP modality is commonly seen as Wolfensohn's main achievement, and indicative of the changes undertaken during his tenure.

## The Wolfensohn Legacy

Among the most prominent issues to Bank staff at the time of my fieldwork was who would succeed Wolfensohn as the next World Bank president. Early in January 2005 Wolfensohn announced that he would be retiring as president, after ten years, or two terms, in office. The announcement came only two weeks after he had triggered the rumour in his 'end-of-the-year' message to all his staff on 20 December 2004: 'I know that there is anxiety regarding leadership succession at the Bank ... We can expect clarity on the situation early in the new year, and I have no doubt that we will make an effective transition'.[5] On 2 January, Wolfensohn formally announced his intention to resign on 30 June, sparking off commemoration of his legacy and achievements among staff and in the media.

In late January 2005, three editorials – in the *Washington Post*, the *Financial Times* and the *Guardian* – all took up the issue of Wolfensohn's successor.[6] The *Washington Post* wrote:

> It matters who takes over the World Bank, because the institution is both powerful and fragile. It is powerful because it pumps out around $20 billion in commercial loans, subsidized credits and grants every year and because its *10,000-strong staff represents the strongest concentration of development expertise anywhere.* This combination of financial and technical muscle has given the bank a lead role in many ventures that affect American interests, from reconstruction in the Balkans and Afghanistan, to the campaign against AIDS, to the *refining of development theory.* (23 January 2005, emphasis added)

On 26 January, Wolfensohn addressed his staff in a general meeting, in one of the larger conference halls on the ground floor. The auditorium was almost packed and the meeting was telecast on B-Span – the Bank's web TV.[7] Such meetings are not normally popular among the staff, I was told. But now, people gathered in excitement as to whether Wolfensohn would say anything about his successor. The official purpose of the meeting, however, was for Wolfensohn to say thank you for the silver collection to the many staff members who had been affected by the recent tsunami in South Asia, as well as to take a provisional farewell, as he would be travelling extensively in the coming months. In celebrating his staff, Wolfensohn quoted the *Washington Post* editorial, emphasizing the part where his staff's development expertise is applauded. He added that among his main achievements during his decade in the Bank was how he and his 'development experts' had substantially changed the way of doing development, and that he had managed to make central the idea that the Bank should be more inclusive and 'listen to our clients – not as policemen or professors, but as partners'. He did not say anything about his successor.

Rumours and speculations about the next Bank president continued to circulate throughout my stay, becoming a good source of information on the current shape of the Bank, how it had developed over the last decade, and what the staff saw as its pathological characteristics and how to effect a cure. Wolfensohn had been instrumental in altering both the Bank as an institution and its aid architecture. He brought to the fore ideas of participation and ownership. By launching the Comprehensive Development Framework (CDF) and Poverty Reduction Strategy Papers (PRSPs) (Wolfensohn 1999; 2005b), part of the Strategic Compact's new inclusive approach towards client governments, Wolfensohn contributed to the resurgence of the state apparatus as a nodal point in development assistance, thus making governance issues central to aid policy. This followed his work on corruption – a highly political theme that had previously been known as 'the C-word' because its too-political connotations were seen as violating the Bank's apolitical mandate.

## Corruption as the Cancer of Development

The Bank recognizes that corruption is detrimental to its activities, but has always had problems in dealing with corruption among its clients because of some fundamental aspects regarding the Bank, which is mandated only to enter lending agreements with governments as the counterpart. This is contingent on trust and consent, which would become difficult to achieve if the Bank were to accuse and address corruption among its counterparts. Moreover, corruption is seen as belonging to the sphere of the client's internal affairs, and the Bank is prevented from engaging in such internal affairs, given its strictly apolitical mandate and because the borrowing governments are necessarily also shareholders, or members, of the Bank itself. Also, corruption is difficult to verify, since 'you don't get any contract or receipt', as one informant said.

After only a year in office, Wolfensohn delivered a pioneering speech at the October 1996 annual meetings of the Bank and IMF. This speech signified a crucial shift in the Bank's policy towards borrowing governments, and dramatically altered how the Bank was to think about partnership and engage with political matters. Although the speech was titled 'People and Development', it is commonly known as the 'cancer of corruption' speech.[8] Up until then, the mere use of the 'c-word' was perceived as infringing on the apolitical mandate, so the Bank usually referred to it as 'rent seeking'. Rent seeking was seen as the main obstacle to growth and efficient use of funds, and, according to one who was present on the occasion of the speech, the assembly jumped in their chairs when Wolfensohn said, 'Let's not mince words: we need to deal with the cancer of corruption' (Wolfensohn 2005a: 50).

> Simply put, capital goes to those countries that get the fundamentals right. And we are working with our clients on those fundamentals … If the new [strategic] compact is to succeed we must tackle the issue of economic and financial efficiency … Corruption diverts resources from the poor to the rich, increases the cost of running businesses, distorts public expenditure, and deters foreign investors … Corruption is a problem that all countries have to confront … The Bank Group cannot intervene in the political affairs of our member countries. But we can give advice, encouragement and support to governments that wish to fight corruption, and it is these governments that will, over time, attract the larger volume of investment. Let me emphasize that the Bank Group will not tolerate corruption in the programs that we support. (Wolfensohn 2005a: 50)

The overall speech illustrates Wolfensohn's two basic feelings on development: the need for the Bank to listen to client governments; and that development hinges on other factors than just economic growth, including corruption, governance and the public sector. The speech acknowledged the problems attached to corruption and opened up the possibility of addressing the issues – even though that might violate the apolitical mandate of the Bank.

Recognizing corruption as a problem to development was not new, but now, in being explicit about the problem and linking corruption to policy conditions and aid disbursement – the 'fundamentals' of good governance policy – Wolfensohn managed to expand the Bank's mandate and scope, if not on the formal level at least in practice regarding how the Bank goes about dealing with these issues. Initially, member states were somewhat reluctant to this shift, but it ended up being fully accepted by Bank staff and the international development establishment – especially among net donors.[9] Although a minor event in itself, the 'cancer of corruption' speech came to signal and pave the way for more comprehensive changes to Bank–client relations, and to political issues.

The reinterpretation and widening of the mandate was a tricky task, but was made possible, Mallaby asserts (2004: 174–206), thanks not least to the inspiration of Scott Guggenheim – an anthropologist working in the Bank's Jakarta office. Guggenheim had grappled with the problem of the Bank's dual intentions of ceding 'ownership' on the one hand while urging for a less corrupt government on the other. The reinterpretation of the mandate was enabled by a simple premise: 'The client need not be the government. The Bank's real clients are the poor people of a country' (ibid.: 202). By recasting its commitment to 'the poorest of the poor' and the citizenry in general – who, through their tax bills are ultimately to pay back the government's loans – the Bank opened a policy space that enabled it to respond to governmental malpractices like corruption.[10] This recasting of the Bank's liability from government to citizens has not been institutionalized – the client government is still considered the Bank's main counterpart – but the idea is prevalent among staff, who use it to justify the need for policy imposition and the use of conditionality towards borrowing governments. As one informant explained to me:

> You know, Jon, our mandate prevents us from engaging in political matters. But our mission statement also tells us to fight poverty for lasting results based on our dream of a world free of poverty [here, the informant points to an official Bank poster in her office with the very same words: 'Our dream is a world free of poverty']. Our work won't last very long if we don't deal with corruption. This very much has to do with building a good principal–agent relationship between government and its citizens, and strengthening government's social accountability ... When we are talking about social accountability, we are not talking about donor-driven processes of demanding accountability. That's not us [the Bank]. Citizens are fed up with bad governance. Citizens are fed up with corruption, and citizens are fed up with failure of performance ... The state needs to be accountable in running its affairs. The Bank also needs accountable counterparts for its lending operations. And governments which don't comply know that Africa is enjoying democracy broadly, governments that continue to get mired in corruption and bad governance and poor performance are asking for an electoral exit or trouble with donors next time around. So there is an internal incentive for governments to work on these issues that is not just driven by donors' potential reward. The donors, of course, they are encouraging the process and say the right things. But it is the choice of the government to listen or not. Not ours.

This quote, from an operational officer, illustrates ambiguities as to who the Bank sees as its counterpart. Dealing with corruption is now integral to the Bank's work, but due to its political character, references to the poor citizens help in legitimizing the Bank's enhanced anti-corruption agenda as part of ongoing public sector reform initiatives. The Bank's mandate as such has not been altered, but the rationale of indulging in political matters has been recast by including 'the poor' as counterpart and recipient on the client side of the donor–recipient relationship. Along this trajectory there has thus been an increase in the Bank's focus on the state apparatus and governmental systems – and where these are weak the Bank is now committed to forging states that are legitimate and accountable to both its donor agency and its citizenry. Still, the prohibition against directly indulging in political negotiations with client governments remains a major concern to Bank staff, who see corruption and weak governance as obstacles to their development efforts. Hence, many refer to the restrictive, apolitical mandate

– and the need to change it – when asked about the main challenges to their work. The corruption speech directed increased attention to the internal affairs of client governments and thereby sparked a process of carving out space to attune the Bank's ambitions to the means available without infringing on its apolitical mandate, thus integrating the recipient state as both means and objective for Bank lending programmes under the evolving PRPS model.

## The Bank's New Aid Architecture

The Comprehensive Development Framework (CDF) and Poverty Reduction Strategy Papers (PRSPs) are the fundamental building blocks of the new aid architecture as conceived within the Bank. The Strategic Compact and CDF are commonly regarded as the philosophical superstructures to the PRSP, while the PRSP is their operational manifestation. PRSPs are the central documents for Bank lending and the formation of partnership. Basic to CDF is a holistic and comprehensive approach to development – comprehensive in terms of policy sectors and actors (Gilbert and Vines 2000; Gulrajani 2007). Together, the CDF and PRPS have dramatically altered the international development architecture as regards both donor and recipient, providing new aid allocation mechanisms based on the idea of partnership. The CDF, which was initiated in 1999 (Wolfensohn 1999), drew on processes underway within the Bank while also explicitly aiming to change how the Bank conducts business, promoting four basic principles: a long-term holistic vision, country ownership, country-led partnership, and a focus on results.

CDF set out to counter earlier Bank lending mechanisms, notably the previously dominant Structural Adjustment Programme (SAP),[11] 'in which loans were proffered in exchange for government commitments to economic reform' (Einhorn 2001: 26). SAP evolved from the late 1970s as a response to the oil crisis and the subsequent global debt crisis, stagflation and economic depression which hit poor nations especially hard. In response, and as the perceived cure, '[the] IMF imposed strict fiscal and monetary discipline on indebted countries as a condition for receiving short-term balance of payment credit … [T]he World Bank stepped in with funds that were conditioned on longer-term, structural and institutional changes that had less immediate impact than the austerity measures required by the Fund' (SAPRIN 2004: 1–2). These adjustment mechanisms were deliberately designed for a general dismantling of the state: opening up markets, privatizing state holdings, and reducing the role of the state in the economy, giving rise to the notion of the 'Washington Consensus'.[12] Einhorn argues that although SAP and the Washington Consensus have been 'caricatured and misrepresented as a symbol for heartless World Bank policies, the reality was much more positive. A Bank study of 1980s adjustment programs in 42 countries found substantial success – with steadier growth rates, lower inflation, and improvements in current accounts and trade regimes' (Einhorn 2001: 26). Positive or negative, this summary nonetheless shows how the policies had an overt and dominant focus on growth and economic issues, as well as being defined by the Bank and not its recipients.

From the mid-1990s, the SAP approach was increasingly criticized by people inside and outside the development apparatus. One critical trajectory focused on the policy content per se, arguing that it was too political in fronting neoliberal ideas with a limited and simplistic focus on economic concerns, as well as providing an a priori one-size-fits-all solution to the multiple challenges of poor nations and people through the systematic erosion of traditional state roles. The other critical trajectory related to how aid was allocated: lending programmes and disbursement of funds from the Bank and the Fund were dependent on the recipient governments' uncritically adopting the policy package of these institutions. Combined, these elements not only gave rise to concerns about client-state sovereignty, they also seriously challenged the Bank itself – of which the recipient governments were members. This created a situation of Bank trusteeship and paternalism in relation to the recipients, as the people and governments most affected by the Bank's policies were seen as having neither the wisdom nor the right to contribute to economic policy debates concerning themselves.

With the CDF, Wolfensohn (1999) set out to counter this system. Although, as he argued, the World Bank had 'contributed significantly to the betterment of mankind … the fact remains that progress is too slow, [and we need] to redirect our institution to one that is result-based and not volume- or procedure-based' (ibid.: 1–2). Compared to SAP, the CDF aimed to 'highlight a more inclusive picture of development' (ibid.: 7).

> What is new is an attempt to view our efforts within a long-term, holistic and strategic approach where all the component parts are brought together. Such development should, in our judgement, be a participatory process, as transparent and as accountable as possible within the political climate prevailing in each country. This is not a return to central planning. It is a holistic approach to development based on country ownership and partnership … It is also a commitment to expanded partnerships, trans-

> parency, and accountability under the leadership of the government. What is new is that the international financial architecture must reflect the interdependence of macroeconomic and financial, with structural and social and human concerns. I personally believe that unless we adopt this approach on a comprehensive, transparent and accountable basis, we will fail in the global challenge of equitable sustainable development and poverty alleviation. We will fail to build a sustainable international architecture for the coming millennium. (Wolfensohn 1999: 30–31)

The CDF is intended to decentralize and convey power over the development process, from planning and policy making to implementation, operation and supervision – from the Bank to the recipient government by presenting a collaborative and holistic approach to development assistance. It stipulates a 'management tool matrix', which illustrates the comprehensiveness of CDF regarding both the actors it involves and the scope of policy. On the vertical axis are the development actors: the client government (on all administrative levels), multilateral and bilateral development agencies, civil society, and the (domestic and foreign) private sector. All these actors are seen as being involved in the policy making and implementation process. On the horizontal axis are various policy measures. Although these are supposed to be the result of government participation and ownership, it holds that certain steps need to be taken before others. The CDF outlines fourteen sectors, grouped into three categories – structural, social and human aspects of development – with an additional residual 'specific strategies' category, all seen as the 'prerequisites for sustainable growth and poverty alleviation' (Wolfensohn 1999: 32). Government participation and ownership are emphasized throughout the document: '[T]he framework should not become a straight jacket' (ibid.: 8), and 'It is also clear to all of us that ownership is essential. Countries must be in the driver's seat and set the course' (ibid.: 9). Although not aiming to be a straitjacket, it is only the fourteenth and final sector that is left open for context-dependent factors, under 'country specific headings' put in brackets.[13] These fourteen sectors are to be achieved through the four basic CDF principles: a long-term holistic vision, country ownership, country-led partnership, and a focus on results.

As part of the Strategic Compact, the CDF is often seen as the brainchild of Wolfensohn, and it was certainly his main footprint on the Bank. The CDF seriously altered both the policy content of aid and its delivery. The scope of the CDF is far wider than that of structural adjustment lending, and it reflects a critical shift from a focus on achieving rapid and sustained economic growth to a broader focus on the social and human aspects of poverty reduction and development under the auspices of sustainable economic growth. However, these changes and the CDF in general should be seen against the backdrop of various contextual and influencing factors, both internal and external to the Bank. Internally, the impetus for change centred on the concerns about the deterioration of social and economic conditions in developing countries deriving from SAP, and recognition of the need to reform the system of aid delivery and ensure that aid was managed and disbursed to alleviate pressures on the poor (World Bank 2003b; Tan 2007). The criticism the Bank repeatedly faced from anti-globalization protesters at international summits and conventions, as well as the rapid increase of private capital and foreign direct investment to poor nations, contributed to weakening the Bank's position as a leading international development agency. Not only did its reputation suffer, but the Bank was also moving away from its hegemonic position at the epicentre of development expertise. The lack of results and the inefficiency of Bank operations provided probably the most important impetus for change – at least from inside the Bank and among its shareholders. Moreover, the CDF reflected the growing normative consensus around partnership and participation within the development establishment. These ideas were not new – they were the very same ones that had evolved during the 1980s and had served as the backbone for the rapid rise in NGOs – but with CDF these ideas became institutionalized on the multilateral level of aid. Wolfensohn's personal influence should, nevertheless, not be underestimated. The appointment of Wolfensohn on 1 June 1995, Pender asserts, was widely regarded as a reaction to the loss of confidence in the Bank as an effective international institution. Bringing with him ideas and experience from the private sector, Wolfensohn saw his mission as being to carve out a 'new role for the Bank, to build a new legitimacy for its interventions' (Pender 2001: 402). Wolfensohn was entrusted with redefining the Bank's mission and of renewing its sense of purpose, and here CDF is the main achievement.[14] The framework has provided the foundation for the Poverty Reduction Strategy Papers (PRSPs), the central modus operandi of CDF and pivotal to the Bank's partnership formation (Brauer 2000; Hopkins et al. 2000; Gilbert and Vines 2000; Pender 2001).

## PRSP

The Poverty Reduction Strategy Paper (PRSP) is the operational manifestation of CDF and the new aid architecture within the Bank. In fact, few today refer to CDF, but rather to PRSP. The PRSP model was officially launched in September 1999, barely eight months after the CDF, and from the very beginning the intention was to embed the CDF principles in the PRSP (Wolfensohn 2005d). 'In short, the PRSP was to be an action plan for the CDF and was to provide governments with the incentives to adopt CDF principles in their development planning and cooperation with donors' (World Bank 2003b: 12),[15] reinforcing the main tenets of the CDF in expanding the development objectives to include poverty reduction and governance issues, as well as the changes it implies for the partnership formation.

Nominally, the PRSP is produced by the borrowing government and outlines the government's overall national development strategy to which both Bank lending programmes and all other external-funded development activities are to adhere. The PRSP plays a paramount role in the arrangement of international aid, due to two decisive factors. First of all, for a country to qualify for World Bank/IMF debt relief, lending and operations, the government must produce a PRSP document outlining national poverty-reduction measures and strategies; this PRSP (although it is a strategy devised and owned by the client government) must then be assessed and approved by the respective boards of the Bank and the Fund. Second, since the document stipulates the country's overall development strategy, all other development actors – local, national and international – operating in that country will have to adhere to and support the national strategy as formulated in the PRSP.

The PRSP approach involves five core principles. First, it is to be *country-driven,* meaning that the policies contained in the strategy should not only be tailored to the specific circumstances and the general context of the country, but the PRSP process should also be a sovereign product of the country itself. Although it is the government that is in the lead role – or driver's seat – of devising the strategy, the latter aspect emphasizes that the process should include broad-based participation of civil society. The requirement that the PRSP is to be country-driven is intended to promote national ownership of the strategy, on the rationale that national ownership and commitment serve to enhance efficiency as well as being a goal per se. Second, the PRSP should be *result-oriented,* with a focus on outcomes – especially poverty reduction and other measures to benefit the poor. This result focus also enables and ensures that outcomes are monitored – a task designated to the government itself, although the Bank has parallel systems and also needs to approve a government's monitoring mechanisms and results. Third, the PRSP is to be *comprehensive,* recognizing the multidimensional nature of poverty at all levels of society (grassroots, private sector, civil society and in government institutions) and in all sectors (structural, social and human aspects of development), which are to be seen together in a complex and integrated whole. Fourth, the PRSP must be *partnership-oriented*, generating a poverty-reduction programme based on the cooperative efforts – and synergetic effect – of national government, domestic stakeholders and the wider development community of external donors. Fifth and finally, the PRSP must be based on a *long-term perspective* for poverty reduction and economic planning, which includes institutional reforms and the improvement of capacity-building focused on good governance principles, anti-corruption measures and accountability in all forms (IMF and IDA 1999; World Bank 2004c; IMF 2005).

Today the PRSP is an integral element in how the Bank functions, internally and externally, and few question or ever think about it. The PRSP has become the air which Bank staffers breathe. Its general underlying principle is to facilitate a country-led development process, as reflected by its integrated ideas of participation, ownership and partnership with other development actors and stakeholder. PRSPs are nominally written by developing-country governments to outline the macroeconomic, structural and social initiatives and reforms they intend to undertake in order to promote growth and poverty alleviation. The PRSP model has triggered dramatic changes in how the Bank engages with its clients. The major overarching shift concerns the deliberate recasting of the donor–recipient relationship, with a shift from a top-heavy to a bottom–up approach. Integral to this new form of partnership are the ideas of participation and ownership among the client government, and thereby a general rejection of Bank-imposed policy conditions. As such, the PRSP has been important in altering the structural set-up of aid relations. But the PRSP is a document that outlines a government's national development strategy: it has no direct linkages to aid disbursement. The Bank is still free to choose which elements of any given PRSP it wishes to support. Although the PRSP needs to pass the Bank's board to become effective, this endorsement does not necessarily mean that the Bank commits itself to supporting *all* the proposed initiatives. That decision is contingent upon other Bank-controlled processes and mechanisms instigated as part of the PRSP model, illustrating how the 'freedom' of the PRSP mechanism is paralleled with the introduction of new governance mechanisms.

## PRSPs and Aid Disbursement

With the PRSP, policy making has become separate from aid financing. Engaging in the PRSP process signals the client state's interest to enter into a partnership with the Bank and thus to qualify for concessional lending within the timeframe and validity of the PRSP – usually between two and five years. As noted, the PRSP instrument is not directly attached to the financial aspects of aid disbursement, but the partnership it facilitates involves other instruments that outline the Bank's business plan and its lending portfolio, namely the Country Assistance Strategy (CAS) and the Poverty Reduction Support Credit (PRSC) respectively.[16] These involve mechanisms that rely on processes separate to the PRSP: while the PRSP is to reflect the country's own strategy, the CAS is the Bank's own programming exercise from which the PRSC – as the Bank's budget support mechanism – is derived. Whereas the government is responsible for and supposed to have ownership of the PRSP, the Bank is in charge of the two other instruments through which it is able to exert control over what it funds and influence the government's own plans. Through the CAS, the Bank stipulates its strategic focus in a country as drawn from its own policy framework and the assessment of priorities within the frame of the country's PRSP. The CAS lays out the dynamic and detailed plans for the Bank's advice, policies, lending and partnership arrangements. Basically the CAS highlights those aspects of a PRSP that the Bank intends to support financially via the PRSC, and indicates the level and composition of assistance to be provided on the basis of the strategy and the country's overall performance in these areas. The PRSC represents the financial aspect of aid relations with the Bank under the PRSP model, and thus answers more to the CAS than to the country's own poverty reduction strategy.

A government's access to loans, or the PRSC, is thus contingent upon producing a PRSP acceptable to the Bank. Yet, the Bank is not committed to supporting all government-proposed PRSP initiatives. An approved PRSP, moreover, is not only a requirement for embarking on the PRSC process involving close policy negotiations between the Bank and its counterpart. It also qualifies the country for debt relief under the Highly Indebted Poor Country (HIPC) initiative, as well as ensuring access to the IMF's Poverty Reduction and Growth Facility (PRGF).[17] Hence, an approved PRSP is more important for what it entails and opens than for the policies it outlines. The PRSP is a precondition for clients entering into partnership with the Bank and thus for gaining access to much needed loans and credits. Hence, the CAS and the PRSC, which come as integral parts of the partnership arrangement, represent important mechanisms enabling the Bank to retain control over the more important means it seemingly surrendered when implementing the new aid architecture as articulated in its PRSP model.

The PRSP's more indirect relation to aid disbursement reflects a basic problem of the new aid architecture. Although the focus is put on government participation in and ownership of the policy-making process and its results, there is no denying the fact that the policy document must have the Bank's approval to become effective and in order for the client to gain access to funding. However, since the financing mechanisms attached to the new aid architecture are still under the Bank's control, it remains dubious whether any de facto conversion of lopsided donor–recipient relations has taken place. Policies are now nominally the domain and responsibility of recipients, but the financial resources for underpinning and implementing these policies remain in the hands of the donor. As aid disbursements are now connected to client performance, the client remains accountable to the Bank for implementing its own policies. The national government is now made responsible for possible failure, being assessed against 'its own' policies – whereas during the previous SAP era, criticism was directed at the Bank and its policies and conditionalities. This shift – made possible by concepts like participation and ownership, being indicative of developmentality – is central to the new aid apparatus, which also has reinstalled the recipient state as both means and objective for Bank-supported lending.

## The Role of the State within the New Aid Architecture: A Field of Contestations

During the structural adjustment era from the late 1970s to the mid-1990s, the state had a diminished role as actor and objective in international development discourse. 'Development' was seen as being a matter of economic growth, to be achieved through the free play of market forces; and here the state represented an obstacle that would have to be overcome. The objective of economic growth was understood in rational and technical terms, but it was nevertheless highly political – as illustrated by the mantra of 'rolling back the state'. Bank policies reflected the worldview of Western elites at the end of the Cold War and the seminal ideological ascendancy of Thatcherism and Reaganomics. This was manifested in international development policy through bypassing the state as a development actor and the objective of dismantling the state, although the state remained the Bank's formal counterpart. The parallel drive towards privatization and state demotion promoted the upsurge in nongovernmental actors as both donors and recipients, leading to a general bypassing of the state throughout the international aid apparatus. The Bank as well the IMF – themselves made up of governments – followed along the same ideological trajectory through policies that sought to dismantle and roll back the state in order to minimize any restrictions to the free play of market forces caused by what were seen as cumbersome, ineffective state bureaucracies. Their promulgation of a pro-market, anti-state approach was highly politicized in the sense that Bank interventions were projected in opposition to economies organized around a state-led model. The state was also bypassed in the policy-making process and thus largely subject to policies drafted by the Bank and the Fund. With the advent of the new aid architecture has come a dramatic revamping of Bank rhetoric concerning the state, its role and its responsibilities on the level of structure and policy – as both actor and objective (see Mosley, Harrigan and Toye 1995; Hatcher 2007).

## The State on the Structural Level of the PRSP

With the new aid architecture, the state has been given a new and elevated role – at least nominally. The state is to be responsible not only for devising its own national poverty strategy, PRSP, to which all development activities in that particular country must relate, but also for implementing it through external financial support. Furthermore, the PRSP – as required by the international financial institutions (IFIs) – should be developed through a broad-based consultative government-led process involving all relevant national stakeholders – civil society, the private sector, and all branches of the state apparatus. This comprehensive approach invokes 'development efficiency', based on the assumption that a country-led process will engender ownership to the process and stipulated objectives, and that where there is ownership the client is perceived to be more committed and thus more efficient in implementing its PRSP. The broad consultative process is, moreover, seen as generating trust and alignment among the various actors involved, thereby enhancing mutual accountability and cooperation between the government and other stakeholders. The new aid architecture thus aims to reinstate 'agency' on behalf of the state, meaning the state moves from a passive to an active client – as illustrated by its role in producing the PRSP whereby the state is made the central node and coordinating actor.

There has been a significant growth in the use of budget support as the main aid modality with the emergence of the PRSP model. Rather than financing specific projects and programmes (with the Bank holding greater operational responsibility), the Bank now prefers the budget support mechanism – not only because it epitomizes the PRSP model, but also because it allows for a closer and more direct policy dialogue with government.[18] Budget support is not a new aid modality, but the extent to which it is used has grown rapidly, parallel to the Bank's overall implementation of the PRSP model. With budget support, the Bank now channels its aid directly into the client government's national budget via its ministry of finance, in support of the government's 'own' policies. Consequently responsibility and monitoring of aid spending are transferred to the government. A corollary to this has been the Bank's increased attention to the state apparatus' internal affairs and practices – the 'nature of the state' (Harrison 2004) – as signalled by the emphasis given to good governance policies, thus making the client state also an objective of its development assistance.

In practice, however, there is a distinction to be made between general budget support and sector budget support. While the former is an aid modality whereby money is given directly and unearmarked to a recipient government to support that government's own PRSP and priorities, the latter earmarks funding to particular sectors. The latter instrument is chosen when the Bank does not fully agree with a government's priorities and spending, or where the government or state apparatus are seen to be weak and fragile and thus subject to the Bank's fiduciary allocation mechanism. Should the Bank–client relation get derailed, or should the Bank deem the client's performance unsuitable for budget support, the Bank can opt for project or programme support – although these are not normally the preferred option, since they imply greater distance to the client's policy processes. The budget support modality, as implied with PRSC negotiations, gives the Bank a unique advantage in close country dialogue. To the Bank, budget support provides important opportunities for engaging in policy dialogue on a wide range of structural issues, especially those related to growth and structural reforms. Consequently, budget support not only implies the Bank's nominal endorsement of a client state's fiduciary and governance systems: it also provides a means for engaging directly in policy dialogue with that government on its internal matters. The better the Bank deems the government, the state apparatus and their institutional capacity, the more likely is it that general budget support will be chosen – and the converse: the worse the institutional capacities, the stronger the operational influence the Bank will seek. As the assessment of a client's governance system is based on highly subjective measures, and budget support is the preferred modality due to the policy dialogue it enables, the Bank might lower the benchmarks on governance to reap the benefits of policy dialogue.

To the Bank, the rationales for the shift to budget support largely parallel those of the PRSP: to move policy decisions closer to the affected beneficiaries, to increase sensitivity to national factors, to entrust the government with the development process, and to build ownership – and thus a commitment to the effective implementation and use of funds – through greater participation. Budget support is also seen as building capacity in the client's state apparatus and enhancing its accountability to external donors and domestic civil society alike (World Bank 1998).[19] The literature indicates two main underlying rationales for the Bank as regards budget support – one that relates to the donor side (see Lawson et al. 2003) and one that deals with the recipient side (see OECD 2006). The rationales largely parallel those of the PRSP in general. On the donor side, the desire for increased development effectiveness is the main rationale. That would enable a more concerted approach and help to overcome the highly fragmented, small ad hoc projects which on the aggregate level fail to deliver the expected results as well as potentially undermining the aid agencies' own objectives. Budget support aims at countering inefficient spending dictated by donor priorities and the high transaction costs deriving from the multitude of different reporting and accounting systems of the plethora of small-scale projects. Such projects are now seen as undermining the state system that aid agencies try to support and build, by creating structures that run parallel to the state itself. Multiple projects decentralized from the state did not, as initially expected, serve to reduce corruption in development management – instead, they nurtured it. The Bank's rationale for budget support relating to the recipient side concerns its contribution to building state institutional capacity and enhancing government accountability to donors and citizens.

The resurgence and elevation of the state as an actor on the structural level is intrinsically related to budget support as a corollary to the PRSP model's increased attention to policy processes internal to the state apparatus. With the PRSP model and budget support as the main aid disbursement mechanisms, the client state has become the fulcrum in partnership relations involving the Bank, after having been reinstated as an active actor by the new aid architecture. The client state is no longer a passive actor bypassed or dismantled by the international aid apparatus. Having been given responsibility for devising its own policy strategy and for managing the financial resources, the state has ascended to a pivotal role within the new aid architecture. The process of including the state as an active agent is interrelated with the inclusion of the state on the policy level as a result of the anti-corruption agenda and the greater focus on good governance issues. The greater the role of the state, the higher are the demands from the Bank. When there is discontinuity between the state's ascribed role and its capacity to fill that role, policies tend to focus on various aspects of capacity-building. The state thus holds the dual role of both actor and objective within the new aid apparatus, both of which depend on the condition of the state: a state the Bank deems weak will be less likely to receive general budget support than states aspiring to the credentials of good governance, which are more in line with the self-governance ceded them under the new aid architecture. States deemed weak tend to be made the objective of assistance in order for them to assume the role ascribed by the PRSP modality. Such state and capacity-building efforts are, in the Bank discourse, termed 'enhancing good governance', 'public sector reform' and 'capacity-building'.

## The State on the Policy Level of the PRSP

The prevalent role assigned to the state within the PRSP framework evolved in tandem with a growing understanding that the state had to be included in all sorts and at all levels of development assistance. This follows the discarding of the rigid economic growth perspective that saw the state as an obstacle. The 1997 World Development Report,[20] 'The State in a Changing World', focused on the role of the state and its impact on development effectiveness – what the state should do, how it should do it, and how it could do it better (World Bank 1997). This WDR was written against the backdrop of Wolfensohn's 'Corruption as Cancer' speech (see above; cf. Wolfensohn 2005a) and raised the profile of governance and corruption issues throughout the international aid apparatus. These issues, moreover, have brought the state to the centre of current development policy. Parallel to the agency entrusted to the state by the Bank on the structural level, the state has become a development objective – contrarily to earlier attempts to dismantle it. Today, and somewhat ambiguously, credible and functional state institutions are not only a prerequisite for Bank partnership with that state: they also constitute the objective of the Bank's ongoing work. This is based on the rationale that if the client government is to be responsible for tasks previously carried out by the Bank, the Bank needs to be convinced that the government and its state apparatus abide by the principles of good governance, as well as having the capacity to manage the processes they have been entrusted. The wide proliferation of good governance and public sector reform policies are thus means to build better state apparatuses and provide them with the basics for managing their own development processes.

The 1997 WDR was instrumental in reshaping the Bank's view on the state. Instead of pursuing policies aimed at dismantling the state, the view now is that a more effective state system is necessary if it is to implement its own policies and to follow the Bank's requirements of accountability for the state to be granted these tasks. This in turn is based on the assumption that countries with good economic policies and strong institutional governance capacity grow faster because they provide a good policy environment for development. And so the state has been recast, from an obstacle to a facilitator of growth.

> Development – economic, social and sustainable – without an effective state is impossible. It is increasingly recognised that an effective state – not a minimal one – is central to economic and social development, but more as a partner and facilitator than as director. States should work to complement markets, not replace them. (World Bank 1997: 18)

The WDR signals a break with the previous era: the objective is no longer 'a minimal state' but an effective partner and facilitator aligned to the Bank's discourse. The report emphasizes two strategies for making the state more effective. The first is to focus the state's activities to match its capability, on the assumption that too many states try to do too much with too limited resources. 'Getting governments better focused on the core public activities that are crucial to development will enhance the effectiveness' (World Bank 1997: iii). The second strategy is to improve state capabilities by reinvigorating public institutions through incentives to deliver better – to 'give public officials the incentive to do their jobs better and to be more flexible, but that also provides restraints to check arbitrary and corrupt behaviour' (ibid.). According to the report, this calls for an agenda of action for good governance and public sector reform.

> These reforms have political implications but do not require the overhaul of institutions … All it takes is the political decision to make the change … This kind of institutional reform involves wrenching changes in the way government agencies think and act … such change is absolutely essential if the capability of the state is ever to improve. The two together – good policies and more capable state institutions to implement them – produce much faster economic development … Reform will also encounter considerable political opposition. (ibid.: 13)

The 1997 WDR marked an early step in the formation of the new aid architecture, altering Bank–client state relations and signalling an eagerness to engage in political reform among recipients – highly unlikely prior to Wolfensohn's 'cancer of corruption' speech. 'Assessing Aid' (World Bank 1998), a Bank report that aimed to grasp when and how aid works best, follows in the same trajectory. Central to the report is the interconnection between ideas and money in development assistance: money can have a big impact, but only when countries have good economic policies and institutions: aid works best in a good policy environment. Money, it is argued, can work once countries reform, and ideas work better than money in generating reform and improving public services. Ideas and the knowledge side of development – donor knowledge creation and dissemination – are seen as critical in helping countries to reform, and in creating states that can effectively provide public services to the citizenry.[21] These ideas were further strengthened through the work of Burnside and Dollar in a Bank working paper on 'Aid, Policies and Growth' (1997, 2004).[22] This work supported the same conclusion – which by now had become mainstream to the Bank – but went further in arguing that not only does the impact of aid depend directly upon the quality of state institutions and their policies, but also that there is no support for the converse hypothesis: that aid has the same positive effect everywhere. These results were incorporated in the Bank's 2004 Global Monitoring Report, which shows that aid in fact acts to reduce growth in countries with 'bad' policies, whereas it contributes to growth in countries with 'good' policies (World Bank 2004b: chapter 11; cf. Ritzen 2005). This gave rise to the Bank mantra that 'good policies matter', meaning that aid is effective only where policies are good, which, to the Bank, translated into a focus on producing good, enabling policy environments in order to increase aid effectiveness. In 2006 the Bank, at its annual meeting in Singapore, approved the 'Governance and Anti-corruption Strategy', which states that the Bank's governance and anti-corruption work 'follows from its mandate to reduce poverty – a capable and accountable state creates opportunities for poor people, provides better services, and improves development outcomes' (World Bank 2007: 4). Framing these ideas within the efficiency regime helped to depoliticize the approach, toning down conflict between the Bank's apolitical mandate and the increased attention given to the internal policies of client states.

Together, these ideas have instilled the state on policy level within the new aid architecture, with the aim of securing good governance and state institutions on the recipient side so that they can carry out the tasks designated by the PRSP model and ensure aid effectiveness. The PRSP framework identifies the state as the prime actor for facilitating the overall development process – but, with the recognition that aid is ineffective and even counteractive in countries with a 'bad' policy environment, this leads to greater attention to state practices and how it manages its facilitating role within the new aid architecture. The proliferating good governance realm seeks to direct the focus to the state's internal workings and its capacity to fill its designated role as a facilitator of development. With the PRSP and the good governance agenda, the state has become both a means and objective in the development process. In consequence, state (re)formation has resurged as a dominant part of the international development discourse.

## Good Governance and the New Aid Architecture

As a concept, good governance made its first appearance in a few World Bank documents in 1989, but it was during the late 1990s that it emerged as a central concept in development assistance (Doornbos 2003; Weaver 2010). As an integral part of both the policy and structure of aid, good governance is at the heart of the current discourse of development. It sets the focus on state processes of decision making, and the processes by which decisions are implemented or not. More broadly, the good governance agenda is integral to, and reflects, the Bank's governance and anti-corruption strategy, which focuses on 'public sector dysfunction (the 'symptom') to assist countries in integrating institutional, regulatory and economic reforms (the 'fundamentals')'.[23] Governance and anti-corruption are intertwined, but are not identical. The World Bank defines governance 'as the traditions and institutions by which authority in a country is exercised for the common good' (Kaufmann 2006).[24] Corruption, by contrast, is traditionally defined more narrowly as the 'abuse of public office for private gains' (ibid.).[25] Corruption is seen as a symptom of bad governance – countries that have got their fundamentals wrong. Corruption, it is argued,

> undermines development by distorting the rule of law and weakening the institutional foundation on which economic growth depends ... Corruption sabotages policies and programs that aim to reduce poverty, so attacking corruption is critical to the achievement of the Bank's overarching mission of poverty reduction ... To reduce the corrosive impact of corruption in a sustainable way it is important to go beyond the symptoms to tackle the causes of corruption.[26]

A corollary of seeing corruption as a symptom and result of bad governance is the Bank's commitment to promote good governance policies through public sector reform programmes. 'A fundamental role of the Bank is to help governments work better in our client countries

... building efficient and accountable public sector institutions'.[27] The Bank does not, however, provide any definition as to what 'good governance' is. Instead, it applies a range of measures – in 2000/2001 these amounted to 194 different measures (Kaufmann and Kraay 2002)[28] – which are compiled into six aggregate indicators concerning the quality of governance of a country to underpin the political, economic and institutional dimension of governance: voice and accountability, political stability and absence of violence, government effectiveness, regulatory quality, rule of law, and control of corruption (World Bank 2006). The Bank sees governance as referring to 'the manner in which public officials and public institutions acquire and exercise the authority to provide public goods and services, including the delivery of basic services, infrastructure, and a sound investment climate' (World Bank 2007: 67). The Bank is clear in its rationale for governance work. The main purpose 'is to strengthen the ability of developing countries to fight poverty' – a rationale which largely parallels that of the PRSP in particular and the new aid architecture more broadly, while also pointing to aspects of developmentality as inherent to the Bank's efforts in state formation.[29]

Governance has become a key concept in the international development discourse, reflecting the enhanced attention to the political dimension of client countries and the transformation in focus from micro-level to macro-level issues (Hyden, Court and Mease 2004). Similarly, bad governance is increasingly regarded as being among the root causes of underdevelopment, which has led the Bank and other donor institutions to tie their aid and loans to conditions of reform to ensure good governance, regardless of the lack of a definition and that the term may mean different things to different people. Hyden, Court and Mease try to make sense of governance, arguing that the multiplicity of views tends to crystallize along two separate lines – 'one regarding the substantive content of governance, the other regarding its character in practice' (ibid.: 12). As to the substantive content of governance, a distinction can be made between those who see 'governance as concerned with the rules of conducting public affairs versus those who see it as steering or controlling public affairs' (ibid.), where the first concerns institutional determinants of choice and the latter focuses on how choices get implemented. As to the character of governance, a distinction can be made between those who see governance as related to results and those who see it related to processes. Cross-cutting these divides is thus the distinction between those who view governance as something static (rules and results) connected to the institutional set-up of governance systems, and those who view it as something that unfolds in practice (steering and process) and related to the practical task of governing. Hyden, Court and Mease sum up governance as referring to 'the creation and maintenance of a system of rules that govern the public arena and thus regulate how state, civil society, and market-based actors relate to and interact with each other' (ibid.: 191). This is, however, a description based on the analysis of governance programmes and interventions in various sectors, and undercuts the normative aspects that donors need to implement governance reforms.

Pomerantz, herself a former Bank empolyee, states that, '[i]n a nutshell, good governance means three things to most donors: increased government transparency and accountability, with checks on corruption and human rights abuses; political decentralisation … [and] multiparty democracy' (Pomerantz 2004: 41). This draws attention to the dual view on governance as referring to both the institutional set-up and the performance of governance systems, as reflected in the Bank's view on governance, both of which relate to the objective of the Bank's reform agenda of establishing new and altering existing institutions and their practices concerning governance.

Good governance came as a result of the general recaulking of aid relations, as granting clients greater operational responsibility brought increased attention to the internal working of recipient-state institutions. The challenging tasks facing the Bank – to maintain the loyalty and consent of African politicians while persuading them to adopt policies potentially challenging their power base (Moore 2007) – thus rest on the ability to craft conditions that can prevent questions from arising about who rules and how. This draws attention to developmentality and the ideological superstructure of the new aid architecture – the general concepts integral to international development discourse of participation and partnership – which in the Bank realm have become operationalized and translated into the PRSP model. This set-up transfers responsibility to clients, but it also includes mechanisms that enable the Bank to retain control, as demonstrated by the importance of CAS – as the Bank's policy response to the client's PRSP – and the PRSC – as a lending mechanism, in the form of budget support, and financial response to the implementation of PRSP/CAS.

The presentation above and the formation of developmentality within the Bank draw on official discourse and a top–down view from the leadership. This makes it possible to consider 'developmentality' as an expression of the World Bank's explicit *intent* of state formation under the auspices of the good governance agenda and by engaging the client in the new aid architecture through the formation of partnership. Developmentality recognizes that the power of the Bank – and of donors in general – is based primarily not on its capacity for direct coercion, but on its primacy over development knowledge, enabling it to frame the conditions under which the recipient's freedom is exercised, as facilitated by various techniques whereby client governments are persuaded to agree to the Bank's discursive realm and aid architecture.

There is no necessary causation or analogy between discourse and practice although they might be interrelated, as per my argument in the introduction regarding the need to analyse both discourses and practices of development. This chapter has discussed and outlined the formation of the new aid architecture within the Bank as a framework and stepping stone for the developmentality concept, showing the intentionality of revamping aid relations and how the new structure granting the recipient greater freedom and responsibility over the development process in form and content are accompanied by other mechanisms enabling the donor to retain control and thereby potentially undermining the new structure itself. In the coming chapters, however, the analytical attention is moved from the discourses and structures of development to the practice. Before that, the following section demonstrates a similar discrepancy between order and practice by drawing on the literature. It thus points to the present chapter by demonstrating the challenges of a verbatim implementation of the bottom–up perspectives nominally championed by the PRSP model, while also foreshadowing next chapter's focus on the epistemic knowledge battles found within the Bank. The section shows the making of the 2000/01 World Development Report (WDR) (World Bank 2000), which involved processes that were intended to draw on the girding ideas of the new aid architecture – participation and bottom–up approaches, as articulated in the PRSP model. In fact, however, the policy-making process was to become an illustration of and challenge to the ideas inherent in the PRSP model, in what Robert Wade succinctly termed 'Showdown at the World Bank' (Wade 2002b).

## How to Attack Poverty

The World Development Report was meant to focus on the girding ideas of PRSP on both structural and policy levels. By being more participatory and inclusive, the WDR was to draw extensively on a consultation exercise with the poor, later known as 'Voices of the Poor'. This was something that the Bank had been running since 1998, involving a collection of voices 'of more than 60,000 poor women and men from 60 countries, in an unprecedented effort to understand poverty from the perspective of the poor themselves'.[30] This structural change was meant to inform the policy level and shift attention 'from growth towards non-income aspects of poverty and from hard-nosed technical subjects such as industrial technology policy and irrigation investment towards 'soft-nosed' issues – education, health, participation, legal reform and cultural projects' (Wade 2000b: 135). In contrast to previous WDRs, and according to the Bank, the preparation of the 2000/01 report 'Attacking Poverty' was to be 'highly consultative, establishing early and ongoing dialogue contact with the main constituencies outside the Bank' (Schech and Vas Dev 2007: 182). From the outset, the report was to embrace the overarching ideas integral to the new aid architecture and the PRSP model's holistic approaches to transferring agency and power to recipients – all of which mark important points in the 'participatory turn in development' (Henkel and Stirrat 2001). A short narrative of processes and challenges in making the report reveals the practical challenges of implementing ideas central to the new aid architecture.

## Making the Report

The World Development Report is the Bank's annual flagship publication,[31] and aims both to consolidate existing knowledge and to indicate new pathways for the Bank. Like most other documents deriving from the Bank, the WDR is not an official policy document, since it is not produced or ratified by the executive board. It does, however, represent the view of staff and management (Kanbur 2000) and thus the general knowledge formation within the Bank.[32] Its message must reflect, and not offend, the ideological preferences of key members, while also being 'backed by empirical evidence and made to look "technical"' (Wade 2001: 1435). The making of the 2000/01 WDR saw the battle between ideas at loggerheads, described by Kanbur as the disagreement between two broad policy constellations within the Bank and their institutional bases of 'finance' and 'civil society' (Kanbur 2001).[33]

Ravi Kanbur was brought in as director to head the WDR team by the Bank's chief economist Joseph Stiglitz. This nomination was approved by Bank president Wolfensohn.[34] 'The director of the WDR has one of the most important idea-controlling positions in the Bank, for the director has the most important say about the content' (Wade 2001: 1436). Both Kanbur and Stiglitz were known to be sympathetic to Wolfensohn's 'civil society' constellation as sketched out in the PRSP model (Wolfensohn 1999) – which mattered for their positions compared to others who argued that such 'anti-poverty' measures would mean slower growth if translated into operational Bank policy. The first WDR draft stated the proposition that 'growth is the engine of poverty reduction', but went on to emphasize 'what is less well understood': that other ingredients are central to poverty reduction, as evidenced by improved poverty reduction even when growth performance is only constant. These ingredients are empowerment, security and opportunity. In contrast to the conventionally dominant 'finance' constellation, the draft version asserted that typical liberal and laissez-faire thinking did not automatically help the poor, and could sometimes worsen their condition. Kanbur's view draws extensively on the Voices of the Poor exercise. This 'civil society' agenda provoked opposition inside and outside the Bank, with critics arguing that it short-changed economic growth and overemphasized the negative effects of income inequality on growth by asserting the positive effects of inequality for growth by strengthening incentives for greater effort and risk taking. Critics were sceptical as to why democracy, empowerment of the poor and making state institutions more accountable were to be given priority over growth: 'get rid of this stuff'; these issues 'pander to noisy and nosy NGOs'; 'the Bank should not be in the business of empowerment' (Bank staff quoted in Wade 2001: 1437).

Yale economist T.N. Srinivasan criticized the report for lacking causal analysis, asserting that its conceptual foundations – security, opportunity and empowerment – could at best be termed diagnostics and at worst three symptoms of poverty, and could thus not provide an analytical engine for poverty reduction (Wade 2001: 1437). Later, when member governments weighed in, the comments of the U.S. Treasury read like marching orders (Wade 2002a). This body stressed the need to emphasize higher economic growth and freer markets as the route to such growth, while demanding less emphasis on the broadening of world income distribution, which was seen as being bad for growth. Then treasury secretary Summers, himself a former chief economist at the Bank, said that 'discussing poverty reduction without emphasising economic growth and open markets was like Hamlet without the prince' (Wade 2001: 1437).

In directing work on the WDR, Kanbur found himself having to try to accommodate the agendas of both 'civil society' and 'finance' – the former reflected by the Bank president, chief economist Stiglitz, the PRSP model and Voices of the Poor, while the latter reflected conventional economist thinking inside and outside the Bank and was the view urged by the Bank's most dominant shareholder. Kanbur and his team, who saw themselves as serious social scientists, were dismayed at having to accommodate interests outside the WDR mandate that was supposed to ensure their complete independence. Kanbur conceded ground to the critics in the second WDR draft by realigning the order of argument and making 'substantive changes in emphasis in the "growth and openness first" direction' (Wade 2001: 1438). He then realized he had gone too far, and tried to bring the argument back to the first draft version. However, by this time Kanbur was without the protection offered by Stiglitz, who had stepped down as chief economist as part of the deal that Wolfensohn had made with the U.S. Treasury to gain a second term as Bank president. Kanbur's senior management now refused any return to the first draft, pushing instead for major revisions, thereby putting Kanbur on a slippery slope with the WDR.

Pressured by the U.S. Treasury and powerful Bank economists, Ravi Kanbur faced the choice of either yielding to their demands for a more 'finance'-oriented report, or fighting to protect his original draft but with the risk that the Bank would dissociate itself from it as 'Kanbur's report', condemning it and sweeping it under the carpet. Instead, he resigned, thereby forcing the Bank to claim 'ownership' of the report as the work of an independent team of social scientists, not toys of the U.S. Treasury.

Kanbur's deputy then took over. Work on the WDR proceeded with the message of the first draft largely intact, although three substantive changes were made in the final version.[35] First, a chapter to show that growth was good for poverty reduction was added. Second, the chapter on market reforms was given a stronger 'finance' twist. Third, the final version severely truncated the argument that the Asian crisis was due to rapid opening of financial markets. All these changes were dear to the conventional 'finance' economists at the Bank, in American academia and in the U.S. Treasury, not least since the Clinton administration had prioritized free capital market as the basis of the world economy (Wade 2001, 2002a, 2002b).

## Listening to Whom?

The original attempt of the 2000/01 WDR to go beyond standard economic analysis, as integral to the PRSP, was contingent on two key inputs: the conceptualization of poverty as a deprivation of basic capabilities rather than merely low income; and the participatory input provided by the Voices of the Poor initiative (Narayan 2000; Narayan et al. 2000; Narayan and Petesch 2002) and the WDR consultation with a global civil society. The Voices of the Poor initiative and its role in the WDR indicate the Bank's well-intended efforts to link participatory approaches with empowerment and the eradication of poverty. Schech and Vas Dev provide an intricate deconstruction of the initiative and the way in which the WDR was informed by a meticulous concern for how 'more than 60,000 poor women and men from over 60 countries'[36] defined 'their needs and interests, and what they consider to be the nature, cause and effects of poverty' (Schech and Vas Dev 2007: 184).

Schech and Vas Dev question '[o]ne of the key philosophical premises of the participatory turn in development … that those most affected by interventions should participate in shaping the character of these interventions' (Schech and Vas Dev 2007: 185). They use the concepts of 'participation' and 'empowerment' as litmus tests when comparing the second volume of *Voices of the Poor,* specially designated to inform the WDR by involving 'open-ended participatory methods' (Narayan et al. 2000: 2), with the 'Attacking Poverty' report. Involving the poor draws not only on their role as 'targets' but also their first-hand knowledge of poverty: 'There are 2.8 billion poverty experts, the poor themselves. Yet the development discourse about poverty has been dominated by the perspectives and expertise [of] those who are not poor – professionals, politicians and agency officials' (ibid.). Despite their lack of education and skills (ibid.: 237) 'the poor are portrayed as being rich in knowledge about their own life' (Schech and Vas Dev 2007: 185–86).[37] Their relevance in giving an authentic voice to Bank processes and policies is thus contingent on two assumptions: first, that the poor are in a position to provide accurate and truthful information; and second, that this information is absorbed and utilized by Bank policy makers (ibid.: 186). Schech and Vas Dev deconstruct both these assumptions by showing the practical disconnect between voice and power. Influence is premised on participation in decision-making processes, and that is not provided by merely voicing and listening to concerns. Rather, they go on to say, agency for change is vested in the powerful, whereas 'the powerless can only hope and pray' (ibid.: 188) for inclusion.

While *Voices of the Poor* was intended to provide WDR policy makers with insights into poverty from the perspective of the poor, the Bank also invited global civil society to comment on earlier WDR drafts. This consultation provides another example of how the Bank understands and utilizes 'participatory approaches'. The Bank invited to broad civil society consultation through an electronic discussion forum, held over the course of six weeks in early 2000. However, of the electronic respondents, only 44 per cent came from the South and 56 per cent from the North, 'and the rural South remained completely silent. Evidently, only the urban elites of the developed and developing world had access to the new technologies required to participate … and the poor remained on the margins' (Schech and Vas Dev 2007: 190). The active participants

– who presented themselves as teachers, researchers, company managers, development bureaucrats, finance ministry officials and agitators – did not reflect the poor or civil society of the South, whose participation was supposed to have been encouraged. Even more devastating was the absence of Bank workers' participation, which effectively dashed any aspirations for an active debate, while also truncating how the consulted voices were listened to and actually used in the policy-making process.

The making of the 2000 WDR illustrates contestation to a verbatim implementation of the new aid architecture and the bottom–up mechanisms of the PRSP. The challenges concern not only the relationship between the Bank and the multiple, diversified poor, but also to knowledge battles between 'civil society' and 'finance' perspectives within the Bank – itself illustrating that one should not take the official discourse as the only version of what is going on and that the formal order does not unambiguously direct or translate into practice. The 'Showdown at the World Bank' demonstrates that the Bank's macroeconomists remain largely hegemonic, although the WDR intended to project the views of the 'usually subordinated minority of non-economist social scientists' (Fox 2003: 522). Schech and Vas Dev conclude their scrutiny of the Bank's participatory methods by stating that 'the decisions and policies at the end of the process do not radically diverge from those previously pursued … [and] by involving the poor in the policies that affect them, the World Bank is able to present its policy recommendations as something the poor themselves request, rendering its own interests, power and agency invisible in the process' (Schech and Vas Dev 2007: 194).

The narrative of the WDR reflects wider concerns of implementing the new aid architecture, not only because of the challenges of restructuring aid relations by flipping top–down approaches bottom–up, but also because of the knowledge this flip potentially conveys and the resistant reception it faces within the Bank's knowledge battlefield, which tends to embrace knowledge of the 'finance' agenda over that of the 'civil society', regardless of whether the 'civil society' perspective is promoted by actors internal or external to the Bank. Similar schisms and knowledge battles were also conspicuous during my own experience within the Bank.

## Notes

1. An illustration: while Bank staff in general were highly attentive to the PRSP model during my fieldwork for this research in 2005, they were less

concerned about it when I later did research for other projects related to the PRSP (see Sending and Lie 2009) with informants questioning its relevance, asserting 'no one speaks about the PRSP anymore'. Tellingly, a friend who worked for two years for the Bank on health issues and fiscal discipline had never encountered the concepts of PRSP, CDF, CAS or PRSC in his work, despite their importance for the Bank's partnership formation and policy processes. Obviously, this change is not only due to temporal factors but is also a result of the scope of my research, and the part of the Bank with which I was engaged.

2. The quotation is from the plaque of the statue in the World Bank. There are four unique copies of this statue, which was donated in 1995 by Merck Pharmaceutical Company who delivered the medicine. Two other sculptures are located at partner institutions of the riverblindness programme – at the Merck World Headquarters in New York, and at the Carter Center in Atlanta, Georgia. A fourth statue is found on a roundabout in the middle of Ouagadougou in Burkina Faso. The one placed in the Japanese Garden at the Carter Center reads, inter alia, 'Now the demise of this ancient scourge is in sight, thanks to a drug'. For the OCP, see http://documents.worldbank.org/curated/en/2014/06/19697609/onchocerciasis-control-programme-ocp-african-programme-onchocerciasis-control-apoc-historical-timeline (accessed 27 April, 2015). There are no pictures of the statue, but several *real* pictures of the *commonplace image* of a boy leading a man. Mallaby (2005) and Ritzen (2005: 136) also make a similar point regarding the statue.
3. None of my informants had given the statue any particular thought before I asked about it. One day, having coffee with one informant in the restaurant next to the statue, we went over to it for her to have a closer look: 'Yes, I see your point. But I don't think either you or the Bank should put too much into it – it's a statue. ... but obviously, it can be read as symbolizing the vagrant and undetermined developing nation groping in the dark in need of a shepherd'.
4. As Marshall notes, Wolfensohn may have been the only president who actively sought the position, and 'with an energy level that few can parallel, set out to make his mark on the institution' (Marshall 2008: 50).
5. Cited in www.washingtonpost.com/wp-dyn/articles/A12326-2004Dec19.html. Accessed 27 April, 2015.
6. *Washington Post* (23 January 2005): 'A Boss for the World Bank'; *Financial Times* (24 January 2005): 'After Wolfensohn'; *Guardian* (25 January 2005): 'Wanted: Big Hitter'.
7. www.worldbank.org/b-span.
8. Reprinted in Wolfensohn 2005a: 45–54.
9. Member countries buy shares in the Bank to help to build its capital and borrowing power. The voting power of each member country is determined by the value of its 'capital subscription'. Net donors are thus those countries paying in more compared to what they borrow.
10. In 1999 the Bank president stated: 'My colleagues and I decided that in order to map our own course for the future, we needed to know about *our clients as individuals*' (Narayan 2000, emphasis added).

11. Also often referred to as Structural Adjustment Loans (SALs).
12. Williamson (2000: 252–53) describes the Washington Consensus in ten points: (1) fiscal discipline; (2) redirection of public expenditure priorities towards fields offering both high economic returns and the potential to improve income distribution, such as primary health care, primary education, and infrastructure; (3) tax reform (to lower marginal rates and broaden the tax base); (4) interest rate liberalization; (5) competitive exchange rate; (6) trade liberalization; (7) liberalization and inflows of foreign direct investment; (8) privatization; (9) deregulation (abolishing barriers to entry and exit); and (10) secure property rights.
13. The first category, *structural,* comprises: (1) good and clean government; (2) justice system; (3) financial system; and (4) social safety net and social programmes. The second sector, *human,* comprises: (5) education and knowledge institutions; and (6) health and population. The third category, *physical,* comprises (7) water and sewerage; (8) energy; (9) roads and transportation, and telecommunication; and (10) environmental and cultural issues. The fourth, a residual *specific strategies* category, consists of: (11) rural strategy; (12) urban strategy; and (13) private-sector strategy.
14. According to Mallaby's biography of Wolfensohn (Mallaby 2004), Wolfensohn himself was thrilled about devising the CDF, but when he first presented it to selected staff, they apparently responded that his framework was actually what they were already doing. Nevertheless, Wolfensohn made the ideas Bank-wide and institutionalized. Wolfensohn's earlier thoughts on the CDF are also reflected in 'The Message of Kampala', an address to the United Nations Economic Commission for Africa on 27 January 1998, which drew on his meeting in Uganda with twelve African heads of state (see Wolfensohn 2005c).
15. Initially there was some confusion over the difference between CDF and PRSP. Both emerged from similar development thinking during the 1990s; but whereas CDF was concerned mainly with poverty reduction and the processes of development, the PRSP was intended primarily to link debt relief – the Highly Indebted Poor Countries (HIPC) initiative – to poverty reduction. In the six months following the launch of the PRSP this was hotly debated in the Bank and the Fund, ending with agreement that PRSP should apply the CDF principles and that the two initiatives were to be mutually reinforcing.
16. The CAS, as a country planning document, was formerly one of the Bank's most tightly held documents. 'Its current form and public disclosure emerged from sometimes difficult negotiations. Not surprisingly, candor has been a casualty of the evolving process and its public face, and the documents of today tend more toward blandness, *with striking similarities in language and issues among countries*' (Marshall 2008: 67; emphasis added).
17. The PRGF replaced the IMF's Enhanced Structural Adjustment Facility (ESAF) as a result of the transition from the SAP to the PRSP era.
18. This latter point is explored at greater length in chapters 5 and 6.
19. The ideas behind the shift to budget support and thus greater involvement of the client state evolved from the early 1990s. Although it was first con-

demned, the World Bank in 1992 released what was to become known as the Wapenhans report, after it was leaked to the public (World Bank 1992). After reviewing 1,800 World Bank-funded projects in 113 countries in the early 1990s, Wapenhans concluded that the World Bank's lending portfolio was under severe pressure, and that this pressure was not transitory but due to deep-rooted problems with project management, which must be diagnosed and resolved. Basically, there was too little return and output from projects, which were seen to deviate too much from the local context. The report criticized the small, highly fragmented and ad hoc projects of the Bank for not delivering results and thereby undermining the Bank's own objectives. The report recommended an increase in country-level performance management over a country portfolio management, stressing local ownership and that the disbursement of aid should shift from loan approval to a system based on performance and project impact.

20. The World Development Report (WDR) is the Bank's annual flagship publication. Each WDR is devoted to specific topics, or fads, of development, and has the twin objectives of consolidating existing knowledge within the Bank on that particular matter as well as stimulating debate on new directions of development policy. The WDR is thus instrumental in reflecting and shaping the Bank discourse on a range of themes. For a list of various WDRs, see www.worldbank.org/wdr. See also next section on 'How to Attack Poverty'.
21. Indicative of the Bank's shift in focus to ideas and knowledge as paramount aspects of development is the 1998 World Development Report 'Knowledge for Development'.
22. The paper was later published in the *American Economic Review* (Burnside and Dollar 2000), and a 'Revisiting the Evidence'-version appeared as a World Bank working paper in 2004.
23. From http://www.worldbank.org/wbi/governance/about (accessed 27 April 2015).
24. This definition includes three dimensions. The first is the political dimension, i.e. the process by which those in authority are selected, monitored and replaced, which subscribes to democratic principles and the rule of law. The second is the economic dimension, i.e. government's capacity to effectively manage its resources and implement sound policies. The third is the institutional respect dimension, i.e. the respect of citizens and the state for the country's institutions (Kaufmann 2006).
25. An alternative, but not yet institutionalized, definition of corruption that seeks to include corruption in the private sector and its implication for the state, reads 'the privatization of public policy' (ibid.).
26. This definition of corruption is from the World Bank's official website, accessed 24 February 2007, www.worldbank.org/corruption (page discontinued).
27. From http://go.worldbank.org/SGO4LFRSS0 (accessed 27 April 2015).
28. The number of measures increases regularly. By 2009, there were 440 different variables. See http://info.worldbank.org/governance/wgi/index.aspx#faq (accessed 27 April 2015).

29. See http://go.worldbank.org/APQ5N1BF30 (accessed 27 April 2015).
30. See http://go.worldbank.org/H1N8746X10. This 'participatory research initiative ... chronicles the struggles and aspirations of poor people for a life of dignity' (ibid.), and has been published by the Bank as a multi-volume *Voices of the Poor.* The three volumes are titled *Can Anyone Hear Us?*, *Crying Out for Change*, and *From Many Lands* (see Narayan 2000; Narayan et al. 2000; Narayan and Petesch 2002).
31. The World Development Report is the Bank's major analytical publication. Each year it focuses on a particular aspect of development, selected by the Bank's president. Each WDR team is headed by a senior Bank staff member, supported by a team of staff and consultants, under the guidance of the chief economist.
32. A review of WDRs over the last ten years is like a review of the evolution of development economics over that period. That is no coincidence, as the objective of the WDR is both to consolidate existing knowledge on a particular aspect of development as well as to stimulate debate on new directions for development policy.
33. Easterly, a former Bank economist, makes a similar distinction between 'searchers' and 'planners' (Easterly 2006: 6). Such disagreement is a prevalent feature internal to the Bank, as illustrated by the contestation between the social development network and PREM network, outlined in the next chapter.
34. Unless otherwise specified, this section draws on Wade's presentation of the contested process of making the 2000/01 WDR (see Wade 2001, 2002a, 2002b).
35. The January consultation draft is available at http://go.worldbank.org/1C4LH5VNO0. Ravi Kanbur's response to the Summary of the final version is available at http://go.worldbank.org/BQSZ0KK3C0. Both accessed 27 April 2015.
36. See http://go.worldbank.org/H1N8746X10. Accessed 27 April 2015.
37. This was Kanbur's rationale for adding 'empowerment' as a strategy for attacking poverty, alongside the conventional security and opportunity already foreshadowed in the Washington Consensus, to the WDR on 'Attacking Poverty' (World Bank 2000).

# Moving beyond Official Discourse

## Interfaces and Disjuncture within the Bank

The empirical focus of this chapter is on two constellations, or networks, within the World Bank that embody distinct knowledge systems akin to the distinction made above between 'civil society' and 'finance' (Kanbur 2001) or 'searchers' and 'planners' (Easterly 2006), largely paraphrasing the ideational foundation of the new aid architecture and the innate discourse of the Bank respectively. As such, this chapter goes beyond the official discourse to explore its renderings from an actor-oriented perspective. It presents different knowledge systems found within the Bank, focusing on the effects of their interface (Long 1989), showing that the new aid architecture not only changed the Bank's external representation but also profoundly altered its internal workings with potentially profound effects for the interpretation and implementation of the new aid architecture itself (see Harper 2005). The internal knowledge battles demonstrate that developmentality and the decentralized and productive aspects of power are just as important for structuring the actions of and within the Bank as for those at the receiving end of the partnership. These knowledge battles are instigated and structured by the Bank's internal matrix organization – itself an imprint of Wolfensohn's Strategic Compact (Weaver and Leiteritz 2005; Nielson, Tierney and Weaver 2006) – in which different knowledge systems compete over winning the favour of the regional-operational departments controlling the purse and the dialogue with client countries. Operational influence demonstrates relevance but also secures the network's funding. But the operational side privileges a particular knowledge – typically legible, quantifiable, generic and abstract (cf. Scott 1998) – which causes the practices installed by the Bank's internal matrix organization to undermine many of the ideas purported by the new aid architecture, which, eventually, affects the Bank's external representation and the partnership formation.

In shifting the focus from official discourse to practices of knowledge/power formation within the Bank, this chapter demonstrates that official discourse and practice are not mutually exclusive and neither should be accorded analytical precedence. To paraphrase Barth: 'formal organisation is [not] irrelevant to what is happening – only that formal organisation is not what is happening' (Barth 1993: 157). As Scott notes regarding social engineering and planned change, the 'formal order … is always and to some considerable degree parasitic on informal processes, which the formal scheme does not recognize, without which it could not exist, and which it alone cannot create or maintain' (Scott 1998: 310). The formal order and informal practices of the Bank should be seen as contextual and interrelated as they can both support and contradict each other. In going beyond the formal organization this chapter portrays a more multiplex Bank, where the staff compete for influence and resources in what is best characterized as a 'battlefield of knowledge' (see Long and Long 1992). Such battles take place between sub-departmental units with differing thematic and operational scopes, and tend to follow established lines as a function of the Bank's internal matrix organization. To put it bluntly, networks represent the Bank's thinkers, and the regions the doers. Thinkers compete for practical influence, while the doers are efficiency-seeking pragmatists. The networks thus compete against each other – arguably being the intent of the matrix organization as this would enhance information sharing and stimulate professional excellence. I experienced the knowledge battles from the perspective of the Social Development group – part of the Environmentally and Socially Sustainable Development (ESSD) network – where I was based while at the Bank. The Social Development family embodies most of the overarching ideas integral to the new aid architecture, but time and again found itself neglected by the operational side and, in particular, overridden and ousted by its nemesis, the Poverty Reduction and Economic Management (PREM) network.

## The Matrix Organization – Networks and Regions

'The Bank is organized in a matrix', a junior staff member explained over coffee, at the beginning of my stay with the Bank. Originally, I was to meet his superior in the Social Development unit, but as he had been granted a meeting with senior operational leadership, our meeting was cancelled. 'As you know by now, our unit is rather marginal. We have to take the opportunities we get to influence the operational side'. This statement, I was to learn, directly concerns the internal knowledge battles of the Bank, which follow from its matrix organization creating both a divide and nexus between ideas and practice (see Bebbington, Guggenheim and Woolcock 2006).

The matrix organization is the product of a major internal reorganization within the Bank in 1997 aimed at strengthening management and overall integration. This reorganization included the creation of five major thematic *networks* to link professionals across the Bank. The networks are organized as units separate from the *regions,* which are the operational side of the Bank. The matrix seeks to enhance the professional skills and development expertise in the networks, and infuse these into the Bank's regional-operational side. Whereas the regions are subdivided on the country level, the networks comprise various thematic units, in Bank jargon commonly denoted as families, anchors, or groups.

My informant illustrated this by drawing a matrix map with horizontal and vertical lines. On the horizontal lines he placed the various regional departments: Sub-Saharan Africa, East Asia and the Pacific, Europe and Central Asia, Latin America and the Caribbean, Middle East and North Africa, and finally South Asia. Each regional department is organized into separate vice-presidential units. The regions are subdivided into country level, and designated country teams are responsible for the Bank's operational work within the particular country. On the vertical lines are the five networks – also organized as vice-presidential units in the larger Bank context – which host the professionals, or 'researchers' as they often are called, involved in Bank work. The networks are clustered around five thematic groups: the Human Development network works on issues such as education, health, population and social protection; the Finance, Private Sector and Infrastructure network focuses on issues of private-sector development, energy, mining, telecommunication, transportation, water and urban development; the Operational Core Services network is a capacity-building network that focuses on generating and disseminating knowledge within the Bank and to borrowing countries; the Environmentally and Socially Sustainable Development (ESSD) network specializes in environmental issues, rural and social development, and the cultural aspects of development; and finally the Poverty Reduction and Economic Management (PREM) network, engaged in countrywide economic policy and cross-sectoral issues of economic policy, gender and development, poverty and governance, and public sector reform (see World Bank 2003b).[1]

Under the management of a country director, country teams are responsible for the Bank's operational work for its designated country, which involves preparing lending portfolios and negotiating policies with the recipient, client government. Hence, the regional side of the matrix holds predominant influence over both money and policies. The thematic networks, however, are detached from the financial aspects of the Bank's lending. Networks are intended to generate professional excellence among the staff and pass this on to the regions, as per operational demand. Networks can also engender their own ideas and approaches, but these will have to be adopted by the regions to influence operational activities. Operational influence is gained when networks manage to transfer and infuse their ideas and policies into the regions' operational activities. As a corollary to this, when a network manages to influence the operational side, it upholds the funds to maintain its activities, to further develop and implement that particular idea: 'to every network manager, operational influence means reproducing its own budget allocation, and should the ideas be endorsed it might even mean an increase', a network manager explained. Operational influence implies access to the supervision budget, and for every network this means continuity of that particular idea and its general work. The utmost objective of any network manager then is to mainstream that network's thinking and ideas throughout the Bank, which would secure the network's relevance, sustain its thematic scope and uphold its financial position. 'This is where the main problem of the matrix comes in', asserted my informant, who was working in the Social Development family under the ESSD network.

> Since we're not directly part of Bank lending operations, we have to make ourselves relevant to the regions and the operational side. We need to create a demand for our services. But that goes for every network, so in fact we compete over the same resources. ... We continuously strive [to make] ourselves relevant. It's a battle against Goliath. It is extremely difficult to persuade those in the regions about our operational relevance – particularly when we have new ideas. Regions tend to be rather inert in that respect.

This statement illustrates two features internal to the networks as an implication of the matrix organization. First, that networks perceive themselves as ideational suppliers to the operational demand side; second, that networks perceive the operational side to be the Bank's locomotive and public face. 'The regions set the course, while networks provide maps', he stated. The internal problem, however, is not merely the distinction between networks and regions, but also between the various networks and which 'map' to deliver and operationalize on the regional side. Networks compete for operational and Bank-wide influence, and their success depends on their ability to infuse ideas into the various regional departments. Although the matrix, which separates the ideas of networks and the operational regions, intends to 'promote and enhance the Bank's professional expertise into becoming an institution of excellence', it also engenders differences between and among networks. 'Goliath', I was to learn, refers not only to the operational side in the regions, but more generally to the economic rationality that prevails throughout the Bank. This, moreover, establishes a schism between various networks depending on their thematic scope. This schism is particularly prominent with regard to the ESSD network on the one side, and the PREM network on the other, as these constitute the distinct realms of 'civil society' and 'finance' respectively (see Kanbur 2001; cf. previous chapter). To generalize, whereas the former comprises social scientists working on social development – often labelled 'soft issues' – the PREM network consists mainly of economists working on issues of economic growth. There is not much interaction between the various networks themselves. Their relational differences get articulated on the regional side of the matrix, which handles the Bank's operational work concerning lending programmes, policies and credit schemes. Networks' competition over operational relevance and input implies that the PRSP-model's bottom–up orientation is undermined by, or at least competes with, processes internal to the Bank. The formal matrix configuration gives rise to internal struggles over knowledge, power, influence and resources – eventually shaping the Bank's external representation.

## The Matrix Seen from the Regions

Among those who work in operational units – that is, country teams in the various regions – the matrix is seen as bringing 'fuzz' and 'disturbances' into their practical work, due to the networks' continuous attempts to install their ideas into the various operational units. In explaining the differences between networks and operations, an operations officer working in the Uganda team told me:

> The operational units are the most interesting part if you would like to see the practical sides of policy making. These units develop programmes together with donors and government, compose conditionalities, and negotiate credits. The research units [networks], on the other hand, are fairly detached from operations, and not that unlike a university – but with plenty of money ... Operations are more hands-on work. It's the place where it all happens.

Those working in operations usually move around a lot in the Bank – 'the matrix infrastructure facilitates that people shift position and office quite often'. This, he maintained, was due to three somewhat contradictory aspects. First it might be due to the need to disseminate knowledge, because if you work in one part of the Bank you gain insight and knowledge on that particular theme or country, which could be of high value to other departments or country teams. This draws on the notion of 'best practice': if you achieve good operational results in one place, you will probably be reassigned to duplicate and implement the same processes elsewhere. Second, the high internal turnover rate is also a means of countering the risk of becoming too dependent on individuals. Third, it prevents staff tunnel-vision and lessens personal attachment to their client counterpart and its national elites. The first explanation celebrates individual merits; the second focuses on the collective, and aims at institutionalizing operational knowledge; and the third reduces country sensitivity, as desired by the new aid architecture. 'Sure, the staff's development expertise is crucial to the Bank's work. It becomes an operational problem if that expertise is lost – either to the Bank in general or to other departments'. To reduce this risk, employees are regularly shifted around – for example, this person who worked in the Uganda team at the time of my first fieldwork in Uganda had been reassigned to the Tanzania team by the time of my second fieldwork half a year later.

There exists no central document outlining how a country team should be organized and composed, nor how it is to work, which many find both problematic and comfortable at the same time. Most notably they find it surprising, 'given the vast bureaucracy and the strict regulation of Bank work'. The lack of a central document to guide the work of country teams is explained by reference to the contextual and complex nature of operations, which requires the team to be flexible to the challenges they may face 'in the field' – that is, when negotiating with client governments. The composition of a country team is not, however, merely the product of requirements and demands on the recipient side – it is just as much a result of processes and knowledge battles within the Bank.

The Uganda team comprises about forty people, in a rather flat structure under a country director and a country manager, which is the common organizational form for country teams. Team members are formally equal, with the exception of the senior country economist, who holds a more influential role by leading and being responsible for the team's analytical work. As regards the Uganda team, the director sits in Tanzania, whereas the manager and senior economist are based at the Kampala office.[2] The 'foot soldiers', which is their self-referential term, are divided between Washington and the Kampala office. Among the foot soldiers are various thematic experts – lawyers, political scientists, economists, resource managers, geographers, planners, and so on. Team composition is flexible and reflects prevailing issues and operational needs. The country director and manager, who are responsible for drafting and appointing new team members, are under great pressure from networks wanting to integrate their ideas and staff into operational work. Consequently, team composition might just as possibly reflect differing knowledge systems internal to the Bank as the operational needs. As a member of the Uganda country team reflects:

> I don't know all in my team. We regularly get new team members. It's confusing coming to internal meetings and you don't know who you're meeting and what they do. Instead of discussing and involving the whole team you end up working with those you share ideas and views with. There are always different people from the networks who seek to advocate their ideas. It is difficult. While we are judged on our operational output, they [networks] are judged on how they manage to influence us. What they say is not always irrelevant, but they tend to be too academic and ideational and less concerned with the pragmatic, practical matters and how we are to implement their ideas, and what the value might be. Although they come here and present new ideas and participate in meetings, they seldom have any significant influence. I don't think their effort matches the effect they have. I end up working with the team members I know. It's much easier. … And when in need of more manpower, we obviously choose those who share our views.

The underlying tension between regions and networks concerns their internal rationale and scope. Whereas the former seek to design and implement projects to maximize output and development effectiveness, the latter produce and disseminate professional excellence and are often, rather patronizingly, referred to as researchers or academics. Although all Bank staff follow the same mission statement – 'to fight poverty with passion and professionalism for lasting results' – there are internally numerous ways of achieving this. Although there is, as will be demonstrated later, divergence between the various networks, the operational units all seem to be driven by the same rationale of operational feasibility and development effectiveness. 'You can almost tell what different people will say depending on which Bank unit they come from', a member of the Uganda team asserted just before we entered a meeting. During the meeting's first session, which started with the ritualistic introduction where people state their affiliation, he signalled me to illustrate his point. In the break, I asked him to elaborate:

> We are continuously approached with all sorts of ideas, and you can tell by their regional or network affiliation what their agenda is and what they will say. They're on autopilot. I do not distrust their intention. Surely they are extremely competent, but everything simply does not add to what we are doing. They do not have the operational approach. You're an anthropologist. I would guess you work with indigenous people. Surely, anthropological input is important, but to us it is not relevant. We

> are planners, and we negotiate with government and seek to strengthen state capacity. Take that social development guy. Surely, he propagates important stuff. But it is difficult to plan in accordance to the whole civil society and all its cultural and ethnic variations. It would, I expect, also be difficult to make the government buy into it. There are too many uncertainties attached. We can't propose a plan with so many doubts. And for sure the government won't sign on to a loan programme when there are so many uncertainties.

Although the matrix aims at producing professional excellence through the networks, regional staff members express problems with incorporating it into operational thinking as it engenders operational complexity – or that it institutionalizes a battlefield of knowledge. Operational staff acknowledge they are guided and driven by a different logic and rationale than the networks. Networks comprise thematic anchors available to the Bank as a whole, far from the operational pragmatism and the political practicalities of Bank–client relations, which make difficult the intended transfer of knowledge from networks to regions of the matrix organization.[3] Networks' operational influence and inclusion – drawing on decisions made largely on the regional side – are premised on their advocacy work towards the regional departments. This gives regional departments great leverage over the Bank's operations and its external representation. Operational staff members are well aware of the position they hold, and they express concern about the multitude and heterogeneity of networks ideas they are subject to, while also acknowledging the predictability of the input from the various networks. Cases in point are the Poverty Reduction and Economic Management (PREM) and the Environmentally and Socially Sustainable Development (ESSD) networks and their respective subunits, the Public Sector Management and the Social Development family. These networks represent two separate knowledge systems. Whereas PREM reflects the general and prevailing economic paradigm of the Bank and is thus more closely attuned to the mentality and objectives of operational thinking, the ESSD – and the Social Development family in particular – involves knowledge that is more marginal to operational activities (see Mosse 2004b).

## The Social Development Family: Institutionalizing a Participatory Approach?

Networks' struggle to make themselves relevant to the operational side takes place both between networks and in relation to the regional departments. This is particularly evident in the part of the networks where I conducted most my research, the Social Development department – commonly called the social development family – which is a group organized under the ESSD network.[4] The ESSD network was formed to promote issues of social development within the Bank and to ensure 'that actions taken today to promote development and reduce poverty do not result in environmental degradation or social exclusion tomorrow' (World Bank 2003a: 139–40). The ESSD network is a de facto manifestation of the new aid architecture within the Bank, as it is intended to deal with sector-wide issues regarding the complex and comprehensive nature of development in general and Bank projects in particular, including participation, empowerment, capacity building, and pro-poor focused approaches. The Social Development (SD) family, as an integral part of ESSD, specializes in processes of transforming institutions for greater inclusion, cohesion and accountability, aimed at empowering poor and marginalized women and men (see World Bank 2005a).[5] Although 1997 saw the formation of Social Development through the matrix organization,[6] the history of social development themes goes back to the early 1970s.[7] A brief presentation of this short history can show the troublesome past with regard to other knowledge systems in the Bank – a feature still found today.

In 1973 the vice president of Bank Operations circulated a paper titled 'A Report with Recommendations on the Use of Anthropology in Project Operations of the World Bank', which concluded 'that there was a need to increase anthropological and social input into Bank projects, and that many Bank staff supported this idea, but did not know how to do it … At the time, the idea was quite radical – unthinkable to most' (World Bank 2004a: 1).[8] From the mid-1970s, the Bank started hiring social scientists on the rationale of adding a social dimension to project operations and working on the 'influence of culture on human behaviour and to point out the social impacts of land acquisition and resettlement, which were major causes of project delay' (ibid.: 2). The social scientists were from an early stage exposed to the Bank's bias of the prevailing economic rationality. Up until the early 1980s the main objective of social scientists was to improve project effectiveness, based on the conviction that economic development would improve welfare and help the poor if projects were well designed. From the mid-1980s to the mid-1990s social scientists concentrated their efforts on devising methods and tools to incorporate social considerations and the views of the poor in project design as the adverse social impact of large-scale structural adjustment programmes became evident. From 1997 social development became manifested through the creation of the ESSD and the matrix organization. Membership in the SD family was initially drawn from non-economic social scientists – usually a subordinated minority within the Bank.

Relevant here is Fox' (2003) study of anthropologists within the Bank, demonstrating how qualitative-oriented social research has succumbed to more quantitative perspectives. Fox claims that anthropologists pursuing a Bank career tend to follow one of three paths. One group 'gets fully co-opted – assimilating the institution's norms and applying their skills to blunting just a bit of sharp edge of what the Bank funds' (ibid.: 523). Second, there are those who are inconsistent in their principled stands. A third and very small group manages to stick to their anthropological principles while still functioning within the Bank by carving out their own niches to promote 'participatory, innovative development projects that are so tiny, by Bank standards, that they don't threaten the rest of what the Bank does' (ibid.). Fox maintains that neither of these groups is particularly large or influential. First, very few anthropologists are actual Bank staff; second, they tend to be involved in small, marginal projects remote from conventional Bank programmes; and third, even if anthropologists do get involved, they are usually ignored. However, as Fox remarks, those anthropologists who ascended to power started to think they knew more about the natives than the natives themselves, in the sense that their innate bottom–up orientation was replaced by one promoting the Bank's views.

With the matrix organization, social development formally became a cross-cutting theme with a group of social scientists. Without its own operational portfolio, the SD group continued to develop methods and tools that would allow it to influence other sections of the Bank. Today, the SD family's self-representation centres on five pillars that are in contrast to what its staff see as the Bank's economic-technocratic paradigm: a focus on people and societies rather than specific sectors or the economy; in-depth country and local knowledge, allowing contextualization and adaptation to diverse conditions; a bottom–up perspective focusing on participation with recipients rather than a technocratic top–down approach; a concern with social systems and not merely the economy; and support for a strong governmental role in transforming societies and institutions to the betterment of project implementation and results (World Bank 2004a: v). Or: 'Rather than advocating universal laws, social development practitioners have been concerned with the particulars of individual societies and the ways in which broad prescriptions must be adapted to fit local contexts – for better and for worse' (ibid.: 1).

## The Social Development Family's Self-Representations

The self-representation of the Social Development group as a 'family' – as opposed to a thematic group or unit, as other networks' subgroups are labelled – should be seen against the backdrop of the historical, and current, context of SD staff's struggle for Bank-wide recognition. Today, the ESSD network hosts the highest concentration of non-economic qualitatively oriented social scientists within the Bank, and the majority of these are found in the SD family. Although some of them are economists, they are nevertheless referred to as 'social scientists'. Similarly, non-economists in economist-dominated networks are often referred to as 'economists'. The designation as 'economist' or 'social scientist' thus refers to the perceived and relative mindset of the network, and not the person's formal professional background. The categories of 'social scientists' and 'economists' refer more to what these individuals do within the Bank and its specific networks than to their actual professional training. The idea of viewing their group as a 'family' derives from the perception of them being at the margins of what is seen as the Bank's dominant economic paradigm.

This self-representation is further underpinned by the many trust funds that finance and facilitate much of the SD's staff and activities. Trust funds are financial arrangements involving Bank member-countries, where the latter entrust the Bank with funds for specific purposes and activities not otherwise prioritized by the Bank over its regular budget allocation.[9] The relatively large share of trust funds within SD indicates a lack of engagement and priority to its scope on the part of the Bank. Trust funds are a means for donor countries to influence the Bank from within, but as these funds are accounted for separately from the Bank's own resources, the donor to a particular trust fund does not gain greater voting power in the Bank, as regular deposits do. That in turn means that trust funds are more guided by their donor than active Bank policy.

> Trust funds are... well, let's say the Norwegian government approaches the Bank and asks it to put more focus on, let's say gender issues, community-driven development or to target CSOs for social engagement. Maybe the Bank is reluctant to include or strengthen those issues, and then it can say, 'ok, we can do it, if you pay'. That is how it works. The Bank is open to include new issues, also issues that are not only about the economy or growth, but it might not finance them.

These words come from a German working in the SD family, but salaried by a multi-donor trust fund. The exhaustive list of trust fund programmes illustrates his point,[10] at least on the surface: none of the trust fund programmes includes the terms 'economy' or 'growth' in its name, whereas many names contain terms like 'social', 'sustainable', 'participation', 'environment', 'health', 'education', 'capacity-building' and 'research' – all of which fit with the SD family's thematic scope. These terms and the name of the trust fund programme tend to indicate where they are located in the Bank organization.[11] Trust fund donors also tend to employ staff of their own nationality. As a result, there are many European social scientists, or likeminded people, working in the SD family, as opposed to economists trained at U.S. universities, who dominate in the PREM network.[12] Trust funds persist either because the Bank does not prioritize these activities over its regular budget, or because the Bank does not fund them because they are already receiving external support. In any case, trust funds are influential instruments through which shareholders can infuse their ideas and shape the Bank from within. SD is one unit with substantial external support,[13] and this affects its thematic and methodological scope vis-à-vis the more regular Bank units.

## SD's Upstream Approach to Topics and Methods

The rationale of Social Development is to mainstream a person-centred approach in Bank projects, starting the development process from the perspective of the poor people, their families and communities. SD's scope reflects the Bank's new business model as outlined in the CDF, and proposes a shift towards a more integrated, multi-sectoral and upstream approach to development. An 'upstream' perspective means a bottom–up approach that sets out to empower the beneficiaries to take control of their own development processes on their own premises – as stipulated by the ideas integral to the new aid architecture and PRSP. Within the SD family, jargon tends to involve concepts like 'ownership', 'community-driven development' and 'participation'. This parallels the ideational foundation of the new aid architecture, but simultaneously stands in contrast to the traditional top–down, donor-driven approach to development, from which the SD family distances itself. Pivotal to this shift is the social development group's identification of inclusion, cohesion and accountability as operational principles, and a greater focus on institutions and how to change them so as to promote better development processes. 'Institutions' in the Bank context refers to the broad set of formal and informal rules, norms and values that operate within society (see World Bank 2005a). Through engaging with and aiming to transform institutions, and not merely focusing on governments being the Bank's official counterparts, the SD family holds the propagating role for bottom–up approaches and its aligned cluster of ideas, such as ownership, participation, empowerment, human and community-driven development. This is illustrated in the words of an SD manager, originally an economist by training, who, when asked what characterized the SD family compared to the Bank in general and the PREM network in particular, stated:

> I think the starting principle for anything we do should be – as we have learned painfully over the years – that if there isn't country ownership things don't work. How do you define country ownership? It depends on the issue. If it's a technical issue, for instance like… how much money should go in through the central bank, there I think you are looking at technocratic solutions that tend to be top–down: you agree with the technocrats on what needs to be done, and these things get implemented. When you move into other areas, which more have to do with institutions – as opposed to the areas with technocrats who usually are educated in the West anyway, speak the same language, understand the same concepts, understand what the Bank is doing and understand more their own constraints. When you start dealing with institutions the approach needs to be very different. For example, concerning primary education in rural areas – that is not something a technocrat solves. Fine! There, I think, is where you have to combine that sort of technocratic top–down with our [ESSD] bottom–up. That is where it becomes critical that you are finding processes and mechanisms by which communities have a voice and then you get an influence, because they are ultimately the ones you are trying to serve. In the past, the Bank – I am talking ten, twenty years ago – you know, would go into the ministry of education, agree with the minister and these technical people on reform of the educational system. And somehow those reforms didn't work. All right? And education I think is a kind of service where you have to combine the two approaches because these are not purely technical solutions. They are about institutions, about people, about incentives, about processes, mechanisms – and all these things need to connect. Therefore we need to integrate a community-driven perspective to Bank operations. And that is equally important in other sectors. Right? If you are not connecting the two approaches, then you will probably fail.

Ideas of bottom–up planning, a pro-poor agenda and focus on institutions serve as gatekeeping concepts in integrating the SD family. This consensus is paralleled by scepticism to other networks that are more closely attuned to the general economic mindset otherwise prevalent in Bank discourse. SD staff see themselves as dealing with social issues and questions of sustainability, which other networks consider too qualitative and 'soft' in comparison to their quantitative and technocratic realm, and thus difficult to integrate in operational activities. Although SD's integration is based on distancing itself from other parts of the Bank, its staff know that influence depends on being able to 'speak the economic and technocratic language' of other dominant Bank units. This was evident at a concept review meeting in the SD family on the role of civil society organizations with regard to the LICUS initiative and how to communicate it outside the 'family'.[14]

## SD's Interface with Operations: Complexity vs Legibility

The LICUS trust fund is anchored within the SD family, and represents an approach to countries that fail to meet the criteria for engaging in a regular partnership with the Bank: namely, a well-functioning state apparatus to hold the role as Bank counterpart and responsible loan signatory – or, in brief, the principles of good governance.[15] The LICUS trust fund[16] allows the Bank to provide modest support and 'efforts to improve the institutions and performance of such countries, and to *help steer them back to the path* of sustained growth, poverty reduction, and debt management and relief'.[17] The help implies governance and institutional reforms aimed at enabling the countries to 'graduate' and qualify for regular Bank lending operations. From an initial focus on general aid effectiveness, the trust fund initiative expanded its scope to state-building in 2005 – to help fragile countries to 'restart state services', which implies an extensive use of non-state actors such as NGOs and CSOs.[18]

The LICUS initiative promotes two main issues. The first concerns the methodological level of aid delivery and policy making, as it seeks to counter the criticism directed at the Bank for not appropriately tailoring anti-poverty relief to the specific needs of recipient countries. Hence the LICUS initiative aims at enhancing donor responsiveness to the particular needs of the borrowers. Secondly, it seeks an alternative approach to state-building in dealing with fragile states, by addressing and transforming institutions outside the state structure rather than focusing its state reconstruction efforts on the government. These two overarching objectives of bottom–up planning and a focus on institutions place the LICUS initiative squarely within the scope of the SD family.

Here let me relate the events surrounding the concept review meeting. I link up with the inviter just prior to the meeting. As we walk along the corridors she tells me about LICUS, which in her opinion is a rather strange initiative, because 'basically, LICUS is about helping those not eligible to borrow from the Bank into becoming so. I mean, isn't the fundamental role of the Bank to help those poorest countries? I think it only illustrates that the Bank is a bank, driven by economist thinking, and not a development agency as it claims', she asserts. Just before we enter the venue, she says: 'This concept review meeting concerns how to integrate the civil society, because when the Bank can't work with the government, we need to go through other actors'.

There are about twenty people at the meeting. Most of them come from the ESSD network, primarily the SD family, and some are involved in the work of the LICUS trust fund. Those few not integral to the ESSD include two from the Human Development network and three from the regional side. One of them, an operational officer, is invited to comment. After the brief and usual round of presentations, a paper on the role of civil society and how to include it in LICUS to strengthen the governance system is presented. The underpinning rationale is that the Bank has a responsibility to the poor, and a weak government that fails to qualify for a loan from the Bank does not relieve the Bank of its responsibility to help – hence the importance of including civil society organizations.

> We need to strengthen the Bank's engagement with CSOs in post-conflict areas and particularly LICUS countries. We need to promote civic engagement to empower people to hold its [*sic*] government accountable and enhance good governance and to build democratic institutions. CSOs can do this. We need a closer link between the Bank and CSOs to improve the Bank's good governance agenda. A vital civil society is crucial for good governance, and it would alter our approach to be more bottom–up than top-heavy – working with the CSOs we would really get a picture of the real needs on the ground. It would make the Bank more responsive to social issues.

A tirade from the invited commentator follows after the brief presentation. The response does not directly concern how to better include civil society in Bank operations, but goes to the very rationale of LICUS and the SD family's commitment to institutions, civil society engagement and how to include them in the operational work:

> First of all, it is not cost effective. There are few evidences that show the effectiveness of going through CSOs and altering institutions. As we have learned from our governance studies, working in areas of weak governance might be detrimental to our overall agenda. But even more disturbing is how you guys neglect the Bank's mandate and its counterparts. We're an organization made up of states, for states. We cannot just channel funds into the civil society just because of a malfunctioning government. Governments are our clients – not CSOs, CBOs, NGOs or whatever you call this plethora … And if we negotiate with government, how likely do you think it is that they will approve to forward the funds

> to CSOs that fundamentally are in opposition to the government? You need to think outside of this box of yours. You cannot approach fragile states only with your network's narrow toolbox. You need to consider how the operational work of the Bank functions and the dilemmas we face when negotiating your ideas with our clients.

Most of those attending the meeting are somewhat taken aback by this harsh response. The chairperson explains that the note was not intended for Bank operations alone, but also to direct other donors as well as borrowing governments. From this point, the meeting becomes a discussion about methodology and how to install the SD and LICUS perspectives at the operational level. 'For this to be relevant', the operational manager retorts, 'it should be presented and discussed in the operational units, and you should add PREM in the loop, not only SD. To gain effect on policy and implementation, the regions – not just the networks – should be included'. Social development ideas – like gender equity, rights and empowerment – that seek to enhance the social dimension of development are dismissed as 'too soft', 'woolly' and generally difficult to relate to in operational work. The operational manager makes a call for more legible and stringent analysis and evidence of effectiveness in order to implement these ideas.

The SD people at the meeting recognize their shortcomings in delivering stringent causal analysis for their perspectives; 'After all, social development is not rocket science,' one participant notes – adding, 'but that does not reduce its importance'. On the one hand, SD staff acknowledge the difficulties in measuring social development issues and thus in providing evidence, stringent models and causal relations between input and output in planning on social development issues. The SD view is that societies and development processes are complex by nature and cannot be reduced to linear or universal models. On the other hand, all agree that in order to spread social development ideas throughout the Bank, particularly on the operational level, it is necessary to follow the causal thinking that, in their view, dominates the general Bank discourse. Later, to questions as to why they are willing to compromise the basic tenets of social development issues – the acknowledgement that complex issues necessitate complex and non-quantifiable approaches – it is argued that the objective justifies the means, and that social development is right, important and a value in itself: 'We need to start somewhere. To install our ideas in operations we need to argue in just as effective a way as the planners and economists do … Once we have instilled our concepts, we can start to hollow them and fill them with meaning'. The SD family sees the Bank as not 'mature' enough to fully incorporate the social dimension in project planning and objectives, asserting that SD's lack of operational influence is due to the perceived newness of social development perspectives.

Thus the meeting. In a later encounter I asked the operational manager who had been invited to comment on the concept note to elaborate on his experience. He replied:

> You know, those are the social development ideas. Sort of, they guide how they do things because that's their policies which they work according to. The way it works is that they do these concept reviews for operations, and then they invite us [operational staff] and we come and sit over to discuss the concept paper and we say 'you know, maybe this is not the greatest idea to do, and…'. But there are no particular measures. Yes, we have been consulted, but that doesn't mean we're listened to – or that we buy into their ideas. Their ideas seem to surpass our operational needs … We also meet with other networks. But at the end of the day we are responsible for mediating and implementing networks' ideas to government.

The operational manager thus underscores the view within the SD family that network ideas are transformed and reformulated by the operational side before being conveyed to the government. The networks' operational influence thus depends on their ability to install their ideas in the operational work of the Bank.

## A Strategy for Influence – Hardliners vs Pragmatists

SD staff acknowledge that in order to disseminate and influence the operational portfolio they need to present their ideas in a manner that can accommodate the internal knowledge system of operational thinking. 'We need to start thinking of the Bank as what it really is – a bank, and not a development agency', an SD manager asserted with reference to the operational units and the PREM network, which to him represent the core of the Bank's economic–technocratic mindset to which SD should align to gain influence. 'They are much better at demonstrating causal relations between input and output. We have a lot to learn from then, rather than insisting on the complex nature of our models', he maintained. Influence is contingent on inscribing the particular ideas into the technocratic–economic rationale that dominates Bank operations. This was evident in connection with the finalization of *Empowering People by Transforming Institutions* (World Bank 2005a), which consolidated the SD group's strategic priorities and approaches. This plan was widely spoken about and circulated within the SD family while being finalized and approved during my fieldwork. Earlier discussions had reportedly focused on the extent to which it should be aligned with PREM's economic and technocratic jargon.[19]

The strategy outlines the core of SD's strategic priorities and scope. The language and underpinning rationale do not comply with the SD family's scepticism to universal laws, technocratic language and economic rationality. Moreover, the document shows that the basic social developmental perspective of putting people first is secondary and subject to the Bank's overarching growth rationale. Social development, it reads,

> promotes better growth, better projects and better quality of life [p. v]. Economic growth is essential for the world … For growth to benefit poor people, development agencies need to invest in human and physical assets … [and] transform the broad set of institutions that determine the quality of growth, service delivery and human development [p. 1] … By transforming institutions to empower people, social development matters for growth and who benefits from it. Growth depends on efficient use of resources [p. 3] … Social development promotes better projects [p. 4] … Given that social development contributes to better growth, better projects and better quality of life, there is global consensus that social development is essential to reduce poverty [p. 5]. (World Bank 2005a)

The strategy reveals an ambiguity between the internal and external representation of the SD family. Internally, SD celebrates the complex character of development – that any development process is uncertain as it inevitably depends on numerous contextual parameters outside the Bank's control. This in fact amounts to a criticism of the general Bank paradigm, driving the SD call for a more people-centred and bottom–up approach to development. Externally, however, this criticism and scepticism to the Bank's growth paradigm are not voiced, as we can see from the quote above.

Drafting the strategy saw tension among various factions within the SD family – the SD hardliners and the SD pragmatists. This tension relates to SD's interface with other parts of the Bank. The hardliners cultivate the SD approach and are highly reluctant to compromise. They have a strong belief in social development, arguing that it represents a radical contribution to all of the Bank's development activities, at the level of both structure and policy, by being bottom–up oriented and people-centred. This somewhat marginal group consists of rather new and young staff who give precedence to 'their idealism or scholarly profession without recognizing how the Bank works', as a self-designated

SD pragmatist put it.[20] He maintained that he, like so many others in the SD family, was once a hardliner, but after understanding how the Bank works internally and in operations, he became more pragmatic. The pragmatists realize their limitations and that the SD approach must be in line with the rest of the Bank if it is to be of relevance to those outside the ESSD network. As argued regarding the SD strategy, 'the board would never have approved it if we didn't comply with their mode of thinking'.[21]

Despite the internal tension between hardliners and pragmatists, they share a firm belief in the approach and policy content of social development, even though these, according to SD's self-representation, diverge from views predominant in much of the Bank in putting people and institutions first – not economic growth and technology. In enhancing social development inside the Bank, SD subjects itself to the growth paradigm by asserting that social development initiatives would inevitably lead to better growth and better projects in the long term. According to the SD pragmatist:

> this might be so, but our main motivation is nevertheless people, to start the development process from the perspective of the poor. This should be based on the community's own perspective, on their own needs. They need to drive the process. Otherwise it's meaningless to talk about social development ... But to have our voice heard, we need to wrap it in the economic technocratic jargon of those outside the SD group. This does not mean that we agree [with the growth perspective]. It is rather a means to communicate and appeal to those outside the SD.

SD's alignment to the economic jargon could be seen as a strategy to enhance perspectives that fall outside the larger Bank discourse. Here the underlying rationale is that it makes people in other networks and those on the regional-operational side more open to social development ideas. Nevertheless, the troublesome reception of central SD issues – like bottom–up approaches, participation, building capacity and institutions and enhancing governance – might seem somewhat strange, as these ideas largely parallel those of the new aid architecture and its manifestation in the PRSP model. The generally concurrent emergence of SD and the new aid architecture has provided no guarantee for SD's operational influence. Rather, the challenges it has been facing indicate reluctance to alter perspectives, policies and approaches similar to those implied with the new aid architecture and PRSP. Such contestation is both between networks and the operational side, and in-between networks – as experienced by an internal Bank course organized by PREM, in which I participated.

## PREM Course on Public Sector Governance and Anti-Corruption

In mid-February 2005 the PREM network organized a four-day core course on Public Sector Governance and Anti-corruption, as that is one of the network's four prioritized areas of expertise.[22] At the time of my fieldwork, issues pertaining to good governance dominated Bank-wide discussions due to two interlinked factors: the preparation of a governance and anti-corruption strategy (see World Bank 2007),[23] and the realization that governance issues had gained relevance because of the greater involvement of their clients in the development process.

The 'course is designed for Bank staff who have to assess and/or confront problems of weak governance and corruption in developing assistance strategies and country programs'.[24] The invitation specifies the course's two aims: first, to 'help staff understand the approaches and tools for assessing a country's governance environment', and second, to provide 'guidance on developing and implementing practical and effective interventions'. The course, a regular event constantly updated to incorporate and reflect current and prevailing PREM ideas, is offered to all Bank employees but is specifically designed to assist the operational side and those responsible for the Bank's dialogue with client governments.

About thirty-five people attended the course in February 2005. The majority were Bank staff, but among the participants were about five from the IMF and three 'independent' ones, including myself. Of the Bank employees, the majority were either from PREM or the operational units. Only a few were from the ESSD or other networks, in addition to three people recently seconded to work for their respective government's executive director. Most participants were rather young and recently employed by the Bank. The participants were seated at five round tables, each comprising groups for coming case activities, since the course is organized as a 'Harvard-style case based on issues that are frequently experienced by staff'.[25] According to the main facilitator, the course focuses on real field experience and how to grapple with various difficulties in negotiating with governments on lending programmes. The course centres on PREM's general thematic scope, particularly its Public Sector Reform subgroup. The invited speakers were, with few exceptions, high-ranking officials in the Bank, mainly drawn from the PREM network itself or the Bank's research department – the World Bank Institute (WBI).

First we were presented with the basic tenets of the Bank's anti-corruption strategy. *Corruption* is conceptualized as 'the use of public office for private gain', whether in the form of administrative corruption or state capture. Administrative corruption is conceived of as 'private payments and other benefits to public officials in connection with the implementation of government policy and regulations'. State capture refers to 'influence of powerful private interests in the formation of laws [and] regulation[s], through illegal provision of private gains for public officials'. Corruption is seen to coincide with weak governments, or bad or malfunctioning governance. *Governance* is understood as 'the manner in which the state acquires and exercises its authority to provide public goods and services' – which opens to define governance as either good or bad. Dealing with corruption implies altering and improving how the state governs itself and its designated affairs, in accordance with certain *institutions* or 'the rules of the game' governing the behaviour of people within a given environment. The PREM network sees corruption and governance as intimately connected, with public sector reform as the prioritized anti-corruption means and way to improve bad governance.

## Shrinking the Journey towards Less Corrupt Government

There was extensive use of PowerPoint presentations throughout the course.[26] The very first slide indicated where we were heading: it showed a mountaineer ascending a steep cliff, accompanied by the text, 'Our difficult climb: initial progress and the ascent ahead'. The course theme was corruption, presented as an obstacle to development and a critical symptom of bad governance – and hence the need for reforming the public sector, so that countries and governments could get their fundamentals right.

A linear infinite graph, illustrating the time horizon, was then presented. Far to the left a big circle was drawn, to illustrate the current extent of corruption. To the far right a smaller circle was drawn, indicating the future and the objective of 'our difficult climb' – less corruption. This was followed by the PowerPoint slide text: 'The way forward – a long journey'. We were told that less corruption is the future, and that governments were starting to realize it: 'Corrupt countries and governments will eventually realize the devastating effects corruption has on growth and development. But it is when governments first realize that it threatens their powerbase that they become willing to reform'. The PREM network sees the Bank's role as one of 'shrinking the time-horizon'. That was the caption for the next slide, on which the smaller corruption-circle had been moved to the left, closer to the present – by making governments understand the consequences of corruption. The path to a less corrupt society was presented as an inevitable and immanent process for every country, with governments 'destined to realize the resources lost in corruption'. The speaker went on to explain: 'As corruption is an ongoing phenomenon that hampers the current development process it needs to be battled. We help countries to become less corrupt. We can't sit still and watch governments waste Bank money. It's an ethical problem in itself, but it also staggers the development process'.

While the first slide presented less, or an 'acceptable' level of corruption as a state in the indefinite far future, the next slides drew it into a more foreseeable time-horizon. Through Bank lending and a push for governance reform in partnership with other donor institutions, the time frame (although accompanied by a question mark) was now stipulated to be twenty-five years. The next slide indicated that it might be possible to shorten this journey to about ten years by 'strengthening the "demand" for reform' and 'improving the "supply" of reform', through 'new approaches' that imply including and even persuading governments to comply with reforms – however, it was also noted, governments tend to be reluctant to engage in public sector reform as this means altering their internal affairs.

The course went on to take up this problem. 'Certainly, it is easy when a government agrees that it is affected by corruption. Then we have a strong base for helping it to reform and tackle corruption. If the government disagrees to our analysis, or refuses anti-corruption measures, it becomes more difficult'. In addressing this, we were told, we must persuade the government to undertake reform – to strengthen the demand side of what the Bank can supply – which is difficult, as the powerbase of weak governments relies largely on corrupt activities. The course offered two approaches. The first was to enhance domestic pressure for reform through assisting and empowering actors outside the state apparatus to infuse and apply pressure for reform. This could be in the form of, for example, assisting and stimulating civil society in monitoring governance performance and reforms, supporting community-based organizations and similar to mobilize the citizenry in favour of increased government performance, and strategically supporting responsible and independent media in advocating anti-corruption measures. The second involved strengthening international pressure for reform, using the international arena to re-energize the agenda, to focus and coordinate pressure with other development actors, and to strengthen global initiatives on anti-corruption towards specific countries.

The PREM network has a three-pronged approach to the supply side of reform: help reformist governments to overcome obstacles; help to tackle political drivers of corruption; and rebuild the ethos of public service. Whereas the first concerns governments that are open to reform and thus directly seeks to help governments to 'better understand and manage the political economy of reforms, … build leadership capacity, [and] change management ethos', the two latter approaches are directed to countries with governments that are reluctant to engage in public sector reform. The second approach addresses issues of party financing disclosure and regulation, work with media and parliament, and targeting reforms that indirectly can reduce corruption. The third perspective is the one least dependent on the cooperative willingness of the state, and includes 'innovative pilots to re-inculcate commitment to public service', support civil society organizations working to transform public-sector values and ethics, and encourage better corporate governance and codes of conduct. 'Encouraging can be difficult,' the course speaker admitted, 'so basically, what it often boils down to is that we need to flex our financial muscles, saying that any loan arrangement is conditioned on reform'.

Although somewhat simplistic, PREM's approaches stand out on two critical aspects concerning the means and objectives of development when compared with the Social Development family. First, SD seeks a participatory bottom–up engagement with recipients, and embraces this methodological process as an objective in itself for strengthening institutional capacity as captured by the new aid architecture. PREM is more top-heavy, guided by objectives of economic growth – the conventional approach that the PRSP intends to demote. Further, PREM's approaches can be classified as either direct or indirect engagement with the government, with the choice depending on the problem – whether 'it is mere corruption, or if government in fact is part of the problem – and of course it's dependent on whether the government participates or not', as the speaker explained. A direct approach is chosen if the government acknowledges that there is a problem with corruption and agrees to deal with it. If, however, the government refuses to embark on anti-corruption measures, the PREM directs its approach through 'allies inside the governance systems or the state, people that can help [to] trigger reform from inside the country'. These are usually referred to as 'champions', and are people internal to the state apparatus who align with the Bank and lobby-proof government officials.

Throughout the course different case studies were presented to illustrate the challenges facing operational activities and in particular how to address political issues and matters pertaining to a state's internal affairs against the backdrop of the Bank's apolitical mandate. With all the case studies, the presenters showed what went wrong by demonstrating various governmental malpractices. The only success stories offered were their own, what they did to 'fix the problems' and how they managed to address governance issues against the apolitical mandate without infringing on the client-state's sovereignty over its internal affairs. The stated challenge is that everything needs to go through the government with its consent. 'And that's where the major problem arises', the presenter told us, 'how to persuade the government to commit to reform itself. That's no easy task. We need to convince government to do the right things and otherwise work through various entry points', or designated champions within the state system already aligning with the Bank. Such 'entry points' are means for approaching a government and installing a reform package without transgressing the sovereignty principle and thereby offending the counterpart.

We can note several common denominators in the various case-study presentations on the course. First, they all focus on when things have gone wrong. Hardly any successful Bank-operation was mentioned, but instead they gave numerous examples of malfunctioning governance systems, corruption, bad management and the influence of vested interests and their negative impact on the society. Second, all the presenters stressed their own successful roles in 'fixing' the various problematic situations they had encountered while working for the Bank, to enhance a good policy and governance environment in their respective cases on the course –Bolivia, Uganda, Indonesia, the Philippines and Ghana, amongst others – arguably demonstrating that success is contingent on individual staff involvement more than on established Bank procedures. Third, in all presentations there was comprehensive reference to and use of data sets, technical analysis, statistics and models to persuade government to initiate reform. Fourth, the presentations neglected the idea of including the recipient in the process.

These elements were all integral to the final part of the course, where participants had to apply in practice what they had learned. Whereas the first three days of the course were devoted to lectures by various key Bank staff members on issues of good governance and anti-corruption, the final day was dedicated to the practical task of simulating the preparation of a Country Assistance Strategy (CAS) for the fictitious country of Uttarstan. Course participants sitting around the same table made up groups, or Bank mission teams, which were to study a particular case and subsequently devise and present their Uttarstan CAS to a panel consisting of the course lecturers in the role of the Uttarstan government. This case, which is used whenever the course is held, was originally drafted by a lead public sector specialist from the PREM group,[27] and thus offers a privileged point for grasping the PREM discourse.

## Preparing a CAS for Uttarstan: Through the Eyes of this Participant

In the introduction to this session we are told that we are to learn and experience – through a role-play that will enable us 'to get a real hands-on feeling with Bank operations' – the difficulties of devising a Bank strategy and later selling it to the government. According to the organizers, this role-play illustrates situations that may occur in Bank–government negotiations, and is 'a real hands-on exercise to prepare Bank staff for operational work'.

The background is that the finance minister of Uttarstan has approached the Bank's country office and urged it to assist with a major public sector restructuring effort. As explained by the country director himself, 'In a letter … the Minister of Finance stated that he was particularly interested in obtaining Bank assistance for strengthening the delivery of certain critical services to the poor (such as primary education and health care), improving governance and combating corruption' (World Bank 2005b).

Each group, or country team, is ascribed the same professional composition as stipulated by the case-study document: a lead country economist, a professor of political science from the University of Uttarstan who is hired as a consultant, a public-sector management specialist from the PREM group in Washington, a public-expenditure management specialist also from Washington, and the Bank's country director for Uttarstan, the latter being the only Bank-employed team member permanently based in Uttarstan.

'Are these the roles we are to play? They are very limited and narrow', one of my team members, based in the ESSD network, sighs. She reacts to the palpable PREM presence in the team which, she holds, reduces the input from other Bank networks, although the finance minister requests help on issues traditionally outside PREM's scope. 'This is so typical. One thing is operational practice… But I honestly thought it would be different in a role play. The Bank always sends the economists and planners in first', she maintains. Others in our group, however, do not seem to agree. Our team consists of five people in addition to myself: the woman from ESSD, one man from the IMF, two from the PREM network and one from the regional department. Although we are to play roles, the group's internal dynamic is driven by the group members' promotion and defence of issues aligned with their institutional affiliation. The IMF representative advocates imposing stronger fiscal discipline. The ESSD representative argues that we should first and foremost respond to the finance minister's approach while we should propose to undertake a baseline survey to gain better knowledge and data before deciding on the diagnosis. The two from the PREM network, as well as the one from the operational side, are, however, and perhaps obviously, more relaxed with and accustomed to the design and content of the exercise, and argue that we can do whatever we like as long as it is convincing, and 'that we manage to convince the government to buy into our plans'. As for my own position in the group, I usually align with the ESSD representative, as this seems most appropriate in view of my affiliation with SD and my academic background.

The case document we are presented with (World Bank 2005b) represents the information that we, the team, have collected over the past two weeks – after the ministry of finance's approach – and serves as the basis for devising the CAS. 'The document', one team member asserts, 'is very PREM-ish. Not strange, given our designated roles.' The background note is divided into four sections. The first three pages concern Uttarstan's social and economic background, with the focus on lexical knowledge, recent IMF-initiated reforms, urban/rural disparities, the political and economic landscape, stagnation in agriculture and industrial protection. The second section, over two pages, concerns the current political situation and the role of the army. Uttarstan has just held general elections that resulted in a new prime minister based on a fragile political coalition, and it is the new government that has apparently called upon the Bank, as fighting corruption – described as endemic to the country – was in focus in the election campaigns of the new leadership. The third section, which is the longest, stretching over almost seven pages, is a summary of the team discussion of the aforementioned information. This discussion centres on the political environment, corruption, governance, institutional accountability and public financial management, and on the economic policy's impact on corruption, with some references to corruption in and patronage of the civil service, the ombudsman and the Anti-corruption and Bribery Agency. The only references here to health and education, issues expressly mentioned by the minister, appear in relation to the last Public Expenditure Review,[28] where the discussion concerns the budget process and not the government's delivery of services. Health and education issues do appear in the fourth section of the paper, which mainly outlines the existing Bank portfolio and previous governance work. Little attention is paid to the requested health and education issues in the document. Instead, the team's discussion is dominated by governance and anti-corruption – both central to the PREM network. The PREM people acknowledge the government's desire for promoting health and education,

> but obviously we must fix the governance system first. There's no point in helping government's service delivery when we know the services won't be delivered properly because of weak state capacity. If you take the PRSP framework seriously, the government should lead the process. But it would be irresponsible [for] us to let a weak and corrupt state system take on these tasks. Governance goes before anything else, and should be a prerequisite for the PRSP and CAS and anything else we do.

Although only one page concerns health and education issues, it is interesting to note how they are dealt with compared to the economic, corruption, governance and political matters. Whereas the latter are dealt with on a macro and structural level, health and education are assessed through singular, micro-events aggregated to signify problems in the health and education portfolios. For instance, the previous CAS sought to address the problem of chronic teacher absenteeism, but 'when teachers showed up for work, they often drank tea among themselves and made no serious effort to teach their classes' (World Bank 2005b: 11). The health programme in the previous CAS also received criticism on micro-issues – like incidents of theft and pilferage of medicines and supplies – that are amplified and thus become crucial to whether the programme is to be extended or not.

The minor attention given to service delivery in the current CAS preparation is due not only to the minimal attention it gets in the background note, but is also a direct result of the country director's priorities – in defiance of the government of Uttarstan's initial intention, a matter that is not highlighted at all in the case document. The country director – who, we are told, is an excellent macroeconomist by training who later discovered institutional economics – has just recently assumed his position. We are also told of his fears

> that a major financial crisis was in the making … This was not something he wanted to happen on his watch. The roots of the problem were institutional and embedded within poor governance, state capture and corruption. It was time for the Bank to move away from its earlier focus upon sector work and to tackle core governance and institutional issues that were at the heart of many problems with project implementation … He was deeply convinced that it was the right thing to do and wanted an improvement of governance to be one of his legacies as country director. (World Bank 2005b: 17)

Against this backdrop, each group is expected to design a CAS to present to selected representatives of the Uttarstan government. Discussions within my group on how to proceed fall into three camps, reflecting different approaches. First, the IMF person wants to 'show that we are serious and impose strong conditions to avoid a financial crisis and show that we do not tolerate corruption in our portfolio'. Second, the one affiliated with ESSD argues there is too little 'empirical evidence', particularly regarding the service delivery issues that the minister wants us to address. The two-week fact-finding mission, she maintains, has not provided thorough or deep enough information to prepare a CAS that can cover both governance reform and help to improve service delivery in the health and education sector. The background paper has a too strong PREM bias, she asserts, which is embraced by and marks the third camp consistsing of the two PREM representatives and the operational officer. As mandated by the paper and argued by this camp, 'we first need to fix the Achilles' heel of weak governance. Everything depends on it. Once we establish a good policy environment, improvements in the health and education sector will follow'. The dysfunctions identified in the health and education sectors drive and legitimize the focus on governance and anti-corruption. In preparing the CAS, we focus on governance reform, but underline the need for more detailed information before possibly embarking on another programme for the health and education sectors. In other words, governance reform must precede a health and education programme.

After finalizing our product, each team presents their CAS to the Uttarstan government, which, for the role-play, comprises the prime minister, the minister of finance, the permanent secretary from the ministry of civil service, the deputy minister for economy, the deputy minister for public works, and a civil society representative. The various roles are played by senior Bank staff active in the course implementation – three from the PREM network and three from the WBI. In the course of the presentations it becomes obvious that all the other groups have struggled with the same problems as we did: the disconnect between the minister's initial approach and wishes on the one side, and the limited case material and the country director's commitment solely to governance reform on the other.

Despite some individual variations, the government's response to the various presentations centres on some common features that, according to the course facilitators, illustrate 'typical government responses to Bank work, which you need to learn how to deal with'. The 'traditional' response is that the Bank is paternalistic in coming with its ready-made plans and policies.

> You come here and expect us to buy into you ready-made reform proposals? We have just had an election and a change in government that illustrates that our governance system works. Why are you so confined to your own understanding of good governance? That much said, we all agree that we have some problems, but they are not limited to governance issues. Whatever happened to the idea of putting us in the driver's seat, as your PRSP model suggests?

The Bank is criticized for imposing too strict conditions and a trusteeship over the client and the formulation of development process and objectives. However, and despite such criticisms of the Bank, the government of Uttarstan acknowledges that it will have to follow the Bank's prescriptions in order to obtain funding. The prime minister speaks:

> Although we might agree there's a need for reform, it might be difficult to carry through. You are asking for critical state-wide changes, which inevitably take [a] long time. First of all, we need fast, visible and effective results to show strength as a new government and to counter the opposition's demand for reform. I might concur with a governance reform and budget cuts, but to do so I first need swift results to convince the electorate and civil servants – to show this government's vigour and efficiency – so they will agree [to] another lending programme and Bank reforms ... Also, when I go to the parliament to suggest your reform plans I would need legible proof and data that the reforms you propose will benefit us.

Although this is a staged setting for the sake of presentation, it shows that staff are accustomed to hearing claims of Bank trusteeship. The facilitators maintain that the case represents a typical Bank–government relation: that the Bank identifies what it believes needs to be done, whereupon it is criticized by the government for being paternalistic. After negotiations and persuasion, accompanied by Bank data and analyses, the government usually concurs, but it needs to have a 'carrot in order to sell it to the electorate and parliament'. This, it is argued, usually takes the form of a quick and effective change backed by the Bank, which serves to increase recognition of the government among the electorate and the opposition. This in turn makes the government more inclined to engage in political reform. In summarizing the course and role-play, one of the organizers explains:

> You now see the difficulties in working on PREM issues, but also the importance of altering corrupt and weak governance systems. Basically, 80 per cent of the challenge of governance reform is to design the plan. The rest is to make the government buy into it. The Bank's analytical tools are important in analysing the situation and presenting the empirical evidences. To hide the disagreement in statistics and ambiguous language is well known to everyone who has crafted a policy document. We all know the devil is in the detail. The technical work is absolutely critical – and

> that's how the Bank is important. It is excellent at technical work, and it enables us to set the agenda in negotiations, also when dealing [with] issues internal to our clients.

This final quote sums up a basic idea within the PREM network: the firm belief in own policy measures and objectives, even when these might diverge from those of the government in question and other networks integral to the Bank. Throughout the course, the PREM network displayed a high level of self-confidence regarding their way of doing things. PREM may adhere to the overarching ideas of the new aid architecture and the PRSP model, but it has an ambiguous relationship to the underpinning ideas of participation, ownership and partnership, which seemed largely forgotten throughout the course. To PREM, governance issues come before other development themes – having a good governance environment is seen as necessary, before engaging in other issues. During the course several remarks were made about 'leaders that don't take governance issues seriously', and how this changed once the Bank had intervened and altered the governance environment. The procedure was referred to as the 'mushroom theory': keeping leaders in the dark and feeding them the dirt.

To illustrate the point, two scenes from the BBC series 'Yes Prime Minister' were presented, showing how state leaders can be opposed and manipulated by the will of civil servants, in Bank parlance known as 'champions of reform'. A further point was made in stating that 'politicians might not necessarily be the problem. It can be just as important to persuade and ally with civil servants and influential permanent secretaries, and frame the information they base decisions upon'. From this follows an elevation of PREM's knowledge and analytical expertise, and its ability to conceal ambiguity – or the devil – in statistics and general terms to obscure complexity and empirical multitude.

This experience shows that, on the one hand, PREM questions 'universal knowledge', meaning that knowledge is seen as a social and cultural product. On the other hand, it also demonstrates a strong belief in the knowledge produced by the PREM network itself – even though this might be challenged by people from other Bank units, as was the case with the ESSD representative who achieved scant recognition for her social development issues among the PREM staff. Throughout the course, the PREM network demonstrated a firm belief in their own means and policies – not least in contrast to the ESSD network. Whereas the ESSD's SD unit bases its work on recognition that development processes and those on the recipient side are multiplex concerns that require local and contextual approaches and solutions through participatory approaches, the PREM staff was seen to have a much stronger faith in solutions devised inside their own network – as illustrated by their work on anti-corruption where PREM, by 'leading the way', seek to shorten the time-horizon towards a less corrupt governance system.

As an epilogue to the role-play, there was a competition between the five groups where the winner was decided by the Uttarstan government's choice of CAS. My group did not win.

## Social Engineering and the Optics of Planning

The empirical material presented above illustrates how the Bank comprises a battlefield of knowledge within, between various departmental units and their representatives. Although the Bank's external representation and official discourse may appear largely homogeneous from the outside, this chapter has shown contestations within the Bank on issues pertaining to the new aid architecture's girding ideas of participation and bottom–up approaches. The internal knowledge battles are a function of the major reorganization of the Bank's internal and external workings – the Strategic Compact – for different reasons. First, it established new thematic scopes and operational approaches in line with and as an expression of the new aid architecture's focus on poverty reduction and partnership. Second, it established new networks, for example the ESSD and thus the SD family, as part of strengthening the implementation of the new thematic scopes and operational approaches. Third, the internal reorganization established the matrix organization, thereby institutionalizing the encounter of different epistemic networks that now compete over influencing the operational side and thereby affecting the Bank's external representation and what meets its partners and counterparts. As asserted by both SD and PREM representatives, operational influence is contingent on the networks' ability to deliver according to operational needs and the requirements of planning. To caricature, while the newer SD family is more in tune with and inclined to address the tenets of the new aid architecture, the PREM network embodies the discursive legacy of the Bank's scope and approaches. Hence, the knowledge battles within are from the outset somewhat skewed as they favour those who are more prone to deliver and serve according to the Bank's operational needs and demands. This begs not only for studying what happens on the receiving end and in the partnership encounter between the Bank and its counterpart (which is expanded upon in the next two chapters), but also for addressing the knowledge requirements for planning and operational activities.

To understand the knowledge battlefields within the Bank and why a particular type of knowledge is privileged by its operational side, I draw upon the work of James Scott who, in *Seeing Like a State*, argues that social engineering and planning are inherently reductionist activities.[29] By focusing on the optical, Scott holds that this reductionism is an effect of the planners' need to *see* their field of intervention in a particular way in order to warrant and enable intervention. This necessity favours a particular form of knowledge, one that limits empirical complexity to the advance of knowledge based on planners' preference for straight lines, legibility and transparency in order to validate intervention. The larger the scheme is the more reductionist the knowledge base becomes. The logics of social engineering is contingent on reducing the complexity of the field – similar to a map that inevitably is reductionist to the terrain it is meant to portray – and thus runs counter to the attempts of bottom–up approaches as this would convey too many empirical uncertainties. What is local and complex becomes standardized and simplified, as social engineering requires legible units to establish causality between intentions, plans, input and expected output. What is seen as empirical fuzz that blurs the model and obstructs planning and implementation is disregarded in favour of the need for legible units. The reductionism inherent to planning and intervention draws on their prerequisite of a sky-high bird's-eye view that manages only to catch simple and relatively homogeneous patterns of the complex – which is the key to Scott's project of understanding 'why so many well-intended schemes to improve the human conditions have gone so tragically awry' (Scott 1998: 4).

How planners see and what they see are highly interlinked, and concern the construction of representations that are crucial in order 'to grasp a complex issue. Observers who want a bigger picture of reality than they can see with their own eyes and from their own vantage point are compelled to construct a series of mediations and proxies between themselves and reality' (Rottenburg 2009: xxxi). Constructing representations, Rottenburg holds, is a matter of translation from what one tends to call 'reality' to its models.[30] This involves a fundamentally reductionist process, as translation merges conventionally separate realms by establishing 'a relation and mediates between multiple elements and makes them compatible and comparable. In this sense, translation also produces commensurability by establishing gauges and metacodes' (ibid.). Translation further involves the interlocking of various knowledge systems and their protagonists, with the result that 'the epistemic community of development experts generally believes that they are standing on firm ground' (ibid.) once the representation – now understood as an objectivistic definition of reality – has been produced. Through the formation of representations, itself a necessity for planning and intervention, 'a form emerges that did not previously exist' (ibid.), which begs the question whether the representation is an accurate translation or whether the meaning has been altered?

To make sense of planning and the construction of representation, Scott identifies four characteristics, or elements, of centralized planning, arguing that the combination of these four leads to failure (Scott 1998: 3–5). Scott writes about the state and therefore not all four elements are found simultaneously in Bank operations. Yet, the elements identified by Scott help us to understand the logic of planning and thus the knowledge interface within the Bank between the different networks and why the operational side of the Bank tends to favour a particular type of knowledge over other competing perspectives.

The first element identified by Scott is an 'administrative ordering of nature and society', which involves simplifying the field in order to get an overview: thus, nature and society are reduced to statistical facts to promote legibility for the planner. Such simplifications – where observations portrayed as being the facts only actually reflect those aspects that are in the planner's interest – share four characteristics: they are *interested*, utilitarian facts; they are nearly always written (preferably numerical) *documentary* facts; they are typical *static* facts; they are *aggregate* facts; and they are *standardized* facts. These 'facts', regardless of their incommensurability, are collected and treated in the same manner, in order to promote comparability and collective, aggregate assessments. The second element is what Scott calls a high-modernist ideology, conceived as firm confidence in scientific and technical progress. The high-modernist ideology implies a rational design of social order commensurate with the scientific understanding of the laws of nature. Planners' approach to nature and society and their overview and simplifications are done in accordance with the high-modernist ideology. This leads Scott to his third element: an authoritarian state able and willing to use the full weight of its coercive power to realize the high-modernist design. In line with the selected representations, or simplifications, planners then set out to form the reality, the nature and sociocultural aspects within their borders of control. The fourth element is interrelated with the third, but concerns the recipients, or the intended beneficiaries, of social engineering, described as a 'prostrate civil society that lacks the capacity to resist these plans' (Scott 1998: 5). As Scott summarizes: 'the legibility of a society provides the capacity for large-scale social engineering, high-modernistic ideology provides the desire, the authoritarian state provides the determination to act on that desire, and an incapacitated civil society provides the levelled social terrain on which to build' (ibid.).

Some points should be added here with regard to the applicability of Scott's work to the present study. Despite ostensible references to the state, Scott's real concern is with the characteristics of planning, and flawed state-initiated interventions in particular. He does not mean to say that the simultaneous presence of the four elements automatically spells failure for any improvement scheme, but notes that all these elements are to be found in flawed interventions. For this study, the third point concerning the coercive power of the authoritarian state may be misleading, as it includes the conventional power of physical force held by the sovereign state over its (element four) prostrate civil society. The Bank does not have the ability to execute such physical force, although it wittingly holds the ability of authoritative coercion through its supremacy in the fields of development knowledge, structures and finance – the new aid architecture and PRSP, as illustrated by developmentality. In such instances it is, with reference to Scott's fourth element, indeed possible to conceive of the Bank's counterpart as a 'prostrate client'.

Scott's work points to the requirements of planning, and how planning is inevitably a reductionist practice that constructs the recipient along lines defined more by the planners' need for legible units to accommodate stringent analysis, than anything reflecting the field's complexity and involving a participatory bottom–up approach, as proposed by the new aid architecture. The empirical material presented above has revealed that the intention of planning is ultimately a headquarters activity concerned with producing representations to establish straight lines and causal relations between development input and results. This demand is both produced by and itself produces discrepancies between various knowledge systems within the planning institution. Knowledge formation within the Bank and the construction of its official discourse and policy to be conveyed to clients evolve through the interface between various systems of knowledge, where the one most attuned to the practices of planning and best equipped to fulfil operational needs seems to prevail.

With reference to the empiricism above, the PREM network would appear to hold a prominent position in this regard, not least in contrast to the SD family. Although official Bank discourse proclaims a PRSP model that champions host government participation and draws on a bottom–up approach as celebrated by the SD group, its internal knowledge regime still seems to prefer the more top–down thinking rooted in the PREM network. The internal knowledge battlefield facilitated by the matrix organization – separating thinkers from doers, constructed horizontally between various networks and vertically between networks and operations – tends to favour knowledge of a particular kind suitable for operational purposes.

There exist various context-dependent regimes of truth within the Bank. The loggerheads situation of PREM and SD bears similarities to the distinction between 'finance' and 'civil society' made in the previous chapter in connection with the preparation of the World Development Report (Kanbur 2001; Wade 2002b). A similar distinction is made by Easterly, a former Bank economist, between 'planners' and 'searchers':

> Planners determine what to supply; Searchers find out what is in demand. Planners apply global blueprints; Searchers adapt to local conditions. Planners at the top lack knowledge of the bottom; Searchers find out what the reality is at the bottom ... A Planner thinks he already knows the answer; he thinks of poverty as a technical engineering problem that his answers will solve. A Searcher admits he doesn't know the answer in advance; he believes that poverty is a complicated tangle of political, social, historical, institutional and technological factors. (Easterly 2006: 6)

The battle between various systems of knowledge within the Bank produces a particular optic and a way of seeing the world to make it comprehensible to operational activity. To caricature, the discontinuities between planners and searchers are akin to those between PREM and SD, and, more generally, between the practices of the old structural adjustment approach and the new aid architecture. As shown by the core course referred to at length above, the planners found in PREM are apparently better attuned to producing the kinds of representations applicable to and needed by the operational demands of dealing with poverty alleviation as a technical engineering problem, to realize a global blueprint defined at headquarters level. SD staff resemble the 'searchers': they are more into open-ended planning without predefined objectives, which rather should be devised through a bottom–up process. The argument to Scott and the PREM group above, and as implied in the Easterly quote, would be that such verbatim participatory approaches would convey too complex knowledge and not facilitate the legibility that planners need for their operational activities. Hence, on a more general level, this points to the difficulties involved in a verbatim implementation of the new aid architecture's ideas of participatory approaches and how internal knowledge battles have effect for the Bank's external activities and its partnership formation in practice.

Development intervention is intrinsically bound to the production of representations and legible knowledge, as functions of how planning works and the requirements of operational activities. Such representations are both produced by a particular way of seeing, as well as they (re-)produce a particular 'development gaze' (Løngreen 2001) – both of which constitute a form of power akin to developmentality.

This chapter has unravelled how various regimes of truth are constructed by attending to the institutional practice taking place within and behind official Bank discourse. By looking beyond the Bank's official discourse and attending to institutional practices and the issue of power as grounded in everyday life, this chapter has demonstrated the complexity and contestation within an entity that from the outside and at the structural level appears largely congruent. Although a post-development approach should not be disregarded in the analysis of larger discourses, by paying attention to actors' conflicting practices within the same institution this chapter has shown how the interface of various actors and discourses entails a knowledge battlefield where meaning is contested and negotiated. The knowledge battles within the Bank are probably not new, but they have gained momentum with the internal matrix organization which both separates and joins various thematic networks and operational units. The internal knowledge battles ramify how the Bank construes its optics or gaze, frames its external representation and thus engages its clients. This draws attention to the productive power associated with developmentality as rooted and manifested within the Bank. Hence, what happens within the Bank may, as a corollary, have repercussions for its external representations and the general formation of Bank–client relationships. That is an empirical question that will be dealt with in the next two chapters.

## Notes

1. See also www.worldbank.org/aboutus.
2. The country director has shared responsibility for operational work in both Uganda and Tanzania. The senior economist had just recently, during my fieldwork, moved to the Kampala office, in line with the current trend of decentralizing Bank staff. According to the senior economist – in a conversation in Uganda – this enhances his opportunity to 'increase his country knowledge, to follow the political situation on a daily basis, and have a closer follow up on operational work'.
3. The networks can be seen as manifesting 'the knowledge bank' (Pincus and Winters 2002) and the aspiration to be a world leader on development thinking – another ambition of Wolfensohn's presidency (Rich 2002).
4. I was allocated an office among the Social Development family, which offered a privileged point for following daily discussions and discourses within that Bank unit. There are obviously more knowledge battles within the Bank than those I happened to encounter and study. Drawing on my fieldwork, the battle between ESSD and PREM is nevertheless most prominent. PREM was the only network that non-PREM staff usually criticized, and it seems most other network representatives share the view that PREM is the predominant network.

5. The Social Development family includes several thematically specialized groups: community-driven development, social analysis, participation and civic engagement, social policy, indigenous people, involuntary resettlement, conflict prevention and reconstruction, and safeguarding policies (see www.worldbank.org/socialdevelopment).
6. I use SD to denote the Social Development group, while their policy scope and themes are denoted and written out as 'social development' – in line to the SD staff's use.
7. The SD group is described in different ways – sometimes as an independent network, other times as a family or thematic group under the ESSD. Davis (author of World Bank 2004a) states the Social Development network was created under the ESSD vice presidential unit. On www.worldbank.org this vice-presidential unit is denoted as 'Sustainable Development', of which Social Development is an underlying thematic group, topic or area of expertise. Sometimes SD is also denoted as SDV, the Social Development Department. There are no formal consistent names for the various sections. In the daily usage, the ESSD and Sustainable Development are similar, and denote the network under which Social Development, as a group or family, is organized.
8. The author of this report, Gloria Davis, became in 1978 the first anthropologist to be hired by the Bank.
9. Bank-wide, there are currently about 850 active trust-fund-financed activities with a total annual disbursement level of about US$ 1 billion (World Bank 2003a; see also https://finances.worldbank.org/trust-funds for a comprehensive list of trust funds. Accessed 28 April 2015).
10. For a comprehensive list of all eighty-two trust fund programmes, see http://go.worldbank.org/CJHIAON6T0. Accessed 28 April 2015.
11. To illustrate, the Trust Fund for Environmentally and Socially Sustainable Development (TFESSD) is obviously located in the ESSD network. The TFESSD is administered by the SD family and is one of the larger trust funds within the ESSD network. It comprises 135 activities in eighty countries, with a cumulative disbursement of US$ 87 million for the 1999–2006 period.
12. The term 'likeminded' refers here to people within the SD family who share values, ideas and approaches. It draws on international development jargon where likeminded has been used to designate the Nordic countries, the Netherlands, Germany and the U.K., which often have joint approaches and programmes due to their common set of shared ideas.
13. One operational staff member denoted the SD unit as 'little Scandinavia' because many of its positions were funded by the 'likeminded group' of northern European countries plus Canada.
14. LICUS, or 'low-income countries under stress', refers to those countries eligible for IDA funding that are in a state of crisis or post-conflict situation. This trust fund was established on 15 January 2004, although it draws on a pilot period following Bank president Wolfensohn's initiative in late 2001.
15. LICUS, as one of the larger trust funds of the ESSD network, manifests the SD approach to state-building, which includes an extensive use of non-state actors as the Bank's traditional counterpart. Countries classified as

LICUS are characterized as having governments too weak to qualify for conventional Bank lending. By initiating activities with other actors, the LICUS initiative seeks to provide basic services and eventually help to establish state structures that can enable Bank lending. In January 2006 the Bank replaced 'LICUS' with the term 'fragile states'.

16. 'LICUS countries' is a common term among those engaged with the trust fund, although it reflects a tautology – 'low-income countries under stress countries' – and thus a reification of LICUS itself.
17. www.worldbank.org/licus (accessed 27 April 2015; emphasis added). Furthermore, LICUS seeks to 'assist them as they initiate the kinds of reforms that would set the stage for arrears clearance and subsequent access to IDA financing and debt relief' (ibid.).
18. Ibid.
19. On 12 January 2005 the document was submitted to and endorsed by the World Bank's Board of Executive Directors.
20. I thank this informant for making me aware of the schism and concepts of SD 'hardliners' and 'pragmatists', thus being not only analytical but also emic concepts.
21. The concept of sustainable development has been instrumental to the pragmatic perspective as it caters to the economic growth perspective while simultaneously seeking to embrace more long-term environmental and social issues (see Bøås and Vevatne 2004).
22. Unless otherwise specified, the quotes in the following section come from various lectures and PowerPoint presentations at this course. The PREM network organizes such courses on a regular basis, sometimes under different names, like the Flagship core course held in April 2003.
23. This strategy was first presented at the Bank's annual meeting in Singapore, September 2006, and was formally endorsed in March 2007.
24. Invitation letter to 'Public Sector Governance and Anti-Corruption Core Course', 14–17 February 2005. Circulated by e-mail.
25. Quoted from the letter of invitation.
26. All these presentations and underpinning documents, largely produced by Bank staff, were given to the participants in the form of a CD-ROM.
27. An Extended Term Consultant, also from the PREM network, had revised the case for the course I attended.
28. Public Expenditure Review (PER) is the Bank's instrument, or tool, when assessing and evaluating the government's budget process and national spending. The PER of Uganda is examined in chapter 6.
29. Scott writes mainly about the state and state planning, but his analysis is applicable to other institutions and agencies devoted to social engineering, as for instance international development aid organizations (see Trouillot 2003; Li 2007).
30. Rottenburg writes that 'translation occurs when an idea or a thing is carried over from one idiom to another, from one culture to another, or when an idea or a thing is connected to another idea or thing in such a way that its effect is intensified as a result (as is the case, for example, with a pulley system or a bicycle chain); or when an idea is manifested in a practice or a thing and vice versa' (Rottenburg 2009: xxxi).

 4

# A Meeting of Partners

## Developmentality as Seen from Uganda

The unfolding of the aid partnership in practice is different from its nominal version. This chapter explores the World Bank–Uganda partnership in practice and how it is instigated by and related to the formal order, thus demonstrating the interconnectedness of the partnership's formal and informal dimensions and the way in which they impinge on each other. Formally the government produces its own development strategy, but after the introduction of the PRSP model the Ugandan strategy has gradually come to resemble any other Bank-supported PRSP simultaneously as it has gradually come to eclipse existing policies and procedures. The Bank's jargon, idioms, procedures and policies increasingly seem to become those of the Ugandan counterpart as the new partnership model settles and entrenches actors at the receiving end (see Harrison 2001b), thus demonstrating the potentials of developmentality.

This chapter examines practices concerning developmentality as articulated in the context of Uganda and in the interface between government bodies and their representatives on the one side, and the Bank and its development partners on the other. The inclusion of development partners – i.e. seemingly likeminded bilateral donors – also demonstrates the expansive features of the new aid architecture and developmentality.[1] This illustrates the Bank's gatekeeping role over the larger development apparatus, thus demonstrating that the Bank is not only an arena where power politics is executed, but also an actor conducting such power politics. The chapter outlines the historical trajectory and the current formation of developmentality in Uganda by examining both narratives and practices of the interface between donor and recipient institutions regarding the evolution and role of the Ugandan Poverty Eradication Action Plan (PEAP), being the Ugandan PRSP. The process of installing the PRSP mechanism as an integral part of Bank–client arrangements has made closer policy dialogue possible on matters otherwise seen as being the sovereign realm of the recipient government. The gradual empowerment of and freedom granted to client governments have been accompanied by an apparatus of mechanisms enabling the Bank to retain control at a distance by making the aid recipient responsible for its own development while remaining accountable to the Bank. The emergence of the PRSP model in Uganda is a story about the Bank's mission creep in practice, and how the new aid apparatus and partnership formation have gradually paved the ground for the Bank's cooption of and increased control over processes previously thought of as beyond the remit of external donor agencies.

The idea of partnership revolves around the participation–conditionality nexus. This dichotomized conceptual pair is central to the new aid architecture and the formation of developmentality. Although emic to development agents, the basic underpinning concepts of the new aid architecture – like participation, conditionality and ownership – are incommensurable in how they ought to anchor and guide practices of partnership, when 'partnership' is interpreted in the strict, formal sense. However, what people say and the representations they provide might not always correspond to what they ought to do or what they actually do. As Olivier de Sardan asserts, development language is 'supposed to address itself to developees while, in reality, it concerns only developers' (Olivier de Sardan 2005: 178). He focuses on the various systems of knowledge present in the encounter between donor and recipient institutions – akin to a focus on interface as the locus for brokerage and knowledge battles (see Fardon 1990; Long and Long 1992; Lewis and Mosse 2006b). Studies of donor–recipient relationships and the knowledge-encounters these entail make it possible to see how heterogeneous strategic groups confront each other and make use of the same concepts and notions by filling them with different meaning.

## The Participation–Conditionality Nexus: Carrot and Stick

The Bank as well as the multiple development partners emphasize different means and objectives in their development assistance to Uganda and the government's PRSP. All, however, stress the importance of national ownership of any development plan involving the government, and that ownership is and should be a fundamental value to any donor effort. Ownership, they claim, emerges from government participation, and engenders commitment and thus efficiency. However, donors' pursuance of different policies and processes indicate contestation not only among donors but also vis-à-vis the government's plan, thus alerting us to the participation–conditionality nexus and how it challenges other gatekeeping ideas, like that of ownership.

There are numerous development actors in Uganda, ranging from small-scale CSOs and NGOs with little direct relation to central authorities, to bilateral agencies of differing size and importance, as well as multilateral institutions like the World Bank, the IMF and the UN. Although these pursue different objectives and employ various means, some work together and thus refer to themselves as 'likeminded' and 'development' partners. Apart from the Bank, this group consists of the African Development Bank (AfDB), the European Commission (EC) and the IMF, and the bilateral agencies of Austria, Denmark, Germany, Ireland, the Netherlands, Norway, Sweden and the United Kingdom.[2] These are all represented in Kampala by their diplomatic mission staff, and, for some, by bilateral aid agencies. Next to the Bank, the British DFID is seen as the most influential donor, drawing on its numerous staff and financial size, as well as diplomatic bonds forged in the colonial era. Development partners who share certain features perceive themselves as 'likeminded'. They meet regularly to share ideas and coordinate efforts; which actors are present depends on the scope and topic of each meeting. Although an influential actor, USAID is noticeable by its absence from this group; they seem reluctant to coordinate and harmonize efforts – or perhaps 'they would like to coordinate, but not be coordinated', as one 'likeminded' phrased it. Other bilateral donors to Uganda with somewhat smaller portfolios include Belgium, France, Canada and Japan, as well as the UNDP. These attend the coordination meetings of the 'development partners' only occasionally.

Formally, the development partners operate within the framework provided by the Ugandan Poverty Eradication Action Plan (PEAP), which is the government's PRSP outlining its national development strategy to which all development actors are to adhere. In preliminary interviews, almost all development partners said they followed this view, asserting that their role was to serve as mere 'facilitators and supporters of the government's initiatives and PEAP'. The concepts of government ownership, participation and partnership were constantly mentioned when I asked development partners to outline the Ugandan aid architecture. Any assertions or questions implying donor paternalism would be abruptly disclaimed. Conditionality was referred to as 'belonging to the past' and 'not relevant to our work in Uganda', although minutes later they might mention the ongoing conditionality review that they found intriguing.[3] It was only when confronted with the effects of a literal application of the participation concept that donor representatives would go into aspects concerning conditionality (see Koeberle et al. 2005). Few, if any, would hold that they do not try to control and influence how their aid assets are managed and spent, calling themselves mere advocates of their respective ministries and guided by their domestic policies, and demands for accountability and audit control. They do not, however, claim this as a form of conditionality, although they recognize that it does not allow for a strict bottom–up process and that the PEAP is not a sovereign product of the Ugandan government.

## Donor Harmonization – Challenging Ownership?

In 2005 donor countries and institutions and recipient countries agreed on the Paris Declaration on Aid Effectiveness, following up the 2003 Rome Declaration on Harmonization.[4] The problems identified and to be tackled were lack of local ownership, increasing fragmentation among donors that was leading to high transaction costs, and insufficient context-sensitive development assistance (Wohlgemuth 2008). In an attempt to make aid more effective, the Paris Declaration stipulates certain partnership principles, such as ownership, harmonization, alignment, managing for results and mutual accountability. The harmonization agenda seeks to bring donor policies and procedures into accord and establish a joint, aligned approach to government plans that relies on the partner country's own mechanisms for implementing projects. A common criticism of the harmonization agenda has been that recipient countries lose out if the donors band together in one grand, concerted approach, as those who hold the purse strings will inevitably override any other, conflicting ideas. The recipient loses the ability to selectively enter into partnership with those donors willing to support its policies, and as such donor harmonization might undermine the processes seeking to enhance participation and ownership.

Already in 2003 development partners in Uganda were embarking on a process of aligning their approaches with the Bank's Country Assistance Strategy (CAS), its triennial response to government's PEAP. This involved trying to harmonize development partners' respective mandates and interests, core competencies and comparative advantages. It took the development partners two years to agree on a joint strategy – the Ugandan Joint Assistance Strategy (UJAS) – that eventually, in January 2006, was approved by the Bank's board. The process was delayed several times and was almost abandoned due to, inter alia, differing donor perspectives and priorities as to how to align, since some would have to abandon their prioritized policies to prevent duplication and overlap. The extent to which political language should be included in the document also drove this battlefield of knowledge, as the Bank – unlike the bilateral agencies – is prevented by its mandate from engaging in political issues.[5]

Development partners seem to have a rather stringent and coherent notion of each others' characteristics, which both drove and became cemented in their harmonization process. For instance, while the Bank is seen to stress good governance and economic and financial management, Norway emphasizes health and education; the Netherlands is seen as dedicated to education and the justice sector; the U.K. prioritizes public sector reform, civil society and democratization; Denmark is understood to be a strong proponent of human rights while also elevating production, competitiveness and income-generating activities on the individual and national levels; Sweden is seen to focus on civil society and democracy; and Japan on infrastructure and road construction. Few informants reflected that the various donors' respective focus could itself be seen to undermine not only harmonization but also government's own priorities and strategies, and thus the scope for national ownership.

While harmonization means those involved should draw on their comparative advantages, the development partners were at loggerheads during the UJAS negotiations over which matters to prioritize. In my discussions with informants, little mention was made of the government's PEAP and the notions of ownership and participation. The more general dilemma was neatly illustrated by a Norwegian diplomat, who said that 'yes, ownership is important', after which she paused for a while before continuing 'but we emphasize health and education'. Although somewhat contradictory, this expression of the conditionality–participation nexus is in line with Norwegian policy and illustrates an ambiguity found among donors in general. On the one hand, Norway has committed itself to ownership and harmonization with other agencies by endorsing the Paris Declaration, by involving itself in UJAS and through a Memorandum of Understanding with the Ugandan government. On the other hand, health and education are areas of concentration for Norwegian development assistance, both in general and in Uganda.

Although the above list is simplistic and based on a generic view that development actors have of each other, they would probably disagree on how they are portrayed, by asserting their complexity and heterogeneity. The list does, however, indicate that different actors emphasize and hold responsibility for different policies and objectives towards the government – itself challenging the very notion of government participation and ownership. To development partners, this division of policies arguably supports the national development strategy, and is commonly accounted for in two ways. First, the plurality is often ascribed to political priorities at the headquarters level of the various actors. Second, the multitude is explained with reference to aid selectivity and a division of labour between the development partners in their joint response to the government's national development strategy. These two points are interrelated. In promoting headquarters' policies, representatives of development partners have not only to negotiate with the client government; they also need to reach agreement within the development community when harmonizing their policies and aligning support to the government's strategy. This concerns the notions of conditionality and participation, and the lack of a stringent division between these concepts. The complex and overlapping use of the two guiding ideas is illustrated by the words of a public sector specialist at the Bank's Kampala office.

> We don't do conditionality any more. That's how we did development a decade ago. Now we've realized that the government needs to own the strategy. We can't impose our plans. It's not the right way of doing it, and it is not an effective way of doing development. Now we let the government participate as a partner and require that they devise their own strategy. This makes them more committed ... But of course we can't accept whatever the government proposes. We also have our demands and priorities.

The quote reveals an interesting comprehension of conditionality. First of all it seems like the specialist is conflating conditionality with the Bank's erstwhile structural adjustment policies. Second, she contrasts conditionality with government participation under the guise of increasing effectiveness. Third, she distances herself from seeing conditionality and participation as a dichotomized conceptual pair. Later in our conversation I return to this seeming ambiguity of how she sees conditionality, and she responds:

> You raise interesting questions. You should have a look at the conditionality review we're [the development partners] undertaking. It elaborates our current view on conditionality. I know the bilaterals want to push it more than us – particularly the political aspects of development. But they know the Bank has its [apolitical] mandate. Still everyone tries to push us on this. They all know that *we have the toughest stick and largest carrot* when it comes to influencing the government.

The latter point refers to donor attempts to influence the Bank in harmonizing their approach vis-à-vis the government. 'It is interesting to note the bilaterals choose to influence us rather than the government', my respondent maintains. Only DFID, she asserts, enjoys somewhat similar influence as the Bank: 'The others are too small alone and need to get their heads together to either influence us or government'. The Bank is used as a proxy for bilaterals seeking to influence government, and that not only creates friction between development partners, but also undermines and challenges the notion of government participation and ownership of processes and policies.

The bilaterals generally share the Bank's ambiguous ideas of conditionality and participation. The main issue on which the Bank and the bilaterals diverge concerns matters of political conditionality. The bilaterals are acutely aware of the Bank's restrictive mandate, but would also like to see the Bank use its leverage to put greater political pressure on the Ugandan government with regard to democratization, human rights, rule of law and governance – which the bilaterals deem important. The requirement of increased conditionality runs counter to the notions of participation and ownership – concepts that the bilaterals tend to celebrate in order to distance themselves from the conditionality concept. Donors thus on the one hand refute notions of conditionality, while simultaneously requiring increased political conditions. This paradox rests on the bilaterals' tendency to equate conditionality with structural adjustment lending – that is, the privatization and liberalization agenda of the World Bank during the 1980s and early 1990s. By prefixing 'political' to conditionality they seek distance from this interpretation. 'So although we are undertaking a conditionality review, this is a kind of conditionality different from structural adjustment. We are not imposing ready-made policies anymore, but we feel it relevant to emphasize certain issues', a representative of the bilaterals explains. This point, as well as the inherent ambiguity between conditionality and participation, is reflected in the minutes of a conditionality review meeting between the Bank and bilateral actors:

> The dialogue on budget support and conditionality centres on political priorities, something the donors must acknowledge. Donors must show respect for national political processes in recipient countries and provide them a certain 'policy space'. Several countries expressed scepticism to political conditionality, but at the same time recognised that *conditionality has a function in supporting positive reformers in a country that does not want reform … We should strive towards finding a term that replaces conditionality* and [that] is a better designation for the current partnership and monitoring based on the countries own poverty strategy.[6]

This excerpt underscores another tension and ambiguity of the conditionality–participation nexus. While the former part of the quote elevates the importance of respecting national processes, akin to ownership, the middle section asserts the potential value of conditionality in countries where there is discontinuity between the government and donors. The latter part proposes finding a less contested term to denote the content of conditionality, which is seen as having too strong connotations to the era when the Bank dictated and imposed structural adjustment programmes. The quote also reveals the dual character of the conditionality concept itself: it is seen as both a particular policy package (although donors claim to have abandoned it) and as a means to impose policies on the recipient. Yet, donors tend to equate conditionality with the policy package of the 1980s, because admitting it as a means to enforce certain policies would run counter to their focus on greater participation and ownership.

Representatives of the government – that is, people employed in the state apparatus and various ministerial bodies – have a somewhat different view on participation and conditionality than the donors. Where the development partners tend to see conditionality as yesterday's policy package, those on the receiving end understand the concept as an attempt by donors to influence the government's sovereign domain of national policy making, or even to enforce certain policies. As an employee in the Ministry of Finance, Planning and Economic Development stated:

> I know donors try to use conditionality, [and] that they tempt with their money to make us buy into their politics. But we don't approve [of] it. We don't like conditionality and being told what to do, so we refuse … Uganda is a sovereign nation … Donors say we should develop our own strategy and that we should have ownership [of] it and be in the lead. So my basic question to the donors when they come with this ownership talk is: why are you here? Obviously they don't trust us and would like to control us, but we decide and we would not buy into any policies if we don't agree to them.

State bureaucrats understand conditionality as a means for donors to enforce policies. One reason they do not equate conditionality with the policy package of liberalization and privatization might be because the Ugandan government embarked on these policy processes from the early 1990s (cf. Museveni 1997; Harrison 2004). Despite the left-wing, Marxist orientation of President Museveni and his government, Uganda embraced the Bank's structural adjustment package of privatization, liberalization and other policy measures of that ilk – allegedly after some arm-twisting by the Bank (Mwenda 2010).

Government officials follow a strict interpretation of the participation concept, arguing that they are sovereign and alone in devising their development strategy, while simultaneously recognizing that development partners aspire to greater influence. The policy-making process is described as a participatory one, 'but we are constantly approached by the donors. They like to influence what we are doing'. This reflects an ambiguity as to how the relationship of conditionality and participation is understood. While disregarding accusations of donor trusteeship and stressing their sovereignty over national policy processes, government representatives also acknowledge donor influence over the policies they fund.

There is no clear-cut, harmonized consensus on the participation–conditionality nexus internal to the various actors involved – the Bank, bilateral donors and government – and even less so among them. Whereas most seem to agree that 'participation' is intended to mean that the government should lead and own externally funded policy processes as the PEAP, there is less agreement as to what 'conditionality' means and entails. Is it a particular policy package, or a means to enforce certain policy? While the Bank subscribes to the former, bilateral agencies and the recipient government hold the latter understanding of conditionality. The above illustrates the lack of a shared understanding of basic ideas inherent to the aid architecture, thus affecting its articulation in Uganda. While all the actors embrace the morally charged concepts of ownership and participation, the idea of conditionality 'is too incriminating, having wrong connotations, being subversive to what we are trying to achieve and runs somewhat counter to basic principles of sovereignty', as a bilateral representative told me.

Recognizing the diverging views on the girding ideas of the new aid architecture and the disconnect between rhetoric and practice, the next section provides a historical account of the evolution of the Ugandan PEAP. This process involved the encounter between the government and the Bank under the nominal circumstances of participation as stipulated by the PRSP model. It describes the historical trajectory of the Ugandan PEAP that, from being a national planning and policy document detached from the Bank's realm, eventually became transformed into a PRSP and thus inscribed into routines and practices of the Bank. The second part looks into such a routine and practice: the Poverty Reduction Support Credit (PRSC) mission, whereby the Bank sends a mission from headquarters level to negotiate its lending programme with the government. Together these parts reveal contestation over the fundamental ideas of the new aid architecture and indicate ambiguities of its direct and strict implementation. What evolved instead are a participation–conditionality nexus and an amorphous aid architecture that demonstrate the workings of developmentality and how the Ugandan PEAP is increasingly being inscribed into the realm of the Bank. This, in effect, questions the ideas of ownership and participation which allowed for the instigation of developmentality in the first place.

## The Formation of PEAP

The aid architecture as spelled out and promoted by the World Bank has its particular and historical trajectory and articulation in Uganda. The Ugandan Poverty Reduction Strategy Paper (PRSP) is locally known as PEAP – Poverty Eradication Action Plan. While the Bank initiated its PRSP mechanism in 1999, this was after the first Ugandan PEAP in 1997. Based on the PEAP, Uganda became a CDF pilot country in 1999. There are ample reference points between the Bank's establishment of a new aid architecture and Uganda as a showcase client with regard to adopting and implementing its CDF and PRSP framework. The infusion of the structures relating to the new aid architecture and thus developmentality followed the institutional trajectory of the first PEAP (1997–1999), largely detached from the Bank, via the second PEAP (2000–2004), which served as Uganda's CDF entry point and thus its first PRSP, to the third PEAP (2004/5–2008/9), which engrained the Bank's PRSP model.

The first PEAP established the policy framework for the eradication of poverty throughout 2017. It presumably draws on a consulting process initiated by President Museveni in 1995, when he mobilized members of parliament, government ministers and donors, and took them to the rural Luwero triangle (Museveni 1997).[7] The trip intended to show the donors the poor state of roads, schools, dispensaries, general infrastructure and the extent of poverty in the region. From this consultative process, the Government of Uganda (GoU) largely managed to align donors to the idea of a national poverty strategy, as formulated in the 1997 PEAP. In 1999, the government formulated a new development plan, 'Vision 2025', with an overview of long-term goals and aspirations, epitomized as 'prosperous people, harmonious nation and beautiful country' (GoU MoFPED 1999). While this provided the vision, the PEAP establishes the policy framework for poverty eradication in the context of a two-decade perspective. From 1999 the GoU engaged in a process of revising the PEAP, allegedly due to its recognition that 'the poor had not been sufficiently consulted' (Isooba and Ssewakiryanga 2005). Following the revision process, the second PEAP was adopted as the Ugandan PRSP. The revision process and the Bank's adoption of Uganda as a PRSP pilot country went unprecedentedly fast. National revision started in December 1999, and a draft version was presented in March 2000. In order to fast-track the pilot-country process, in May 2000 the Bank and the IMF approved a *summary* of the revised, second PEAP as the Ugandan PRSP.[8]

To most donors (notably the Bank) and government representatives, the historical trajectory of PEAP and in particular its precedence to the Bank's PRSP model have somewhat different meanings. To the donors it means there is strong national 'leadership and ownership' of the PEAP document with regard to both devising and implementing it. The PEAP is praised as 'homebrewed' and a 'sovereign product of a government showing willingness to reform and commit itself to development', as a Bank staff member recalled. This view commonly arises when donors are faced with criticism of trusteeship, of superimposing their own policy and of undermining the sovereignty of the recipient state. Among government officials the same historical trajectory is read as Uganda being seminal and conducive to the Bank's PRSP model – that it 'in fact was us and not them who came up with the idea of a comprehensive national strategy for poverty eradication', as held by a GoU representative involved in the PEAP processes.

I met this informant several times. The quote above is from our first meeting, which was interrupted when he had to attend to the donors who had suddenly requested a meeting. When I returned to his office a week later for a rescheduled meeting, he was busy and reluctant to talk, feeling I ought to have sufficient information on the PEAP process from our previous meeting. He was not interested in a long conversation, but was open for succinct and practical questions. Feeling dejected at once again being rejected by an informant who others deemed highly central, I asked a rather open-ended and critical question regarding the PEAP trajectory: why is it that the PEAP over time has increasingly come to resemble any other PRSP and Bank document? After a brief silence, my informant provided a very comprehensive answer, quite against his self-imposed time constraint. The presentation below draws on his response.

In transforming PEAP into Uganda's PRSP, he noted, the first PEAP revision started in December 1999; the Bank's CDF/PRSP framework had been launched the preceding January. The May 2000 approval of PEAP as PRSP was based on a summary of the former. This fast-tracking and bypassing of regular, more rigid Bank procedures was possible because there was a shared understanding between the government and the Bank that Uganda should be a CDF pilot country, with effect already from 1999. While a driving factor for the Bank was that it needed pilot countries – preferably showcase countries that had already demonstrated a willingness to comply with Bank policies[9] – the government of Uganda was eager to become a pilot country, as this would mean support for processes already undertaken by the government;

moreover, the PRSP meant inclusion in a much-coveted programme of debt relief.[10]

While the second PEAP was fast-tracked in the Bank system into a PRSP, the revision of PEAP II was much more extensive and typical of the traditional Bank–client country interface. Although the second PEAP was to run throughout 2004, the revision process had already started in November 2002. First was the formulation of a Poverty Status Report, now installed as a biannual event undertaken by the Ministry of Finance, Planning and Economic Development (MoFPED), as the body responsible for overseeing and implementing the PEAP, to present evidence on progress towards the targets spelled out in the PEAP. This revision included contributions from NGOs because of the Bank's demand for increased participation of civil society and grass-roots organizations. Second, driven by the rationale of both maintaining control over the revision process and creating a node for internal (domestic actors) and external (with donors) PEAP communication, the MoFPED established a PEAP secretariat to ensure it was on the top of the PEAP revision process. The revision process officially started in mid-July 2003 with a 'stakeholders' workshop' from which, inter alia, a new design for further decentralized consultations emerged. Consultations were now to be held at the levels of central government, local government, private sector, and within civil society. The central government-led consultation was divided into fourteen sectoral working groups, each with at least five CSOs. The inclusion of sub-government levels, civil society and the private sector is directly in line with the intentions spelled out in the Bank's original CDF document – which also divides the various activities into fourteen sectors. Gradually we see how the Ugandan PEAP became inscribed into the Bank's realm, although my informant probably did not intend to demonstrate it.

The inclusion of CSOs made the PEAP revision more extensive, comprehensive and challenging. This largely served to impede progress. Although the PEAP secretariat had outlined a strict timeframe for preparing PEAP III by the end of 2003, it was a year before the revision process was launched and a year and a half after consultation before the third PEAP was finalized (see also Ssewakiryanga 2005). Whereas government representatives argue that they included CSOs in the process for it to be more 'comprehensive' and 'participatory', CSO representatives recall how they had to struggle to be included. After failing to convince the government, they approached the Bank to advocate their case with reference to the seminal PRSP idea of an inclusive and participatory planning process involving the CSOs. As a Ugandan civil society representative involved in the process writes: 'Due to donor aid influence and conditionalities, participation is becoming central. It is also becoming increasingly fashionable for CSOs to describe the approach to their work as participatory. The scenario that has emerged, especially between CSOs and government, is best described as the politics of participation' (Isooba 2005: 44). This parallels the narrative of the government representative involved in the PEAP drafting process who argued: 'We cannot ignore donor conditionality. If they want us to enhance the civil society involvement, we need to do so. Although a condition, we don't necessarily oppose it'.

The process from PEAP I to PEAP III has brought to the fore a strategy that increasingly bears the Bank's stamp in terms of procedure, structure, result and jargon. The first PEAP outlined various general prioritized programme areas.[11] By the second PEAP, when it also became accepted as the PRSP, these were renamed 'pillars', being in line with common Bank parlance and its PRSP set-up. Pillars represent broad goals for national poverty eradication, of which PEAP II contains four.[12] PEAP III renamed and expanded the number of pillars to five.[13] These renamed pillars now appear in a language that is closer to that of the Bank and its designated knowledge networks: 'directly improving the quality of life of the poor' is now 'human development'; 'creating an enabling environment for sustainable growth and transformation' is now simply 'economic management'.[14] Note also that none of these themes was explicit in the first PEAP. In the second version the themes appeared, and in the third PEAP the Bank's labels are in place.

On the policy level, the most important change relates to *good governance*, referring to the process of decision making and the process by which decisions are implemented or not. Good governance is thereby a qualitative measure of the governance environment referring to certain characteristics like participation, greater government transparency and accountability, political decentralization and multiparty democracy (Pomerantz 2004). Hence, good governance concerns the internal workings and practices of the recipient state, and as such also involves the PEAP process. It is interesting to note that in Uganda's first PEAP, which did not imply Bank involvement, there was no mention of good governance. Good governance became increasingly prominent in the PEAP parallel to the Bank's growing involvement in the process. While totally absent in the first PEAP and lumped together with 'security' in the second, good governance was singled out as an independent pillar in the third PEAP. There might be various reasons for this. Although the Bank's governance agenda dates back to the mid-1990s it was not until about 2000 that it started to gain momentum and become a significant part of the Bank's lending portfolio. This follows the trajectory of budget support and the PRSP model. With the PRSP model the Bank removed itself from micro-managing a host of different Bank-controlled projects, instead transferring responsibility to the client to devise its poverty eradication strategy, to which the Bank would provide budget support. To maintain control, or at least minimize misuse, of finances and the policy-making process, the good governance agenda made it possible to deal with the state apparatus' internal procedures of checks-and-balance systems, aimed at improving the governance environment, decision-making processes and economic management in order to increase efficiency.

Good governance has evolved parallel to the resurgence of the state as a means and objective of development assistance: the greater the role of the Ugandan government in the policy-making and implementation process, the more emphasis the Bank puts on internal procedures and the ability to conduct these tasks. The good governance pillar is inward-looking, focusing on the government's institutional capacity to devise and manage its own strategy and finance transfers from the Bank. Likewise, refocusing the PEAP II pillar from 'creating an enabling environment for sustainable growth' to 'economic management' also demonstrates the turn from the state's productive role in the economic domain to an inward-focus on the state's own policies and procedures. The better the governance system, the less is the Bank's hands-on involvement.

Another rationale for the Bank to separate 'good governance' from 'security' is that issues pertaining to the latter are deemed to be too political and thus beyond the Bank's mandated scope and core competencies (Lie 2008b). The association of good governance and security issues under the same pillar had restrained the Bank from involvement with the former. Informants on the Ugandan side assert that the original security and governance pillar of PEAP II was meant to address the security situation in northern Uganda and the Lord's Resistance Army. Arguably, singling out good governance as a separate pillar in PEAP III meant reduced capacity in the northern region and an increase in external scrutiny of the central state apparatus.

Although the government is responsible for both preparing and implementing the PEAP, from the above we can see that the formation of PEAP has increasingly come to bear the mark of Bank influence and has become inscribed into its model. Nevertheless, both government and Bank staff maintain that this is a government-driven process in which the Bank has, at most, been 'consulted'. In their arguments, the Bank fears being associated with conditionality, while government representatives are reluctant to indicate reduced ownership and demoted sovereignty over national policy processes. Hence it is difficult to assess *how* influence, or consultation, takes place – not least due to the diachronic character of the above. In the section below, mechanisms available for the Bank to exert influence over a client's domestic policy process are presented. This rests on the PRSP being merely a policy document and not directly linked to aid disbursement. The crux of Bank influence derives from its policy response to the client's PRSP and its financial instruments at hand.

## Responding to PEAP

The PEAP is nominally the sovereign product of the Ugandan government. This means the Bank is formally detached from the process of making and implementing it, although the inclusion of other stakeholders in the process – like civil society and private actors – came as a request from donors. The Bank applies other instruments in relating and responding to the PEAP, of which the Bank's Country Assistance Strategy (CAS) and Poverty Reduction Support Credit (PRSC) are the most important. Whereas the CAS is the Bank's policy response to PEAP, PRSC is the Bank's financial commitment and is deducted from its own CAS, not the government's PEAP.[15] A CAS spells out which parts of the PRSP the Bank is willing or able to finance:

> The CAS takes as its starting point the country's own vision for its development, as defined in a Poverty Reduction Strategy Paper or other country-owned process. Oriented toward results, the CAS is developed in consultation with country authorities, civil society organizations, development partners, and other stakeholders. The purpose of the CAS is to set out a selective program of Bank Group support linked to the country's development strategy and based on the Bank Group's comparative advantage in the context of other donor activities ... The CAS includes a comprehensive diagnosis – drawing on analytic work by the Bank, the government, and/or other partners – of the development challenges facing the country, including the incidence, trends and causes of poverty.[16]

The CAS thus holds a prominent position in determining how and what the Bank chooses to fund of the policies proposed by government in its PEAP. Conventionally CAS is a document devised primarily by the Bank, but it might consult government and its development partners.[17] In the current Ugandan context the bilateral donors have been included, and the CAS has been renamed the Ugandan Joint Assistance Strategy, or UJAS. The formation of UJAS involved a challenging battle of knowledge between development partners who disagreed on aid selectivity – which development partner to spearhead which thematic sector – and the extent to which political conditionality should be included. This battle lasted for two years, so UJAS was not endorsed by the Bank or made operational until 17 January 2006. Although UJAS was not active at the time of my fieldwork, the term was already in common usage.[18]

The official version states that it was the government who called upon the development partners to harmonize their approach in UJAS, in order to reduce the budgetary procedures and transaction costs that came from each donor demanding that the government subscribe to individual and diverse reporting routines. The government, and some bilaterals, have questioned the relationship between PEAP and UJAS: 'why should we prepare a PEAP when it is inevitably the UJAS that means most to the Bank?' and 'why was the Bank so eager to transform the PEAP model into a PRSP?' On the Bank side, the arguments involve the intention to maintain control over the lending portfolio – 'we simply couldn't detach ourselves to the extent the PRSP model initially proposed' and 'the UJAS instrument not only enables us to maintain a certain degree of control, but also allows us to focus on our core competencies'. The UJAS involves a process in which donors 'cherry pick' among the wide range of PEAP issues. This cherry picking draws on what the various donors deem most pertinent to their own competency and scope – or what has been designated to them through donor harmonization. Since 'everything is in the PEAP', as a Bank staff member claimed, the cherry picking involves more contestation between donors than between donors and government. The importance of UJAS, however, rests in its links to finance and disbursements of funds, which is provided through the PRSC.

The PRSC is one of several arrangements and instruments implied with Bank operations and its partnership modality that indicate developmentality. The PRSC credit arrangement is the Bank's mechanism for direct budget support and, in line with the PRSP model, grants to the government the resources and responsibility for implementing its policies as selected by donors in UJAS. Budget support is privileged to both government and the Bank: it allows the government control and priority over funds and spending. To the Bank, it provides important opportunities to engage in close policy dialogue with government on wide-ranging structural issues, especially those related to growth and structural reform. Budget support makes possible such policy negotiations on an annual basis. While UJAS parallels the PEAP as a triennial exercise, the PRSC involves annual negotiations between government and the Bank where performance is assessed vis-à-vis policies stipulated in UJAS. Bank staff refer to these annual discussions as 'PRSC missions'. The first Ugandan PRSC came in 2001, the year after Uganda got its PEAP accepted as a PRSP.[19] PRSCs 1–4 (from 2001 to 2004) have all amounted to US$ 150 million in budget support. PRSC5 negotiations – which took place at the time of my fieldwork and are presented below – originally aimed at maintaining this level, but it was eventually reduced by 10 per cent to US$ 135 million, due to 'disagreement on the attainment of stipulated prior actions', according to one Bank staff member.

The notion of prior actions is central to the debate on conditionality – and indeed the formation of developmentality. Discarding structural adjustment lending led to a decrease in the number of binding conditions imposed by the Bank. This decrease has, however, 'been accompanied by a sharp upturn in the number of benchmark or "soft" conditions' (Wood 2005: 1), i.e. 'prior actions'. The Bank does not see prior actions as imposed conditions since they have been defined and agreed upon by the Bank and government in the annual PRSC negotiations. The Bank sees prior actions as 'policy actions that the country agrees to take before the Bank's … Executive Board approves a loan' (Bull, Jerve and Sigvaldsen 2006: 4). Prior actions do not necessarily entail clear unambiguous quantitative measures – they may be highly qualitative and thus subject to severe controversies. Compliance with prior actions and their stipulated benchmarks is required before funds are released, as the Bank needs to be convinced that 'satisfactory progress' has been made (see Wood 2005) and that there is a conducive policy environment where future assistance will yield results. These highly subjective measures are discussed during the annual PRSC missions.

## The Bank's Mission in Uganda

The PRSC is the Bank's mechanism for budget support operations. The PRSC mission involves a forum for policy dialogue and negotiations between government and the Bank and its development partners.[20] For the mission to Uganda taking place during my fieldwork, negotiations focus on whether government has achieved previously stipulated objectives, and on jointly formulating new 'prior actions' – subject to scrutiny for next year's mission – with the objective of determining the scope and size of budget support.

> Every year there is a new PRSC mission. That's how the project cycle works. This mission is the fifth. It indicates that Uganda has good relations with the Bank, and that it has come a long way in incorporating our

> [the Bank] routines. They now realize how we operate – which makes our job much easier. I believe this mission will go rather smooth and easy, as missions tend to do. We only need to agree with government.

This quote is from a Kampala-based Bank employee who was reflecting on the PRSC mission team soon to arrive from headquarters in Washington DC. Smooth partnership and cordial negotiations, he indicates, depend on those on the receiving end having incorporated the routines and realm of the Bank. A slightly different view was offered by government staff who see the PRSC model as undermining the long-term thinking of PEAP: 'It's not only a result of the PRSP model, we also want to plan in a long-term perspective but the annual PRSC exercise makes it difficult'. The state bureaucrat refers to the PEAP's triennial outlook which, although being endorsed by the Bank, only receives financial support on an annual basis. 'Our performance is evaluated annually, although our objectives and vision exceed the three-year cycles we are destined to plan according to'. The informant was here referring to the first PEAP's policy outlook towards the year 2017 and the government's 'Vision 2025'.

Government staff also complain about the extent and frequency of Bank missions. 'Now, when they come, they'll stay for over two weeks. We want and need to meet them. They provide funding and invaluable input. But expecting us to take part in all meetings and discussions distracts us from doing our job – which is, at least partly, precisely what they evaluate'. There is scepticism towards the Bank, which expects 'us to drop whatever we are doing to accommodate them once they're here'. PRSC missions are extensive exercises that follow a certain Bank-stipulated ritualistic form.

> Well, first we have an *identification mission,* where we look into needs, intentions and possibilities. Then later comes the *pre-appraisal mission* where we review results and attained achievements. Subsequently comes the *appraisal mission,* which is a continuation but involves increased dialogue with the government to agree on the assessment that forms the basis upon which the Bank will tailor its next PRSC loan. The final step is *negotiations* – between government and donors. Negotiations are more technical in character, on how to disburse loans, to which sector, and so on. The most important part is the appraisal. That's when the Bank mainly conducts its analytical work, and that's where we assess previous prior actions and stipulate new ones.

This cycle is repeated every year. The concept of 'prior action' refers to a new disbursement tactic from the Bank's side – 'but this should not be seen as a new form of conditionality', I was told. Disbursement of PRSC funds is conditional on the government implementing and fulfilling certain defined 'prior actions'. Traditionally the Bank authorized loans before the country had begun implementation of structural and policy reforms, under the pretext that the funding should cover the reforms. Now, funds are released after the government has fulfilled the stipulated conditions and demonstrated satisfactory performance. This move – which in the Bank vocabulary is phrased as one 'from *ex post* to *ex ante* conditionality', as said by the informant who minutes earlier had rejected prior actions as 'conditionality' – came along with the PRSP model to comply with the highly criticized conditionality of policy-based lending.[21] This evolved from the Bank's recognition that government 'participation' and 'ownership' are paramount to produce results. The rationale of why the informant rejects conflating prior actions with conditionality is that prior actions 'are not something we impose on government. We formulate and agree on the prior actions together, drawing on the PEAP and government's own policy'. Consequently, the government is seen to own and be responsible for the prior actions. At the PRSC mission to Uganda, discussions of prior action came to the fore.

## Bank–Government Interface

The World Bank's PRSC5 'appraisal mission' to Uganda took place from 2 to 17 May 2005. What government and Bank staff initially thought would be a 'business as usual' mission, where they would quickly agree upon the context and framework, turned out to be a period of considerable turmoil and political discussions. This is evident if we compare the 'kick-off' and 'wrap-up' meetings that marked the formal start and end of the PRSC mission. These meetings are commonly perceived by staff of the Bank, government and other donors, to be boring, and without particular interest or value. 'They are only a formal exercise – nothing happens. So if you want to attend, be my guest', my inviter, a government employee, said.

## The PRSC Kick-Off Meeting

The 'kick-off' meeting is held at the Office of the Prime Minister (OPM),[22] where the Bank's mission team – having come from DC – meet government representatives, notably permanent secretaries, technical officers and bureaucrats. I am invited to sit in and am told in advance, by an OPM senior officer, that 'this is regular formal procedure. Nothing really happens, but it illustrates how the formal diplomatic links work. The interesting stuff takes part in other, more informal meetings'. This is confirmed by Bank staff. For instance, just prior to this meeting there was a 'mission brief' for selected GoU and Bank officers. Allegedly that meeting was planned from 9.00 to 11.30 AM, but discussions kept them busy until the kick-off meeting at 2.30 PM. I arrive on time, but there is still hardly anyone present because the mission-brief meeting is running over time.

As people gradually enter the room they all position themselves strategically around the big hardwood table. The state bureaucrats, most of whom I recognize from previous meetings and interviews, seat themselves – as I do – beyond the table itself. 'This is politics', I am told. 'I am not a politician. I'm a technocrat. Those around the table do the politics.' Members of the Bank's mission team sit at the head of the table, on the same side as its development partners who attend as observers, while the permanent secretaries sit on the opposite side. The seats at the very head of the table, however, are reserved for those who attended the mission brief. Once in place the meeting's chairperson, a permanent secretary, delivers the formal welcome remarks, in which he also speaks of the prior actions negotiated in the preceding pre-appraisal mission.

> As you are aware the successful implementation of these prior actions is a useful indicator to our development partners of [the] government's policy reforms, and enables them to make decisions to support our poverty efforts through budget support ... At the end of the pre-appraisal mission three out of eleven prior actions were identified to be either at risk or off track ... [We will] work with the mission and show evidence that the situation of the performance of those prior actions that are categorized as either 'at risk' or 'off track', is not as bad as they appear. We need to show the progress that has been made since the pre-appraisal mission on those three prior actions ... the mission also intends to work with government to fine tune the PEAP.

Much attention is given to the prior actions, particularly by the Bank. The Bank's mission team leader, who sits at the top end of the table, declares – after the usual formalities and with reference to the ritualistic PRSC cycle – that

> we won't move into *negotiations* if we don't see progress on the prior actions. As the pre-appraisal mission showed, we are not in tune with prior actions. This mission is important for both PRSC5 and 6. The whole PRSC5 depends on government's progress and compliance with the prior actions. It should be needless to remind you that you have agreed to them. I recognize some are difficult but you still need to show commitment. I cannot emphasize enough that we cannot continue, or move into PRSC5

> negotiations, [until] we have agreed upon the performance, implementation and progress of the prior actions we defined last year. We also need to settle on the prior actions for next year, for the PRSC6. All this needs to be done before we can continue progress and start negotiating the PRSC.

The team leader hands out a sheet of paper showing the status of the prior actions, based on Bank staff's assessment and consultation with government representatives. The paper shows the eleven prior actions attached to four of the five PEAP pillars.[23] 'As you all see, there is a huge disconnect between anticipated actions and actual performance on at least three prior actions', the team leader maintains.

Prior actions involve highly subjective measures, where the Bank would like to see 'improvement', 'progress' and 'satisfactory implementation' of the eleven stipulated prior actions. Prior actions are classified hierarchically as 'off track', 'at risk', 'on track', 'partially met' or 'completed'. Of the eleven prior actions, three are assessed as 'completed', five as 'on track', two as 'at risk' and one as 'off track'. The prior action deemed to be 'off track' relates to the PEAP's good governance pillar, and concerns the Inspector General of Government (IGG). This anticipated prior action (no. 5) deals directly with the state apparatus' internal practice, i.e. good governance: 'IGG verifies asset declarations of Ministers and appropriate action is taken by relevant authorities in accordance with the law', the distributed note reads. In the space for comments is written: 'There has been limited progress with only 10 declarations partially verified out of the agreed 64 … Implementation is off track'. The two anticipated prior actions considered to be 'at risk' are no. 2: 'Expenditure for Public Administration in 2004/5 should be within the agreed allocations for budget 2004/5', and no. 8: 'Increased alignment of budget allocations of [eight ministries] to PMA review undertakings'.[24] These prior actions relate to the PEAP pillars 'Economic Management' and 'Enhancing Production, Competitiveness and Income' respectively. After presenting the note and the assessment of the various prior actions, the team leader repeats that 'we won't move into negotiations before we have agreed on the prior actions and defined new prior actions for next year's mission'. Later he explained that he had said this to underscore the seriousness of the matter.

Those attending the meeting are disturbed by the note. A government representative asserts: 'You exaggerate the problem. Your analysis is based on old information. Much has changed since the identification mission and we have, by and large, accommodated all the concerns you raise'. Another representative questions to what extent the Bank updates its analysis, since 'we agreed on the prior actions last time. For us that means we have committed to meet your requirements. I believe you should update your data set and make a new assessment of the prior actions'. The increased tension is suspended by the Bank's team leader when he says, 'Very well. We'll look into what you have done. Achieved progress is one thing, but we also need to be convinced that the government still is willing, committed and capable to deliver in the future. You did agree to the prior actions, so you should demonstrate that you own them … It is crucial that we determine this in the coming weeks'.

As the meeting fades out I turn to the bureaucrat who had originally invited me in. He deems the meeting as boring and as expected:

> I knew precisely what they would talk about. In fact, I was just listening to myself. I wrote the opening address note, and I had been communicating with all actors in advance. This is only a shadow play. They [the Bank] don't mean to be so strict. They can't be. Those guys are playing politics, but it is in fact technocracy. They always start hard, but they never put leverage behind their critique.

Leaving the venue I am approached by a Bank employee I had met in Washington DC. As part of the country team, he travels to Uganda regularly. He says it is good to see me again and he is happy that I have established relevant contacts in Uganda who can enable me to follow the mission. 'So, what do you think of the meeting?', he asks. I respond that it was interesting compared to my expectations, as I had been told it would be a boring formalized meeting. 'Well, Jon, you should not put too much into this. We're all just trying to consolidate our position before we get the mission rolling. This is normal. We raise our concerns, and they respond.'

A technical officer central to the government's dialogue with the Bank offers a somewhat different view on the meeting:

> You know, these guys don't know Uganda and what we are doing here. They come here on and off. They never stay long. They should know that if we say we will do something, we do it. That they haven't updated their prior actions assessment shows that they don't pay enough attention to what we do. Once they realize what we have done since their last visit I don't think there will any problems reaching an agreement. But they need to see. Seeing is believing. So it is good they're here … We are used to the Bank pushing for what they want. Of course, that's their job. My job is to ensure that we get what we want. But we are not used to this harsh tone. It is not very diplomatic considering our coming meetings. But I know that guy [the team leader]. I think Uganda is new to him. He knows the Bank, but not Uganda.

The government representative asserts that the harsh rhetoric is due to the Bank moving in a more political direction and that it has bought into the bilaterals' judgemental attitude to domestic political matters. 'I understand the bilaterals. They can be political – but not the Bank. Second, they do not understand our system. We, like anyone else, are allowed to direct our own politics.' He claims the prior actions are on track; and he is convinced that once the Bank does its analytical work, the updated assessment and meetings between government and donors will settle the dispute before the concluding wrap-up meeting – which, he claims, has the same ritualistic form and function as the kick-off meeting.

## Contextualizing PRSP Negotiations

The meetings he referred to are the extensive interfaces between donors, with the Bank in the lead, and government representatives, conducted under the umbrella of PRSC negotiations. Prior to the mission, people on both the government and donor side had given me the impression that I would basically have unrestricted access to most of these meetings. However, come the mission, the situation changed. I was notified and invited into only a small portion of them. Both my own understanding and my informants' explanation of this change point to the political tension between development partners and government, as well as between bilateral actors and the Bank, that escalated in-between the kick-off and wrap-up meetings. It also became somewhat difficult to catch up with informants, and arrange meetings and interviews, since most people seemed busy with the PRSC negotiations, particularly the Bank staff only temporarily in Kampala for the mission. Whereas the Bank's mission staff were generally occupied with meetings, ministerial employees were more open to talk, as long as they were not 'requested for by the Bank'.

Mission staff and resident representatives of the Bank and bilateral donors tend to meet after working hours, in what is called 'the 5.30 meetings'. These meetings are held daily throughout the mission period and provide an informal venue for information-sharing and discussions. This facilitates discussions among donors on their joint progress and dialogue with government. I hoped to sit in at this venue, but disagreement among development partners on their joint government approach and the extent to which aid should be used for political means obstructed my participation.[25] Government representatives are invited to these 5.30 meetings, but they seldom attend. One of my informants preferred to spend time with his family after working hours, and held that the expat community's lack of family obligations and the visiting mission's dictates were reasons for the inappropriate scheduling of these daily meetings.

The political tension between the Bank and government soon leaked to the press. During the mission, the media provided daily references to or leakages from the negotiations. These usually concerned either donor paternalism or the revelation of government mismanagement of public monies. On 17 May people in Uganda woke up to a news headline in the government-owned national daily *The New Vision*: 'World Bank may cut aid'.[26] This piece was based on a report commissioned and then condemned by the Bank, 'The Political Economy of Uganda: The Art of Managing a Donor-Financed Neo-patrimonial State', also known as the Barkan Report after its main author, Joel Barkan (Barkan et al. 2004).[27] The report had been commissioned by the Bank to advise and aid in comprehending the wider political context of its Uganda operations, but it was later condemned. I was made aware of the report in an informal dinner conversation attended by Bank and donor representatives. It was a bilateral representative who first mentioned the condemned report, whereupon a Bank employee asserted that the Bank had to condemn it: the report was too political in recommending the Bank to cut its budget support due to allegations of severe government corruption and uncertainties regarding democracy and the political system. When I later asked if I could see a version of this report I was first told that they regretted having mentioned it to me, and that 'the report was condemned because the Bank did not like the method and style. We condemn reports all the time, so you should not put too much into this'. Since the report had been rejected just prior to the mission, it received considerable attention while the Bank team was in Uganda. According to a Bank employee, 'there has hardly been so much attention and interest in a Bank report before. It's sad these are the circumstances'. Although the denounced report was kept confidential it soon started to circulate, creating rumours among development partners that the Bank was changing course vis-à-vis the government. Then, at one point, I was provided with a version and development partners started to approach me to get a copy.

On 17 May, *The New Vision* cited from the report which, inter alia, states that 'The Bank should plan for the possibility of a "low case" lending program in Uganda during the period of the forthcoming Country Assistance Strategy (CAS)'.[28] The distinction between low, middle and high cases refers to the Bank's assessment of a borrowing country's policy and institutional framework. The diagnosis has implications for the type and amount of aid, with the basic rationale that the lower the assessment the higher the risk is of deteriorated efficiency and effectiveness of loans and investments. Designating Uganda a 'low case' would thus mean a drastic reduction of aid and a move from budget to project support – something neither the government, which depends on foreign aid, nor the Bank, already planning according to a given budget, were keen on.

A brief note needs to be made here of the political context. The Bank mission came at a time when the general donor community had been voicing their concerns about the current regime and the development of Ugandan politics. The context, commonly referred to as *kisanja*[29] or 'political transition', developed in 2005 when President Museveni revealed that he might change the constitution to lift the limits that restricted him to only two terms in office. Museveni was celebrated by donors when, after ten years of autocracy, he devised and passed the 1995 constitution which reintroduced democratic presidential elections and limited the presidency to two five-year terms. *Kisanja* would allow for a third period in office – much to the disappointment of donors who now saw him as 'yet another African leader intending to rule for life'. Development partners also criticized the announced referendum to decide on the transition from a non-party to a multiparty system, because it was an expensive affair and no one really opposed this transition.

All this involved a more general donor reconstruction of Uganda, from being a 'donor darling and a development success story' to a 'worst-case scenario of political mismanagement' (see next chapter). What was relevant for the mission was how the bilateral donors attempted to push the Bank to engage in these political matters and employ political conditionality in its policy dialogue with government. The Bank, however, rejected these calls with reference to its apolitical mandate. Nevertheless, the Barkan Report, *kisanja,* and development partners' concerns about Ugandan politics derailed the mission, impeding relations between the government, the Bank and bilateral donors.

## The Wrap-Up Meeting

In contrast to the poorly attended kick-off briefing, the wrap-up meeting is packed. Extra chairs are needed to accommodate everyone. The drastic increase in participants is due mainly to more donor representatives attending the meeting after the news columns had triggered their interest, excitement, rumours and tension. There is also a change in the composition of participants, with more from the senior level, and the Bank too has a heightened presence. The team leader has moved one chair down the table to make room for the Bank's country manager at the head of the table, next to the permanent secretary representing the government. The change to more senior and diplomatic attention from development partners is not paralleled by the government side, however. The same permanent secretary heads the meeting, but there is an increase in the number of government bureaucrats present. While waiting for the country manager, I talk with two government employees sitting next to me. One, working at the Office of the Prime Minister, has been engaged in the mission's meetings and is surprised to see so many present, which, as he says, is unprecedented at these routine meetings. The other person works in the Ministry of Gender, Labour and Social Development. She had not planned to attend, although the ministry had appealed to her to represent their unit: 'We're always sent to different formal donor meetings. Like everybody else, I usually abstain. But today's news headlines made it a bit more appealing'.

The meeting starts when the Bank's country manager arrives. She is the very last one to arrive, according to protocol, I am told. Following the formal welcome by the chairperson, the country manger is given the floor. She regrets that the Barkan Report, with its suggestions of a cut in aid to Uganda, has been circulated and quoted in the media, and disclaims that it has any association with the Bank: 'It is not approved by the Bank and as such it should not be read as a Bank product'. She underlines that the Bank is committed to collaboration with the Ugandan government and she hopes that the present mission and discussions have been fruitful in terms of devising the PRSC5, as the first Bank support package for the third PEAP.

In line with protocol, the mission's task team leader continues by expressing gratitude and thanking the government for facilitating and hosting the mission, after which he gives a brief outline of the mission's work.

> Compared to other PRSC countries, Uganda is much more developed and acts maturely to budget support. We have a rather good impression. There are, however, some issues of concern we feel pertinent to address. These relate to governance, transparency and corruption. Governance has been and still is our key concern. We have identified serious governance issues during the mission, and there is too slow progress ... We are also disappointed with the IGG.[30] It lacks the capacity and will to act on issues it should respond to. This we believe is because government and IGG [are] too interconnected ... We also need to express our concern with the public administration reform. We see improvement related to the prior actions, but progress is too slow. Government is not performing well enough. In general we believe that although many results have been achieved, the underlying processes are not good ... The mission has focused on establishing agreement on new prior actions [for PRSC6]. We have not intended to redefine those currently at risk. We believe the Republic of Uganda should stand by its commitments and fulfil previously

> agreed prior actions. There is dialogue and we are moving forward in agreeing on both former and future prior actions. These must be complied with by the 15th of July when we are to finalize the negotiations and reach an agreement on PRSC5 before presenting the agreement to the [Bank's] board. It should be unnecessary for me to stress the importance of meeting the stipulated measures before that.

The permanent secretary responds that he regrets that the Bank is left with the impression of a derailed governance environment, as, in his view, that is not the case. He maintains that the government will provide an update as to what is being done to comply with and meet the prior actions, asserting they will be finished by the end of May. He, moreover, reproaches the Bank 'for not having read, or misunderstood, documents we did provide you with. I find it peculiar you say they are missing as we have produced them and sent them to you. These would have given you a clearer picture of the situation'. In response to the concerns over IGG, governance and corruption, another bureaucrat refers to the Ugandan leadership code, which 'was established as part of PRSC1, when anti-corruption measures were part of the prior actions'. He outlines that under PRSC1 government passed two anti-corruption bills, the first establishing the IGG and the second being the leadership code bill, both of which have later been re-enacted to secure relevance. Together, these aim to fight corruption by ensuring public access to the assets declarations of government leaders and to investigate allegations of corruption and abuse of government office. 'As you are aware, the two bills address the concerns you raise on governance and corruption', he maintains. A third government employee continues in a more diplomatic tone, calling on his employees and colleagues in the ministries to thoroughly 'study the prior actions and performance indicators to stay on track and improve the possibility to deliver duly and as expected. Our main aim hereafter should be to fulfil the prior actions by May 31 as we previously have agreed upon'.

The Bank's task team leader expresses appreciation for the response, adding that 'the government's commitment to fulfilling the prior actions is decisive if we are to land the PRSC successfully once we move into negotiations'. The assessment of the prior actions is still subject to discussion among the development partners, and the team leader states they will submit their assessment as soon as their work is done and consensus on the diagnosis has been established.

Compared to the kick-off meeting, the wrap-up session is much more cordial than anticipated, given the news column on a potential aid cut. Apart from the increase in the level and number of those attending, this meeting is later described as being much more like traditional official protocol meetings between the government and the Bank and its development partners.

## The Mission Revisited – Cutting Aid over Politics

It is only at a later stage, after the wrap-up meeting and in conjunction with finalizing the PRSC5 document, that an updated assessment of the prior actions is provided. To the delight of the government, the Bank has now looked into the prior actions, and all have been deemed 'completed', including those previously assessed as 'at risk' or 'off track' – with one exception. Prior action 1, on 'budget execution',[31] has been downgraded from 'on track' to 'partially met'.[32] The Bank assesses it as being only partially met because 'one important element of this prior action went off track': namely, that public administration expenditures exceeded budget.[33] Despite this, government representatives seem satisfied, with one stating:

> This was just as expected. We knew they would upgrade the prior actions once they looked into the facts … The remaining condition on budget execution – well, we also saw that one coming. We knew we exceeded the budget, but that is related to extra costs with other reforms we are undertaking … I don't see it [as] crucial, and I don't think the reaction will be too strong.

The exceeded public administration spending is explained with reference to extensive reform programmes pushed for by donors, but also the extra expenses caused by the 2005 census, preparation for the referendum on whether to reinstall a multiparty political system, preparations for the following year's general elections, and operating costs to the Electoral Commission.[34] According to one informant, much of this can be attributed to donor demands, which seem to be 'based on the assumption that any increase in public spending can be covered through rationalizing. But they forget that these reforms to improve efficiency themselves cost money'. Another government staff member opines that the mission and meetings were more or less as expected – apart from the attendance at the wrap-up meeting.

> It's always like that. The whole setting is just a charade and pretence. They [the Bank] start hard, to set the agenda, but we all know that everybody is interested in reaching an agreement. And we know the Bank can't push too strong conditions since they need our consent when working through government. And political conditions would be against their mandate … The bilaterals are different. They tend to be more pushy – also on politics … You don't say no to a donor. But saying yes, or not

> saying no, does not mean we agree. I remember one donor asking us to fix [a] procurement system for sixty-eight districts. We knew that would be impossible within the timeframe they gave us, but we said yes. When they returned to make the assessment we had only managed eight districts. We told them if we were to make all sixty-eight we would have to outsource the task, which would be unconstitutional. 'So why did you say yes to it', she asked me. I tried to explain about power politics and following the power of the purse. It is easier to ask for forgiveness than ask for permission. If we had said right up we couldn't do it, they would [have] made it a condition. Now we were criticized for not performing well enough and asked to improve efficiency instead ... I talked to my friend in the ministry. He knew all along they couldn't prevent exceeding the public administration budget given the costs they were facing.

There is an ambiguity as to why the budget was exceeded. While some in the government explain it by referring to reform programmes and other conditions emplaced on the public sector by external donors, Bank staff assert it was simply due to bad financial management and that the government lacks the capacity to monitor and control its own budget. 'Budget control and execution are difficult technical tasks, so I understand their problem given their severe lack of capacity', one Bank staff member told me. According to another, however, the public administration budget was exceeded because of government corruption. Last year it was revealed that the army payroll included thousands of 'ghost soldiers' – non-existent soldiers whose salaries went into the pockets of military officers or government officials. This year the public service has come under scrutiny – warranted by the recently conducted census – to check for any phantom civil workers on the government payroll. This check is part of the public sector reform initiated by development partners. Initial 'ghost-busting' revealed around 9,000 (out of 230,000 individual records)[35] as ghost workers.[36] In terms of finance, this means that about US$ 1 million each month was shelled out of the budget into corruption. 'Why should we support a corrupt government? To make government really act we can't just push for soft reforms, we should also give a clear statement that we don't tolerate financial mismanagement', the Bank representative went on to say. If the decision were up to him, he would cut aid. Another argued that the role of the Bank is precisely to monitor budget performance – 'that's part of our main competencies'. He asserted that such monitoring was particularly important, due to the increasing shift from project and programme support to direct budget support, 'and had we not pushed these reforms and government undertakings of these public sector reforms, we – and probably not government either – would never have revealed these ghost workers'.

The bilateral actors are happy about the unmasking of budgetary mismanagement as they also put vast resources into the government's budget: 'Obviously we don't tolerate financial mismanagement, but what's revealed results largely from lack of capacity and not a lack of willingness to scrutinize these issues'. Excess government spending concerns the bilateral actors, but in reviewing the mission just about everyone mentions the difficulty in raising concerns about the political system and transition as most disturbing. The inability to flag these issues is due to the Bank's apolitical mandate. Just as the Bank works through government, the bilateral actors need to work through the Bank to have a say, since the Bank is seen to have a longer stick and a bigger carrot. 'Bilateral discussions are difficult, almost bound to fail, if you don't have the backing of the Bank', one person states. Several representatives of the bilaterals point out that they independently face difficulties in influencing the government's priorities, and so they seek instead to influence the Bank. The exception would be if the bilaterals managed to agree amongst themselves on a joint approach, but as they all emphasize different issues regarding Uganda's PEAP it is difficult to establish a shared approach that would enable momentum and leverage towards the government.

An important part of the mission was also to determine anticipated prior actions for the forthcoming PRSC6. In fact these prior actions were rather easily agreed upon. According to one government representative, the Bank more or less stipulated what they wanted as prior actions for the next PRSC, and the government concurred: 'I would say the new conditions are well targeted. They address issues also we see as important. As such I would say we're happy with the prior actions. But I wouldn't say we agreed on them'. The main concern that was raised related to the continual increase in the number of prior actions: while PRSC4 had eight prior actions, PRSC5 had eleven, and for PRSC6 13 anticipated prior actions were suggested.[37] 'We do what we can to fulfil the Bank's demands, but when each year we receive an increase in number, I get the feeling we'll never finish', bemoans one informant. On the Bank's side, the devising of new prior actions is seen in terms of diligent government participation and partnership 'through building a shared understanding of future challenges to the government'. The Bank expresses satisfaction with both the process and the result.

The PRSC5 document, as the output of the mission, was originally planned to be presented to the board of the World Bank for consideration and approval on 6 September 2005.[38] This presentation was postponed several times, due to delays both in finalizing the PRSC5 document and agreement, and in establishing consensus among development partners regarding the UJAS – the Ugandan Joint Assistance Strategy. The PRSC5 document was, in fact, not presented to the board until 17 January 2006. This meeting approved both the CAS (or UJAS) and a credit and grant to Uganda for the PRSC5 in the amount of US$ 135 million. According to a Bank statement following the board meeting, in addition to approving UJAS:

> The Board of Directors also approved the PRSC5, which provides external resources necessary for the execution of the Government budget and supports the economic and institutional environment for the sustained implementation of PEAP reforms, including budget execution, rural development, public service reform, decentralization, anti-corruption, public financial management and human development (education, health, water and sanitation). *The Directors approved a ten per cent reduction of the PRSC5 amount to US$ 135 million to reflect their concerns about expenditure overruns in the public administration budget. The Directors expressed concern that this trend might further escalate during the current fiscal year if no initiatives are taken to mitigate over-expenditure in this sector.*[39]

The 10 per cent reduction in aid – which equals US$ 15 million – came as a surprise to most of the actors involved. Government representatives were surprised that exceeding the public administration budget triggered this harsh reaction that means they must probably make cuts in already planned activities as spelled out in the Bank-approved PEAP. Bilateral representatives welcomed the cut, although some felt it was due to the wrong, official reason – political and not economic mismanagement was what warranted the cut. Bank employees obviously knew that aid cuts had been proposed and discussed in Washington DC, but were not sure of the outfall. The bilateral actors, I was later told, did use their representatives at headquarters level in Washington to argue for aid cuts, wanting the government to improve the political environment in Uganda. Nevertheless, the official reason for cutting the credit and grant by one-tenth was couched in terms of budgetary technicalities and excess spending, and not politics. The cut inevitably sent out political signals and caused effects, since it would force the government to cut its expected budget and plans.

The narratives and processes involved in why aid was cut and the role of politics will be dealt with more thoroughly in the next chapter. For now it is important to recognize that Bank aid to Uganda was in fact cut following the mission's assessment of government performance on prior actions. Through the liberal concepts of participation, partnership and ownership, the Ugandan government became accountable to the Bank after it had been granted the freedom and thereby installed with the responsibility for the PEAP and its affiliated mechanisms of PRSC negotiations and prior actions. The client government's nominal ownership of and responsibility for the processes and objectives of these provided the contingency for the Bank to respond. As explained by a Bank official, 'the prior actions are owned by the government, and consequently failure to attain their stipulated objectives is a responsibility exclusively to be borne by the government itself'. As such, mechanisms integral to the new aid architecture involve the process of responsibilization in which the receiving end is made responsible for the policies and their implementation, regardless of the Bank's involvement, influence or imposition. The process of responsibilization is found in the nexus between conditionality and participation, and points to developmentality working as a means of indirect rule. While the Bank transfers to its client governments greater responsibility and freedom, it also seeks to retain control and orchestrate the 'conduct of conduct' through other means and instruments. Prior actions, as an integral part of the PRSC instrument, represent such a mechanism, which in practice makes it possible to juggle between the concepts of participation and conditionality.

## Conditionality and Participation in Bank–Uganda Relations

Conditionality is strongly associated with the concept of prior actions, as shown by the Bank's decision to cut aid to Uganda by a tenth following what it assessed as derailed public sector management compared to what had been envisaged in the prior actions. The case of the Bank's mission to Uganda and the role of the prior actions elegantly illustrates the ambiguity inherent in the conditionality–participation nexus and thus developmentality: although the Bank has nominally transferred responsibility to its client, the recipient government, for devising and implementing its own poverty eradication strategy, the Bank still maintains its own presence in and influence over the process, only now in a more subtle, indirect manner. The concept of prior actions circumvents the intended architectural shift immanent in the PRSP model, if the notions of participation and ownership are to be interpreted and applied literally.

The case of the Bank's PRSC mission to Uganda and the role of the prior actions have demonstrated the workings of developmentality in the practical encounter between the Bank and its Ugandan counterpart. We have seen the practical unfolding of the new aid architecture and the ways in which the Bank is able to retain control over its development portfolio and influence over its counterpart, despite, at least formally, having transferred to the client responsibility for the whole planning–implementation–reporting process. The Bank's ability to influence these processes rests not only on the main architectural set-up of aid relations – participation and the PRSP modality – but also on the unfolding of its sub-architectonical structures and mechanisms in its particular context, like the PRSC, prior actions, and UJAS and donor harmonization. These are techniques and mechanisms implied by and affiliated to the new aid architecture, and facilitate practices that allow the Bank to preserve the asymmetrical knowledge/power formations it ostensibly aims to alter. Under the Bank's orchestration, the unfolding of the new aid architecture in Uganda hints at a process whereby the government's poverty alleviation efforts have gradually been inscribed and come to resemble the Bank's realm. Through an apparently free and liberal concept of partnership based on recipient participation, mutual complicity is constructed, with the client made responsible for policies and processes instigated largely by the Bank. Developmentality is thus contingent on the Bank's ability to make its policies those of the recipient.

As seen from the Bank and the general donor community, what are known as 'prior actions' are derived from the government's own PEAP strategy. The stipulation of prior actions is based on the shared expectations – established through negotiations facilitated under the PRSC mission – between government and the Bank. As a Bank official argued, 'the elaboration of prior actions by nature is participatory and builds on Uganda's own poverty strategy'. This statement illustrates the official understanding of the new aid architecture and the mechanisms it involves as seen from the donor side. However, the practices pertaining to the new aid architecture as outlined above tell a different story. In practice, what is supposed to be the equal partnership based on government participation involves a donor–recipient relationship with the notion of conditionality apparently still prevailing.

Whereas the formal representations and rhetoric of partnership lean on participation, their actual practices resemble conditionality. However, my informants did not always have a consistent view on the role of prior actions with regard to the conditionality–participation nexus and whether to view conditionality as a particular policy package or a means to enforce policies. Their stance on this seemed to depend largely on their temporal and spatial situation. One of my informants, who during my fieldwork represented a bilateral development partner, would constantly refute any allegations of conditionality by her institution or any other donor agency, including the Bank. Later and after my fieldwork, however, she co-authored the Uganda case study as an input to the report 'The World Bank's and the IMF's Use of Conditionality to Encourage Privatization and Liberalization' (Bull, Jerve and Sigvaldsen 2006). In the Uganda case study she equates prior actions with conditionality. As the case study reads, it mainly builds on their 'experience and observations from participating in PRSC missions over the last two years' – which means the PRSC5 mission scrutinized in this chapter.[40] The study goes on to say that prior actions 'can be seen as conditions in the sense that they have to be fulfilled in order for the program to be presented to the World Bank's board'. Although none of the Ugandan prior actions seemed to concern privatization or liberalization – the conventional understanding of 'conditionality' as a policy package – the report states that 'conditionalities in the PRSC5 come primarily as Prior Actions' (ibid.: 37), the number of prior actions reflecting the number of conditions the Bank puts on Uganda.

Another informant, who by the time I returned for the second part of my fieldwork had left the ministry, said that if I now asked the same questions as we had discussed earlier – government participation and whether there was national ownership of the PEAP – 'I would now definitively answer 100 per cent no!' This, he claimed, was not only because he no longer represented the government, but because the government's ownership had been constrained by the Bank during its recent mission. A similar discrepancy is found among development partners, whose informants in formal settings tend to praise government participation and ownership of the processes and policies they support. However, in informal settings – like in dinner conversations, or over a drink – ownership and participation are refuted and instead described as labels pasted onto their initiatives. Arguably, government servility to donors draws on two broad and mutually reinforcing aspects. First, government lacks the necessary capacity – it needs both the financial and technical support of donors. Second, donors pursue their own agendas based on their respective competences, and that guides what they see as Uganda's challenges. This latter point is in focus in the next chapter.

It thus appears that both sides of the donor–recipient chain find it feasible to insist on participation, ownership and other concepts of that ilk aimed at guiding aid partnerships. They seem to both recognize and reproduce the disconnect between ideas and practice, discourse and its representation or the new aid architecture and its implementation. For a government to say it does not own the policies it implements but that these are crafted by external donors would be to undermine its own sovereignty and control over domestic affairs, and to admit to have fallen prey to the influence of external actors. And if the Bank and other development partners should insist they are the ones who call the shots in driving the policy-making processes, that would undermine their own mandate and role, fuelling allegations of trusteeship, while also making them responsible for failure.

Yet, as we have seen throughout this chapter, there is something happening against or behind official discourse, found in the structures of the new aid architecture, indicating that the Bank exerts arm-twisting as regards its government counterpart. Although this might be intentional, it is just as much an effect of and interrelated with how aid relations are organized and the emphasis on efficiency, accountability, effectiveness, governance and improved partnership. Donor obsession with results, coupled with the discourse asserting that development aid is most effective in areas with good governance and a conducive policy environment, translate into a bureaucratic management by objectives that embrace effectiveness and rationality. It is to grasp these mechanisms and processes found in the nexus of conditionality and participation that I apply the developmentality concept. Developmentality alerts us to the indirect mechanisms of power constituted by and identified in the interface of the structures and practices of the new aid architecture as well as the wider objectives of development partnerships aimed at producing self-governing clients able to develop themselves, with the Bank retreating to a more withdrawn position from which it conducts conduct and governs at a distance.

However, the friction between the Bank and its Ugandan counterpart in agreeing upon the prior actions has revealed a jarring partnership and the failure of the Bank to merge different realms properly and establish consensus. This, moreover, points to an inadequacy of developmentality, showing that it is not an omnipotent modality of power and that there is room for resistance. What the friction over 'prior action' reveals is that the various modalities of power as outlined by Foucault (1991) are not mutually exclusive but can operate interchangeably. When the government of Uganda refused to comply and the Bank could no longer rely on the indirect power of developmentality, it applied a more direct form of coercion – backed by the spectre of aid cuts – to gets its way. The fact that the Bank indeed did cut aid can thus be read as the Ugandan government refusing to comply with the Bank despite being subject to both indirect rule and direct coercion and thereby maintaining, at least in symbolic form, its own independence and sovereignty. This in turn serves to show that the Bank's power, be it in the direct or indirect modality, is not total or hegemonic, and that those engaging in Bank partnerships do have the chance to refuse. However, as we will see in the next chapter, in this case the Bank's aid cut was not only a matter of disagreement around prior actions or other measures integral to Bank–Uganda relations. The decision influenced and was influenced by processes and knowledge battles among the wider group of development partners. This shows that developmentality is not only something between donor and recipient institution, but also relates to the interrelationships of development partners; and that signals the gatekeeping role of the Bank over other development actors, through its central role in the new aid architecture.

## Notes

1. Involving the bilateral actors draws on several factors. First, they are formally required to sustain the country's own strategy, i.e. the PRSP. Second, the global donor community intentionally seeks to harmonize and coordinate efforts to increase efficiency and prevent duplication. The idea of 'harmonization' draws on the Rome (2003) and Paris (2005) declarations on harmonization and aid effectiveness, respectively. Although donor informants claim it was officials of the Ugandan government who requested them to harmonize, government staff say they were asked to request this from donors, as implementation of the two declarations was to be based on government ownership and not imposed by donors. Third, the Bank and the bilaterals in Uganda have collaborated for a long time, although on a more informal basis. There are numerous intersections and cross-references between them in situ that necessitate involving them when analysing developmentality in Uganda.
2. These are represented by their diplomatic missions and embassy staff, or their bilateral aid agencies which are then subject to the policies of their respective ministries of foreign affairs. In Uganda, these often share premises and staff, since development cooperation constitutes their main diplomatic involvement there. Austria's bilateral agency is ADA, Canada's is CIDA, Denmark is represented by DANIDA staff, Germany by GTZ, Ireland by Irish Aid, Japan by JICA, Sweden by SIDA, and the U.K. by DFID – Department for International Development. The Netherlands and Norway are represented by their embassies.
3. See http://go.worldbank.org/6UF9OQDJO0 and http://www.actionaid.org.uk/doc_lib/what_progress.pdf. Both accessed 27 April 2015.
4. In brief, the Rome Declaration on Harmonization is a treaty to enhance development effectiveness through aid harmonization. It was ratified in early 2003, with heads of multilateral and bilateral development institutions and their partners (i.e. client countries) as signatories. Two years later countries across the world reaffirmed the Rome principles when endorsing the Paris Declaration on Aid Effectiveness in early 2005. Aiming to reaffirm the international commitment to eradicate poverty and promote sustainable development, the Rome declaration's 'deliberations are an important international effort to harmonize the operational policies, procedures, and

practices of our institutions with those of partner country systems to improve the effectiveness of development assistance' (see www.aidharmon isation.org). The Paris 2005 meeting builds on these ideas but aims to be more comprehensive in realigning the way donor and developing countries interact based on principles of partnership.

5. The process and dilemmas of devising UJAS, which itself amounted to a battlefield of knowledge among development partners, are examined in greater depth in the next chapter.
6. Minutes from 'World Bank Conditionality Review: Practitioners' Forum on Budget Support'. Cape Town, 5–6 May 2005. Emphasis added.
7. Luwero is a district in central Uganda, just north of Kampala. The Luwero triangle is known as the site of fierce fighting during the Ugandan civil war (1981–1986). The war is commonly known as the 'bush war', as Museveni, in his ascent to power, 'went into the bush' to amass troops and wage war against the government of Milton Obote and later Tito Okello.
8. Relevant to the notion of 'ownership' and the degree of 'homebrewedness', it should be noted that although PEAP precedes the PRSP model, the PEAP relates to another decree of the international community. In 1996 the UN established the Decade for the Eradication of Poverty (see UN 1996 A/RES/51/178) which 'recommends that all governments formulate or strengthen integrated poverty eradication strategies and policies and implement national poverty eradication plans or programmes, in a participatory manner, to address the structural causes of poverty, encompassing action on the local, national and subregional, regional and international levels, and stresses that those plans or programmes should establish, within each national context, strategies and affordable time-bound goals and targets for the substantial reduction of overall poverty and the eradication of absolute poverty' (ibid.: paragraph 13).
9. Bolivia, Ghana, Romania and Vietnam were also enrolled as CDF pilot countries, alongside Uganda.
10. Notably the Heavily Indebted Poor Countries (HIPC) initiative, started in 1996, which made the cancellation of previous debt conditional on having a Bank/IMF-accepted PRSP. IDA lending (World Bank 'soft loans') was later also to be premised on PRSP acceptance.
11. PEAP I prioritized programme areas were: primary health care; rural feeder roads; primary education; provision of safe water; and modernization of agriculture.
12. The four PEAP II pillars were: creating an enabling environment for sustainable economic growth and transformation; promoting security and good governance; directly increasing the ability of the poor to raise their income; and directly improving the quality of life of the poor.
13. The five pillars of PEAP III: economic management; production, competitiveness and incomes; security, conflict resolution and disaster management; good governance; and human development.
14. The rephrasing into 'economic management', moreover, means that the Poverty Reduction and Economic Management (PREM) network of the Bank receives its relevant pillar. Similar is the renaming of 'directly improving the quality of life for the poor' into 'human development', as the

responsibility of the Human Development network. See chapter 5 regarding the matrix organization of the Bank.

15. In Uganda the CAS is named UJAS – Ugandan Joint Assistance Strategy. The UJAS involves several donors – not solely the Bank – and is intended as a means of harmonizing donors and reducing governmental transaction costs. It apparently took donors two years to harmonize and agree upon this document, which was approved by the Bank's board in January 2006. UJAS will be covered in detail in the next chapter.
16. See http://www.worldbank.org/en/projects-operations/country-strategies (accessed 27 April 2015).
17. The Bank makes an important distinction between 'consultation' and 'negotiation'. While 'negotiation' means that all involved parties need to agree on the end product, 'consultation' implies non-committed discussions.
18. Draft copies were circulated from early 2005; the final, approved UJAS document covers the period 2005–2009 (UJAS 2006).
19. PRSC1 was finalized and accepted in 2001, PRSC2 in 2002, PRSC3 in 2003, etc.
20. The PRSC mechanism is interlinked with budget support, both of which provide important means for country policy dialogue. The importance of PRSC is reflected in the current Ethiopian CAS, where the Bank – having discontinued budget support since 2006 over political concerns – reflects on the advantages of PRSP: 'Budget support provided an important forum for dialogue, especially on issues related to growth and structural reforms' (paragraph 51) and 'important opportunities to engage in policy dialogue on wide-ranging structural issues' to address 'key structural issues that hinder more robust growth of the private sector' (paragraph 60) (see Ethiopian CAS 2008–2011; available at http://go.worldbank.org/ZBCG9IF761).
21. Contrary to previous *ex ante* conditions, prior actions are *ex post* conditions in the sense that reforms must be undertaken, or at least initiated, before any finance is provided.
22. OPM is mandated to lead government business in parliament, and to ensure efficient and effective implementation of government policies and programmes. It is functionally responsible for coordination, monitoring and evaluation of all government policies, programmes and projects, and to ensure that the national policies and programmes being formulated are internally coherent and consistent with the overall national strategy (PEAP) and in accordance with approved government plans. OPM holds the role of coordinating the government's internal affairs and its relation with external development actors (GoU OPM 2006). Due to the heavy focus on financial matters the latter has traditionally been the responsibility of the Ministry of Finance, Planning and Economic Development (MoFPED). Desire among government and donors to have a more comprehensive focus entailed OPM regaining its seminal role of coordination, which it had largely lost when the presidential post was initiated as the head of state. After years of diminution, the resurgence of OPM in 2003/4 was in line with its original mandate, but came at the cost of reducing the scope of the MoFPED.
23. The third PEAP pillar, 'Security, conflict resolution and conflict management', is exempted due to the Bank's apolitical mandate.

24. PMA – Plan for Modernization of Agriculture, part of government's broader strategy of poverty eradication as contained in the PEAP.
25. Somewhat ironically but frustrating as it happened; one informant said that had the Bank or the Norwegian embassy signed the letter referred to in chapter 1 above, I could have attended the meetings by being associated with them – although, as stated in the introduction, the letter said that I was an independent researcher and *not* affiliated with them.
26. *The New Vision*, Tuesday, 17 May 2005. Vol. 20, No. 117, pp. 1–2. Available at http://www.newvision.co.ug/ D/8/12/435022.
27. The following week the other national daily, the *Daily Monitor*, printed extensive excerpts from the report.
28. As a not too irrelevant curiosity: on 17 May each year Norway celebrates its Constitution Day, and 2005 was the 100th anniversary. Before the wrap-up meeting I attended the embassy reception; several people in the Norwegian diplomatic mission were highly interested in the two daily newspapers. I was soon to learn they did not pay too much attention to the front page with Bank rumours. Due to lack of resources, the Norwegian embassy had appealed to its partners – NGOs, civil society, private companies and other organizations it supports – to contribute to an announcement to mark the 100th Constitution Day. The result was, to the astonishment and ambiguous satisfaction of the embassy staff, not just an announcement, but one insertion in each of the dailies – totalling about thirty pages – with greetings from Norwegian and Ugandan organizations that had received funding through the Norwegian embassy. A Norwegian diplomat was really happy at this, but at the same time a bit overwhelmed by the extent. Few of the people I spoke with showed any particular interest in the 'World Bank may cut aid' story. In comparison, the USA marked its national day, 4 July, with a one-page announcement in each of the newspapers.
29. The term *kisanja* actually refers to dried banana leaves, which symbolize Museveni and his policies. Dried banana leaves are usually seen at pro-Museveni political rallies, and embellish welcoming parades when Museveni returns from abroad. During the political transition, *kisanja* came to mean 'third term'.
30. IGG is the Inspector General of Government, and as a prior action it was deemed 'off track'.
31. This prior action is commonly referred to as 'budget execution', but reads, in full, 'In the public expenditure review, Government has agreed with donors on the medium-term expenditure framework (MTEF) for 2004/05–2006/07, and has executed the 2004/05 budget consistent with budget allocations'. See 'Table 4: Status of Prior Actions for PRSC 5', page 21 in the PRSC 5 document.
32. This prior action was not assessed simultaneously with the others because it relates to budget performance. As the fiscal year runs from 1 July to 30 June, the verification of this prior action was set to 22 July.
33. The assessment reads: 'One important element of this prior action went off track – combined expenditure for Security and Public Administration was to be held within the approved budget. While the Security Sector performed at 100.2%, Public Administration was above target at 112.9%'.

34. After a decade of autocracy, Museveni introduced a no-party democracy in the 1995 constitution, meaning that candidates running for presidency could not represent a political party. This prohibition was justified by being a means to prevent ethnic conflicts, since partisan politics organized around ethnicity have been a feature of Ugandan political history.
35. See www.dfid.gov.uk/casestudies/files/africa/uganda-ghosts.asp (accessed 31 July 2008).
36. Later estimates suggested Ugandan 'ghost workers' represented about 20 per cent of the workforce. See www.blog-pfm.imf.org/pfmblog/files/public_expenditure_tracking_surveys.ppt (accessed 31 July 2008; now unavailable).
37. Anticipated prior actions for PRSC6 relate to budget execution; investment climate; rural development; public financial management (general); public financial management (procurement); anti-corruption (general); anti-corruption (IGG); public service reform (new phase of ongoing reform); public sector reform (staffing and wage bills issue integrates with budget process); decentralization; education; health; and water and sanitation. See PRSC6 document, Annex 4: pp. 74–109.
38. There is no mention of Uganda in the board's minutes of 6 September 2005. According to the report from the meeting, this meeting lasted only three minutes (12.33–12.36 PM) and involved accepting Bank loans and credits for Mexico, Brazil and Pakistan totalling US$ 319.51 million. See www-wds.worldbank.org/external/default/WDSContentServer/WDSP/IB/2005/09/22/000090341_20050922092447/Rendered/PDF/33617.pdf. (accessed 31 July 2008, now unavailable).
39. Emphasis added. See http://www.worldbank.org/en/news/press-release/2006/01/17/uganda-joint-assistance-strategy-and-world-bank-approval-of-us135-million-for-fifth-poverty-reduction-support-operation (accessed 27 Apri 2015).
40. The quote is taken from the Uganda case study, which does not appear to be openly available. The main report (Bull, Jerve and Sigvaldsen 2006) provides only excerpts of the cases. Although the table of contents lists the case studies as part of the annexes (nos 2–5), they are not included in the online version (see www.regjeringen.no/globalassets/upload/kilde/ud/rap/2006/0164/ddd/pdfv/300495-7final_conditionality_report.pdf (accessed 27 April 2015).

# Developmentality and the Politics of Harmonization

The ideas and practices of aid harmonization and alignment emerged as part and parcel of the new aid architecture, but refer more to how donors conduct their affairs than to the government.[1] In brief, harmonization means donors should harmonize their policies to prevent duplications and inconsistencies. Alignment means that donors should align their harmonized policies with those of the government. The idea of harmonization concerns the donor more than the recipient. It involves altering the generic practices of donors by establishing a joint approach towards the government. The idea of alignment, however, suggests that this approach should be aligned with that of the government. This is easier said than done, particularly when donors pursue their individual and sometimes conflicting objectives, when they disagree about the problem and thus the cure, and when they disregard or disapprove of the government they are supposed to be aligning their policies with. This chapter explores the practices pertaining to and emerging from the notions of donor harmonization and government alignment.

Indeed, harmonization processes are better described as knowledge battles than cordial and orchestrated joint ventures. Harmonization is intended as the instantiation of development partners' joint approach to government, but the social practice it institutionalizes in the encounter between different actors seems to reproduce existing schisms more than bridge them, even if those involved share the overarching idea and objective of harmonization. In this respect, harmonization efforts recall Ferguson's work (1994) on how development projects fail to reach their objectives but instead keep on producing the same effects, even though those involved are acutely aware that the specific targets are not being reached (Lie 2007). One reason might be the social dynamics of policy making, where – as Mosse suggests (2005b) – new policies, as the product of complex social relations and interests, end up reproducing and legitimizing the existing establishment instead of instigating new practices, which is policy making's nominal objective. Neumann (2007) makes a related point with regard to speech writing at the Norwegian Ministry of Foreign Affairs in asking why speeches written by diplomats, as official representatives of a country, always sound the same and never bring any new insights. Part of the answer draws on discursive reproduction as inherent to bureaucratic culture and organizational life, in which the credo of negotiations is that making concessions means conceding defeat. Similarly, donor harmonization as a form of cooperation involves building trust and solidarity. As Douglas asserts in *How Institutions Think* (1986), cooperation and solidarity imply rejection and mistrust. 'Solidarity involves individuals being ready to suffer on behalf of the larger group' (ibid.: 1), something that proves difficult as the ratiocination seem to be based on sustaining 'the institutional thinking that is already in the minds of individuals as they try to decide' (ibid.: 4) on matters of cooperation and solidarity – or harmonization, which this chapter is all about.

The inevitable debate on whether aid is or should be used for political purposes challenged donors' harmonization and alignment efforts in Uganda. Donors' ambiguous relation to politics is epitomized by how they responded to what they saw as a mismanaged Ugandan political system. The government at the receiving end, however, is acutely aware of the discord among donors, and the challenges and opportunities this discord provides for the formation of partnerships.

Bilateral aid is channelled through and managed by donor country embassies or designated agencies, and is thus de facto political, being integral to political structures – although the bilaterals' development rhetoric plays on the liberal, altruistic rhetoric of the new aid architecture. In contrast, the Bank is a member-based organization with both donors and clients, and needs to operate with the consent of the host governments, which makes political activity difficult. The Bank's apolitical mandate prevents involvement in the internal, political affairs of the client country. Needless to say, the turmoil that came with the 2005 Ugandan political transition made an important backdrop in understanding the dynamics of donor harmonization and government alignment. The debate over political aid came to the fore, giving rise to severe challenges for the interrelationship of development partners, who now found themselves between a rock and a hard place as to whether to respond to the worsening governance environment or whether to respect the Ugandan authorities' self-determination. This impaired the donors–government relationship as well as that between donors, as illustrated by donors' attempts to provide a joint public statement on the Ugandan national budget and the challenges in harmonizing around the Bank's CAS structure in what was to become the Ugandan Joint Assistance Strategy (UJAS). The cases demonstrate the seminal and pivotal role of the Bank regarding both the new aid architecture and the partnership formation. While the idea of harmonization was novel and embraced by development partners and government alike, the process of devising joint approaches proved to be far from harmonious. It resembled a battlefield of knowledge where development partners were gradually inscribed into the new aid architecture as orchestrated by the Bank, thus illustrating the Bank's gatekeeping role and the ramifications of developmentality outside the Bank–client relationship.

## The Political Transition: Rock Homos and Dictators

What was referred to as Uganda's 'political transition' became a growing headache to the development partners. Almost everyone assessed it as a deteriorated and mismanaged process that revealed structural flaws in the Ugandan governance system and a lack of commitment to democratic principles on the part of President Museveni. The term 'political transition' referred to three interrelated processes. The first was the president's desire to alter the constitution, with its two-term limit on the presidency, to allow him to run for a third period in office. The second was the issue of the referendum on whether or not to reinstate a multiparty democratic system. The third was the general and presidential elections planned for early 2006. The political transition had brought critical challenges to development partners' harmonization agenda. These processes evolved and coincided during the first half of 2005, and the shifting political terrain made it difficult for donors to establish a joint approach.

During Easter 2005 there were two public rallies in the streets of Kampala – one for and the other against the pop singer Bob Geldof, who since arranging Band Aid (1984) and Live Aid (1985) has become better known for his political activism than his music. The demonstrations came in response to Geldof's statements at the launch of the Report of the Commission for Africa, or the 'Blair Commission for Africa' as it was known since it was chaired by U.K. Prime Minister Tony Blair. Geldof was amongst the seventeen commissioners, most of them being (former) politicians, nine of whom were from Africa.[2] At the launch of the report on 11 March 2005, after first saying 'I hate politicians' and 'I can be emotive, I don't have to be empirical', Geldof stated: 'The President of Uganda who implemented poverty measures and AIDS measures that all worked with debt relief, and now he is trying to be president for life. Get a grip Musevoni [*sic*], your time is up, go away'.[3] While international media reported that Geldof had spoken up for the people of Uganda, people in Kampala took to the streets condemning Britain and

Geldof. On 21 March, hundreds marched to the British High Commission on Parliament Avenue, handing over a petition and a statement, before continuing to the Parliament, outside which appeals were held. The demonstration was organized by the Makerere University Students Movement Supporters. Several demonstrators had draped themselves in dried banana leaves, *kisanja* – as previously noted, the symbol of the campaign supporting Museveni's bid for a third term in office. Appeals made a point in legitimizing *kisanja* by pointing to Blair's ongoing preparations to call for a new election which, if won, would secure *his* third term as prime minister.[4] Demonstrators protested against what they called 'unfriendly remarks against the sovereignty and independence of Uganda'.[5] Placards addressed the donor community, reading: 'We say no to recolonialization', and 'Keep your donations, we retain our freedom'. Other posters were addressed to Geldof: 'Geldof, sober up and shut up', and 'NO to drug addicts and rock homos'.

Two days later a counterdemonstration was organized by a group called the 'Popular Resistance Against Life Presidency'. This rally had initial problems in getting authorization from the police and the government, which the donors saw as deliberate attempts by the government to silence political opposition. After an intensive media debate in which the political opposition received backing by the donor community over concerns related to freedom of speech, good governance and democratization, the demonstration was eventually allowed. This pro-Geldof demonstration was larger than the preceding one, but received limited attention by donors and international media, as the demonstration's late approval caused it to be held on Maundy Thursday, when many expatriates had already left Kampala for the Easter holiday. When I arrived at Constitutional Square in central Kampala where the demonstrators had congregated I was approached by several attendees who pleaded with me to 'write home what you see' and 'let the world know about our suppression and Museveni's dictatorship'. In addition to the numerous national media, a few international reporters were present to cover the demonstration and the march towards the Parliament. The crowd was huge, with opposition politicians in the lead being celebrated like rock stars, standing on the back of a lorry driving down Kampala Road. There were placards reading 'Lecture Museveni about democracy!', 'Thank you, Bob', 'Geldof for president', 'Donors save us', 'No kisanja', 'Donors: stop supporting dictatorship' and 'Cut aid to help Ugandans'.

The pro-et-contra responses to the Geldof case showed the existence of popular support for both sides of the political transition and *kisanja*. This partition was reproduced and articulated in most other conflicts relating to the political transition, the main points being to alter the constitution to lift presidential term limits, the referendum on a return to the multiparty system, and the run-up to the general and presidential elections.[6]

The Ugandan constitution limits the presidency to two terms of five years each. When Museveni first assumed office in early 1986 after a five-year struggle against the ruling Obote regime (1981–86), he was endorsed as a freedom fighter and celebrated by the donor community for bringing peace to the country. He soon became the darling of the donor community for adhering to their structural adjustment programmes of privatization, liberalization and cutting government spending. In 1995, after a decade of autocracy, Museveni introduced a new constitution involving the return to democracy – albeit in a non-party version – with a two-term limit on president tenure as a system of checks and balance to prevent accumulation of power around a long-serving leader. The non-party system was intended as a means to prevent partisan politics being built along ethnic lines, which Museveni saw as the reason for earlier power struggles and civil wars in Uganda. This eagerness to reform and adhere to international principles made Uganda a favourite among donors. Museveni won both the 1996 and 2001 presidential elections with landslide figures. After the 2001 elections, supporters were already proposing amending the constitution to allow Museveni a third term in office. In late 2004 these rumours were confirmed and heard by the international community, subsequently becoming a major concern to donors in Uganda, particularly those who provided the government with budget support. After popular allegations of nepotism and rumours of bribes and corruption of parliamentarians, the Parliament, on 28 June 2005, voted in favour of the bill lifting the ban on presidential term limits. The amendment was proposed by MPs who supported *kisanja* and not Museveni himself. Popular criticism, media commentators and donors all pointed to well-established bonds of patronage. Nevertheless, the official construed version became that Museveni was acting on behalf of the people, and that he saw it as his duty to run for a third term when called to do so by the people.

The return to a multiparty system also required amending the constitution. Opposition and international donors found it ironic that this was put to a referendum whereas the lifting of presidential term limits was not. Moreover, there was virtually no resistance to a multiparty system. Although lawyers claimed the constitution allowed certain changes if no opposition was voiced, Museveni now insisted that this should be decided by the people, who, he asserted, owned the constitution. Holding a referendum is very costly. Donors argued it would exhaust the

Uganda Electoral Commission's budget and consequently jeopardize the February presidential election, unless funding could be replenished. Donors were against this, and read the excessive spending on a sudden and unnecessary referendum as a signal of weak public administration. In the multiparty referendum held on 28 July 2005, 92.4 per cent voted yes and 7.6 per cent no to the question 'Do you agree to open up the political space to allow those who wish to join different organizations/ parties to do so to compete for political power?' Turnout was close to four million, or 47.3 per cent of the registered voters, in a country of 22 million citizens and about 11 million eligible voters, although only 8.5 million of them were registered.[7]

The run-up to the general and presidential elections of 23 February 2006 saw numerous challenges to the free press and the political opposition – notably involving the main opposition candidate Kizza Besigye of Forum for Democratic Change (FDC). Besigye had returned from exile in late October 2005, having fled the country in 2001 after disputing the presidential election, which he lost, and was later accused of treason. In the prelude to the 2006 election, Besigye was regularly imprisoned and taken to court accused of treason, concealment of treason, and rape. After being granted bail by the High Court he was imprisoned by the military, who invoked court martial due to allegations of terrorism. The government banned all public rallies, assemblies and seminars relating to the trial of Besigye. Although released from prison by the High Court, he was nevertheless detained in Kampala, as he was obliged to attend his own court sessions. International actors and political opposition saw these incidents as attempts to truncate political opposition and restrict it to Kampala, while the incumbent used government resources to travel the country campaigning for re-election. It was against this backdrop of a 'political transition' that development partners sought to get together and harmonize their various policies, strategies and structures in order to produce a joint approach to be aligned with the government's own system. The political tension, and conflicting donor assessments and responses, meant challenges to donor harmonization.

## The Harmonization Agenda

The new aid architecture is not limited to aid relations involving the Bank. Associated ideas have also emerged on the global level in an attempt to improve relations between development partners and to better their joint approach to the government counterpart. At the international level there have been initiatives to enhance coordination of donor agencies so that they can align their harmonized policies, strategies and structures with those of the client government, illustrating the ramifications of ideas integral to the new aid apparatus and their gatekeeping effects beyond the singular Bank–client relationship.

As a global initiative central to the formation of the aid architecture, the heads of multilateral and bilateral development institutions and their 'development partners' – here meaning aid recipients – in 2003 met in Rome to discuss how to increase development effectiveness. The Rome Declaration on Harmonization focused on

> unproductive transaction costs … [and] partner country concerns that donors' practices do not always fit well with national development priorities and systems … Partner countries are encouraged to design country-based action plans for harmonization, *agreed with the donor community*, that will set out clear and monitorable proposals to harmonize development assistance. (Rome Declaration 2003; emphasis added)

The main output of the Rome meeting, however, was the decision to reconvene in Paris early in 2005, this time on the ministerial level, involving ministers from donor and recipient countries in addition to the participants of the Rome meeting. This resulted in the Paris Declaration on Aid Effectiveness (2005). The declaration stipulates certain partnership principles for making aid more effective, and for bringing donor policies and procedures into accord, to facilitate their alignment with government's plans. As Rakner and Wang assert, the official rhetoric of the declaration 'demands donors to "step back" and harmonise and align aid, as well as foster ownership of the development agenda. Advancing nationally determined development strategies means that development partners – i.e. donors – must subordinate their aid programmes to partners – i.e. recipient – national policy preferences' (Rakner and Wang 2007: 1). There is thus a chance that recipient countries might lose out when the donors band together in one grand, concerted approach, since those who control the purse strings have the potential to both override and restrict alternative ideas. Harmonization requires that the donors actually manage to team up and harmonize their myriad and kaleidoscopic approaches. This has the effects of not only centralizing knowledge/power formations but also reducing variety and complexity. As particular knowledge systems gain hegemony, alternative perspectives become ignored (see Hobart 1993a).

The rhetoric of the Rome and Paris declarations on harmonization and alignment has overarching objectives akin to the Bank's PRSP model: to increase effectiveness and efficacy by fostering and strengthening client-country participation in and ownership of its national development processes. Additionally, the harmonization agenda is aimed at reducing transaction costs, preventing overlap and duplication of efforts amongst donors, and avoiding the creation of structures parallel to existing ones. The harmonization agenda is thus bold and novel, and represents a critical input into the continuous reconfiguration of the international development architecture driven by ambitions of transferring more and more responsibility to the client government. There is, however, a potential ambiguity in this that parallels the ambiguity pertaining to the participation–conditionality nexus. On the one hand, development partners seek to harmonize among themselves and align with government priorities, thereby 'stepping back' and transferring responsibility to the client. On the other hand, development partners uphold their analytical work and assessments that have evolved as requirements in tandem with increasingly more aid being channelled as budget support. Rakner and Wang note the 'need to acknowledge that the Paris Declaration and the growing process of assessing governance may be two largely contradictory agendas' (Rakner and Wang 2007: 1). This contradiction may undermine the notion of country ownership, which, according to the Paris Declaration, is achieved when 'partner countries exercise effective leadership over their development policies and strategies, and co-ordinate development actions' (Paris Declaration 2005). Effective leadership, however, is premised on a good and conducive policy environment – and what constitutes a 'good policy environment' and 'effective leadership' are highly contested and subject to negotiations with no objective standards, making measurement difficult and highly subjective.

While alignment concerns the relationship between development partners and client government, harmonization involves the relationship between donors and their formulation and selection of policies. Donor harmonization in Uganda centres on the Ugandan Joint Assistance Strategy (UJAS), as an extension of the Bank's Country Assistance Strategy (CAS) that includes the wider array of development partners in a joint approach to the Ugandan government. Bilateral donors attune to the Bank's realm and policy mechanism through UJAS, which illustrates the gatekeeping role that the Bank holds not only over government but other donors as well. Devising UJAS saw the development partners at loggerheads: the idea of UJAS was conceived in autumn 2003 but did not materialize until the very end of 2005.[8] The reason it took the donors such a long time to produce a joint approach was because harmonization proved unexpectedly challenging in terms of deciding who should do what, and because the donors could not agree on how to respond to Uganda's political transition, with which they all were dissatisfied. Given the challenges that the political transition made for donor harmonization, it became difficult for development partners to align with the government.

## Disharmonious Partners: Donors' Working Groups

During my fieldwork much attention was being paid to the Rome and Paris declarations, since the Paris meeting had only recently been concluded, in February 2005. However, that donors put their heads together was not something new from these declarations, nor should it be seen as an imposition or strategy employed by the donors. In the first PEAP (2000), the Government of Uganda (GoU) outlined ideas for its relationship with donors. In 2003 the government and key donors agreed on certain partnership principles to guide the government–donor relationship, including donor harmonization to enhance joint policy approaches and uniform routines vis-à-vis the government. This gave rise, inter alia, to joint sector working groups, sector-wide approach programmes and joint funding mechanisms. Donors met on a regular basis in various sector working groups. Although this was described by donor representatives as resulting from the government's call for donor harmonization – recall the informant who said the government had been asked by donors to make this call – donors had been meeting long before this request, because holding regular meetings is 'the best way to share information and plan strategically', as asserted by one Bank staff member.

These thematically focused working groups largely correspond to the PEAP sectors, and comprise topics such as health, education, water, decentralization, agriculture, JLOS (Justice, Law and Order Sector) and PRSC/macroeconomic group. The groups have a flexible organization, and participation is voluntary and interest-based. The different groups compose 'the likeminded', as they call themselves. Members are representatives from the multilateral organizations (the Bank and the IMF), bilateral aid agencies and diplomatic missions tasked with following up their respective countries' aid portfolio. Usually, if a donor country is not present through its governmental aid agency, the embassy assumes this role. The most active actors are reported to be World Bank, the U.K. Department for International Development (DFID), the Netherlands, Norway, Ireland and Swedish SIDA. These institutions send representatives to most of the group meetings. Denmark, the IMF, the European Commission (EC), Belgium and Japan also participate, but only in a selection of the groups. The USA, via USAID, is more reluctant to harmonize and does not participate, although it is one of Uganda's largest donors.[9] Most of those attending the various working groups hold diplomatic status, but claim that 'our discussions are purely at the technical level', and not the political level. Development-focused embassy staff usually see themselves more as development technocrats than as diplomats.

There is one anomaly among the sector working groups. The Donor Democracy and Governance Group (DDGG – later renamed PDG, Partners for Democracy and Governance) is explicitly concerned with political matters. It was set up in order to 'deepen democracy and facilitate the transition to greater political pluralism ... [and] promote human rights and good governance' (DDGG 2002: Article 2.1). DDGG, however, has a more recent and ad hoc character than the other groups. It was established in mid-2002 to strengthen processes aimed at reinstalling multiparty democracy in Uganda by supporting civil society initiatives and constitutional and legal reform, and was to be terminated in 2006 after the Ugandan presidential election. The political character of DDGG thus necessitated that it be more formalized than the other working groups, so a memorandum of understanding (MoU) was formulated by the parties to ensure transparency with regard to the GoU. Instead of meeting on the technical level, this group brings together thirteen ambassadors of various diplomatic missions to Uganda, as well as the official accredited representative of the EC and UNDP. Due to its restrictions on political scope, the Bank does not participate in this group. The DDGG parties, however, recognize the importance of the Bank and its lending mechanisms and instruments to their work. Hence, the MoU states that DDGG might support specific interventions on, for example, 'good governance as appropriate within the framework of the Poverty Eradication Action Plan (PEAP), the Poverty Reduction Strategy Paper (PRSP) and the Poverty Reduction Support Credit (PRSC)' (DDGG 2002: Article 3.2), all these being instruments and models introduced by the Bank.

The Bank's involvement in harmonization processes and the various sector working groups depends on whether the topic is perceived as being political or not. The Bank's apolitical mandate and the fact that it needs host government consent for its operations put restrictions on the Bank's thematic scope and outreach, and, by implication, the topics on which it can harmonize. As such the DDGG is indicative of a wider problem of donor coordination, since what is considered political or not has implications for actors' ability to involve themselves in harmonization processes. At the same time, most development partners subscribe to the view that 'we can't do anything without teaming up with the Bank', as a Dutch representative asserted. Bank staff agree with this view, as expressed by their repeated statements on the Bank's great 'stick and carrot' – the leverage achieved by coercive measures or incentives. Although the Bank is not part of the DDGG, the latter inscribes itself into the Bank's realm by connecting its involvement in good governance to the PEAP and the PRSC – both of which are Bank-induced mechanisms. Thus, donor harmonization becomes contingent on whether the scope of the various sector working groups is framed as technical or political. Whereas the DDGG is explicitly political, there are no clear-cut distinctions with the other groups, as illustrated by the economist group convening to prepare for the Public Expenditure Review (PER) meeting. The PER, or budget conference, is part of the PRSC instrument, being an undertaking demanded by the Bank to take place during the PRSC mission outlined in the previous chapter.

## Donors' Economist Group Meeting

On 12 April 2005, representatives from DFID, the Netherlands, Denmark, the IMF, the African Development Bank (AfDB), Japan, Norway, the EC, Ireland, Sweden and the World Bank meet for the donor economist group meeting. The Dutch embassy chairs and hosts the macroeconomics group. I have been invited to the meeting to get a sense of the general dynamic between donors and 'to learn more about the coordination system and the situation we are facing', as stated in the email correspondence prior to the meeting. My inviter has asked me to come to her office an hour prior to the meeting for a briefing on the topic and the various coordination groups and forums in Uganda. Arriving the fashionable five minutes early I learn she is busy preparing for the meeting, and will have to cancel my briefing. Later, however, when driving to the Dutch embassy, I pick up on our email correspondence to enquire about the 'situation they are facing'.

The 'situation', I learn, regards donors' general dissatisfaction with the Ugandan political transition and concerns over President Museveni's aspiration to alter the constitution to allow him to run for a third term. The 'situation' concerns whether, and the extent to which, development partners should respond to what they see as a deteriorating political process: 'As you will experience in today's meeting, the area of tension is just as much the relationship between the Bank and the bilaterals as between donors and government. We all agree it is an alarming situation, but we are not sure how to respond'. She has to cancel our briefing because she has to clarify political standpoints with her superior before the meeting.

The meeting starts with the mandatory presentation round, and then the Dutch chair introduces the agenda: 'to discuss the Ugandan government's proposed budget for the next three years' and to prepare for the big budget conference, the Public Expenditure Review (PER), in which the development partners will give a joint statement. The meeting is started off by those attending going through the National Budget Framework Paper for fiscal years 2005/6–2007/8, which is the context of the upcoming PER, which GoU submitted to the Parliament on 31 March. The economists go through the budget from the top, initially just making brief comments to the various posts.[10] At one point, the AfDB representative interrupts the presenter, asking what 'N' and 'NR' mean.[11] 'Well, frankly I don't know', he replies, turning to the IMF representative: 'Perhaps you know what it means? You ought to be familiar with these terms?' The IMF representative replies that he thinks he knows what the abbreviations mean. 'But are you sure?', another asks. 'Not totally; only 95 per cent.' The group starts to laugh, one person remarking, 'That's good enough for me – it's not rocket science we are doing'.

The government's budget strategy for 2005/6, which the macroeconomists discuss, rests on three main goals: implementing rural and industrial development strategies; enhancing good governance and the provision of security and basic social services; and maintenance of macroeconomic stability. 'Ah. They still don't get it. We cannot support military and security issues. It is too political!', a bilateral representative exclaims with regard to the second main objective. To the Bank representative, the linking of governance, security and service delivery in one goal is read as having a disregard for the overall partnership dialogue underpinning the formulation of the third PEAP. In the transformation from the second to the third PEAP the Bank requested the government to split the second PEAP pillar of security and good governance, and thus increase the number of PEAP pillars from four to five, in order to facilitate Bank involvement in good governance without challenging its apolitical mandate. As the Bank representative argues:

> If nothing else, the upcoming PER is an exercise in budget discipline. The government should know by now that listing security with good governance and service delivery politicizes the objective and hampers our chances to support the mere technical sides of governance. It is totally unacceptable that we should support any reallocations in the defence budget.

The government's defence spending is the only budget post that is kept concealed from the donors, which makes the IMF representative anxious: 'The government's defence expenditures are still too high.

We should use our leverage to turn this trend. Otherwise I am concerned we will end up supporting Museveni in allocating 10 million to two months of banana research'. Although this is said sarcastically, and spurs laughter at the meeting, the reception among the development partners indicates the underlying gravity. Last year they criticized government's proposed rise in defence spending, which made donors unable to fully support the government's budget allocations. They are concerned that such a reallocation of defence expenditures into agricultural research is only a means to conceal what the money is used for. There is also general concern that the government has still not understood the importance of keeping the security realm separate from good governance – 'if they would like to resume support for governance reform', as the Bank representative phrased it. The DFID representative follows up: 'That might be so, but my contact in the Ministry of Finance says that there is real concern about donor influence. She says that "the IMF and the Bank are crawling all over our books". The government thinks we are too active in monitoring and controlling its budget'. Referring to the conditions of budget support, the IMF representative asserts, 'But they have agreed to that [laughter again]. We are mandated and allowed to look into their budget'. The chair interrupts, saying this debate leads to the next point on the agenda, on the development partners' joint statement to be delivered at the PER meeting. 'We must have in writing what we are thinking', he says. 'Yes, but what are we thinking?', the Bank representative retorts.

Little discussion is needed to establish consensus on pressing the government to detach security from good governance – all agree on 'the need to depoliticize governance reform', as the DFID representative puts it. Among the rationales for donor scrutiny of the Ugandan budget is to ensure that it satisfies the requirements of a well-formulated budget targeted at the challenges and objectives stated in the PEAP. To the donors, the government's continued merging of security and governance is seen as undermining governance reform – one calls it 'misconduct in the budget process'. The donors are all concerned about the governance situation in Uganda – particularly with regard to the political transition – and in order to fully commit themselves to reforms it is essential that the security realm should be removed from any other policy discourse. Problems arise, however, when the meeting discusses how to respond to the government. Some hold that a statement in the upcoming budget conference would be sufficient, while others suggest that donors should consider reducing aid to Uganda. A bilateral representative argues, 'although this budget has its flaws, it's a much improved version compared to the one we discussed a year ago'. The

Dutch chair asserts that 'at least the government's intentions are good'. 'Yeah. Right. I've heard that one before. After all, our budget support is based on performance. Taking the performance-based allocation system seriously, we could consider cutting aid. Or reallocate some budget support into regular programme support', replies a representative for the multilaterals, again causing laughter.[12] It seems they laugh because they find it unlikely that anyone would in fact impose aid cuts.

They settle for giving a joint statement at the upcoming budget conference, in which they intend to send a strong signal to the government that 'we need to be convinced that the government is committed to the PEAP ... why shouldn't they? It's their strategy', the chair states. The development partners agree that they should voice their concerns to the government before the PER meeting to allow the government to prepare and demonstrate PEAP ownership at the budget conference. They are not, however, able to decide who is to convey the message to the Ministry of Finance, or who is to deliver the joint statement. On the latter, the majority propose that the Bank should deliver the macroeconomist group's joint statement, but the Bank representative is reluctant, arguing it should be the responsibility of the working group's chair – 'not least since the political language we are adopting could be counterproductive to our mandate'. The chair agrees, but adds that 'if nothing happens [after first informing the Ministry of Finance] we'll take it one step up and let Grace [the Bank's country manager] deliver it'.

The discussion on their joint PER statement then touches on the notion of politics. Development partners become agitated, some even stating 'it is revolutionary that we now, finally, discuss politics and address the real challenges'. However, once this topic has been raised the debate shifts focus to a more general level as to whether aid should be political or not. A participant asserts that the economist group used to be very technical but that recently it has assumed a more political character as a corollary to the increase in budget support, the harmonization agenda, and the Ugandan political context. Another bilateral representative holds that 'to a large extent we are the focal point of politics as we deal with budgetary issues', since this conveys influence over all other sectors. The macroeconomists inform and are informed by the performance of most other sectors, like health, education, energy and public administration. Operating in the mediating crux of sectors between donors and government, the macroeconomist group sees itself as the most important working group. Representatives of the nonbilaterals, however, are rather quiet during the meeting's wind-up debate, only noting that they are governed by the non-political mandate that prevents them from taking a formal standpoint on politics.

## Public Expenditure Review Meeting

The Public Expenditure Review (PER) is a Bank requirement that comes with the PRSC model and budget support. The rationale is to foster public scrutiny of the government's spending of foreign aid so that it may be held accountable to its citizens and other tiers of the government system. The PER is a mechanism integral to the Bank's country economic assessment and sector work. It is inscribed into the Bank's PRSC project cycle, and has evolved in scope and importance as development assistance – from the Bank and bilateral donors – increasingly becomes channelled as budget support. PER has evolved to become the Bank's main vehicle for analysing government performance in budget formulation and execution, and enables the Bank to assess macroeconomic concerns. The PER also enables the Bank to check on government political priorities, as articulated in the budget, in relation to the PRSP. The Bank's self-presentation of PER reveals a kind of trusteeship – 'a PER is undertaken to assist the borrowers in understanding their development problems and potential solutions as well as help illuminate the World Bank's own country assistance strategy'.[13] The PER feeds into the PRSC cycle's assessment and stipulation of 'prior actions'.

On 10 May 2005, Ugandan government ministers, ministry staff, members of parliament, local council (LC5) chairmen,[14] city mayors, civil society organizations, private sector representatives, the diplomatic community, and representatives of multilateral organizations all assemble at Speke Resort Munyonyo, about half an hour's drive from Kampala city centre. Arriving early, I sit down in the bar and order a coffee. As the participants start arriving, an informant from the Office of the Prime Minister joins me. He tells me that the choice of venue is due to a lack of proper facilities available in the city as these are all being renovated in preparation for the 2007 CHOGM.[15] 'But that's the official version', he adds. When meetings are held in the capital, the LC5 chairmen and other district officials attending tend to disappear, to 'go shopping at the market, spend their allowances, and visit friends and families'. This apparently happened the year before, creating unrest at the meeting and engendering dissatisfaction among the donors, who complained to the government, since one of their PER rationales is for district representatives to hold the government accountable.

Eventually people arrive at the venue, and I recognize several from previous meetings. Before convening for the Ministry of Finance, Planning and Economic Development's (MoFPED) welcome remarks, I engage in small talk with some whom I have met before. A general impression is that while government employees see this as a regular donor-installed exercise where 'we just have to go though the motions', the development partners are much more tense, still making preparations and discussing 'the tone of our address'.

Three sessions are planned. The first session includes welcome remarks by the MoFPED, a keynote address by the prime minister, and an outline of the budget strategy and government priorities for the fiscal year 2005/6. After a coffee break, session two starts by addressing increase in productivity with a case from the agricultural sector, followed by a brief discussion, before the mandatory statements from the private sector and from civil society organizations. Session three comprises a statement by donors, a statement by parliament, and a more comprehensive discussion, before the final closing remarks.

## Moving out of Script and into Politics

All the statements have been handed out upon registration, with few exceptions – including the statement by the donors. All statements start with the customary mentioning of all groups present – from honourable ministers down to the distinguished guests, ladies and gentlemen. There is only one deviation from protocol: when one minister interrupts his own recitation by asking 'Will this list never end?', to general laughter. Similarly, all presentations are recitations from well-prepared manuscripts, continuously checked against delivery, particularly by donor representatives, in order to take note of any deviation from the script. Also here there is one exception. It occurs during the prime minister's keynote address, and results in extra attention.

After welcoming the participants, the prime minister sets the agenda by listing:

> a number of cross-cutting issues which are critical to the development of our nation, namely good governance, effective public administration and conflict resolution ... Ladies and gentlemen, allow me to turn to governance issues. Government is committed to promoting basic values and good leadership by ensuring that the democratic process of elections, constitutional review and the wishes of the people are respected. I am pleased to inform you that Parliament has decided to request the Electoral Commission to hold a referendum concerning the change of Political System in accordance with Article 74(1)(a) of our Constitution. Before Uganda adopted the Movement Political System, the people were consulted through a referendum and they approved the adoption of the Political System. It was logically necessary to consult them concerning the change of the Political System.[16]

At this point the prime minister interrupts himself, departing from the manuscript, and turns to the donors, who have all assembled in a cluster to the left of the rostrum. He accuses donors of being paternalistic and inconsistent: on the one hand, he says, the donors talk about ownership, enhancing good governance, reintroducing the multiparty system and implementing public sector reform – all with a focus on budget balance – while on the other hand they are opposed to the planned referendum because they think it is too costly. 'If we are to change our constitution, it should be up to the people. You always criticize us for being undemocratic, for having a dictator as president. But when we now turn to the people for advice, you oppose it… I find it strange.' He then calls upon the donors to support the referendum – morally, politically and financially. The referendum is reported to cost 30 billion Ush[17] – 'and I hope you will maintain your commitment and financial pledge to help [to] facilitate enhanced good governance and the reintroduction of [a] multiparty system'. He continues with a pro-et-contra deliberation on the political and economic costs of the referendum and the political transition, asserting that the political costs of not consulting the people would be higher than the economic costs of holding a referendum. He also addresses media claims indicating dialogue and connections between donors and political opposition, and that opposition parties have asked donors to withdraw budget support, in order to push for democratic reform, whereupon he reminds the donors that it is the government, not the political opposition, that are their counterpart.

Although the remaining manuscript recital touches upon some political aspects relating to decentralization, public administration and expenditures, these appear rather uncontroversial to the donors. While reading the remaining text, donors start sending notes to each other, and some also leave the meeting room to talk together. In consequence, the next presentation, where the MoFPED outlines the budget strategy, receives less donor attention. During the ensuing break there is intensive meeting activity among the various donors, which I end up observing from a distance after they reject me taking coffee with them as 'we need to organize and coordinate our response'. It is the donor macroeconomics – those from the working group at the Dutch embassy – that meet. The group is now augmented by the Bank's country manager and a recently arrived Bank employee, who that morning had been introduced to me as the next Bank country economist 'who has a larger swimming pool than the country manager'. They all group around a laptop, revising and amending their joint statement. They do not appear to be quarrelling, but there are serious gesticulations, only interrupted by people leaving the group to make phone calls. When walking past me to make a phone call, one of the bilaterals apologizes for turning down my coffee invitation, but 'this caught us a bit by surprise. We didn't expect such political language by the government' – before he moves on.

When we reconvene for the second session I enter the venue together with a Bank employee. He was originally based in DC, but is now in Uganda as part of the PRSC mission. I ask if they (the Bank or donors) have prepared any questions for the upcoming discussions section, on the basis of the previous political welcome remarks. He reveals that that section, and the PER in general, is not for the donors, but for the local representatives (LC5) to hold the government accountable – 'but surely I hope they address the costs of the political transition as it inevitably affects their budget and allocations'. He is, however, to be disappointed. The short half-hour Q&A session involves questions from the LC5s. These mainly concern complaints over lack of roads, infrastructure, schools, health systems and, generally, that the government has not delivered what they anticipated or promised. There is no discussion. On the one side, the district chairmen complain about all the things listed in the previous PEAP that 'we don't experience in our districts', and, on the other side, about all the issues that are lacking in the current PEAP, as when one chairman complains that 'everybody seems to have electricity, water and roads. In my district, we have nothing. Why is my district not mentioned in the PEAP?' Other chairmen react, saying that they too have no access to the facilities he mentions.

Halfway into session two, I go for a break and a cigarette. Outside I meet another acquaintance from OPM. He is not too amused by the PER in general and the district chairperson's complaints in particular. This is common routine, he asserts, the only difference this year being that the LC5s have not left already, since the meeting is being held outside Kampala, so we will probably witness even more complaints this year. Also he was surprised at the prime minister's political tone this morning, and expects donors to react in their statement. He sees them working on their statement, but assures me that government representatives also prepare a rejoinder after the donors' statement.

In the break preceding the third session – which is to commence with the donors' statement – I join some of the donor representatives for lunch, during which they discuss their upcoming statement. The conversation confirms the suspicion that some donors were not satisfied with the statement and wanted a tougher tone, particularly after the prime minister moved away from his script. Consequently, the statement was modified, although to the Bank's discomfort. The development partners are still discussing who is to deliver their statement. The economist group meeting a month ago had suggested the Dutch representative, by virtue of chairing the working group, but since then it appears they have settled for the Bank's country manager. Now, however, she seems hesitant, since the statement, after today's recalibration, has been instilled with political language stronger than she is comfortable delivering as Bank manager. She manages to persuade one bilateral representative to deliver the statement, but he is refused permission by his superior, the ambassador.

When we reconvene for the third session, the joint donor statement – now in printed form – is handed out to all participants. The hard copy does not indicate who is to read the statement – neither does the workshop programme, which merely states that the presenter will be a representative of the donor community. After the participants have taken their seats, the Minister of Works, Housing and Communication addresses the audience, asking for silence, and then introduces the Bank's country manager, who will deliver the statement on behalf of the joint donor group.

The country manager starts by praising the government for spearheading an inclusive process: 'Uganda was the first among African countries to adopt a structured and participatory process in the formulation and execution of the national budget'.[18] She adds that 'good progress has also been made in reflecting PEAP priorities in the FY2005/6 sectoral budget allocations. A year ago, the donor community was unable to support the budget allocations in the 2004/5 BFP [Budget Framework Paper],[19] due to the proposed large rise in defence spending and the corresponding compression of planned spending on PEAP priority sectors. This year, we welcome the decision to limit defence spending to the levels of the earlier MTEF,[20] and to allocate additional resources to PEAP priority sectors, notably agriculture'. As such, the development partners endorse the reallocations – although only one month earlier they had criticized putting money into 'banana research' – which, in the MoFPED's statement, was highlighted as one of the main means to increase domestic revenues, enhance exports, and secure rural development. She goes on to state that '[f]urther progress, however, is needed in reducing the rate of growth of spending on public administration. And, we see a strong case for assigning a somewhat larger share of total funding to the Justice, Law and Order, and Accountability sectors'.

The donor statement contains fourteen numbered points that all deal with various aspects of Ugandan politics, budget performance, and development strategy – and the linkages between these. The points include budget allocation, budget process, PEAP priorities, defence sector, budget sustainability, pay reform, the execution of the previous fiscal year's budget, supplementary expenditures and budget allocation for fiscal year 2005/6. Interestingly, almost all the points start with an 'acknowledgement', 'note', 'recognition', or 'welcome of government efforts and achievements' on the various matters – subsequently followed by a disclaimer starting with 'however', 'but', 'although', 'it is worth noting', or 'we are concerned that'. This formula is paralleled in the overall structure of the statement. After the brief and initial praise of the government's achievements and progress over the last year, the Bank manager takes on a more restrictive tone:

> Past accomplishments, however, are no reason for complacency. We are concerned that the budget dialogue is not as effective as it needs to be in order to ensure the credibility of the budget and its linkage to the desired development outcomes in Uganda. The following areas require further attention: (1) many of the issues that arose in the past have not been adequately addressed in this budget; (2) the National Budget Framework Paper is not strong enough on outcome orientation; (3) the extent to which sector and local government budget framework papers are reflected in the proposed allocation is not very clear; and (4) dialogue around the formulation of sector plans and budgets could still improve in line with the Partnership Principles ... We note that the National Budget Framework Paper aims to orient public expenditures towards achieving the PEAP objectives, but more work is required to strengthen the link to the PEAP priorities ... The 2003 Defence Review highlighted the need for rationalization of the sector and its expenditures, but we feel that the progress has been slow. We welcome the recent formation of the Defence Sector Working Group and the release of the Defence Corporate Plan. But it is disappointing that it took so long for the Government to act on the commitments made this time last year ... We support the Government's plans to pursue a path of gradual fiscal consolidation. It is worth noting that sustained reliance on donor inflows is not the cause but rather a symptom of inadequacy of domestic resources and inefficiency in public expenditures. In particular, we would urge the Government to act decisively in eliminating wasteful spending and low priority activities from its budget ... Although Uganda has increased its revenue performance over the last decade, it remains low by the standards of its peers ... Progress towards instituting a comprehensive public sector pay reform and effective payroll management is slow and undermining the integrity of the budget ... While we welcome the resolve of the Government to limit supplementary expenditures only to unforeseen emergencies, we are concerned about the frequency and size of the supplementaries in the recent years ... This seriously damages the integrity of the budget process, and undermines the parliamentary oversight ... Even more damaging, the frequent use of supplementaries can, over the long term, dilute the Government's commitment to enforce budget discipline on spending units and undermine the credibility of the budget process ... While the

> broad allocations suggested in the National Budget Framework Paper reflect the need to adequately fund the revised PEAP, we believe that there are several expenditures categories ... that are of concern.

The latter refers to donor concerns at the budget allocations of the Ugandan government, and addresses specifically the categories of public administration, decentralization, insecurity in the north, the justice sector, special directives, agriculture, and the energy and industrialization funds. With regard to public administration, it is noted that:

> The increasing size of the expenditure for this sector goes against the stated Government commitment to streamline and rationalize the sector. Of the increase of the Ush 40 billion for the sector since the November 2004 MTEF, only Ush10 billion is attributed to increases in the estimated cost of the upcoming referendum and election. The rest comes from the expenses required for payment of salaries of local political leaders, hosting of the Commonwealth Heads of Government Meeting, and additional funding of Parliamentary commissions. Furthermore, we believe that public funding for the Movement Secretariat should be discontinued if the Constitutional Amendment adopts a multiparty system.

The 'banana research' issue is addressed in connection with agriculture:

> The increased budget allocation to agriculture to enhance productivity in the sector is welcome. However, the limited proportionate increase in resource allocations to the priorities identified in the Plan for the Modernization of Agriculture [PMA] is a concern. Interventions such as seed and cotton subsidies, microfinance and banana wilt prevention need to be based on solid analysis and integrated within the overall PMA objectives.

One might have expected the Bank's country manager, in representing the wider donor community, to return to diplomatic protocol in the final remarks. The critical tone, is, however, maintained:

> We are committed to working with the Government in effectively addressing the various issues and concerns highlighted above. On behalf of the Development Partners, I wish to encourage the Government to further align the budget and the MTEF to the priorities identified in the revised PEAP. We would welcome the Government's reaffirmation to continue implementing key reforms that are needed for the long-term sustainability of the budget. We see this as a basis for continued donor support to the budget for achieving the PEAP objectives.

Before leaving the rostrum she thanks for the audience for their attention. After some polite applause, the chair introduces the next speaker, the chairperson of the Parliament's budget committee, who will present the final statement. During the MP's statement, there is some activity among government representatives. Some – apparently private-sector representatives and government officials – start leaving the venue, as it is now after 3 PM with only the MP's statement and a discussion session remaining before the closing remarks and subsequent cocktails. My acquaintance from OPM also leaves, together with other informants from, inter alia, the OPM, the MoFPED and the Ministry of Foreign Affairs. These have a hands-on relation with the PEAP formulation and Bank negotiations, so I assume that they are leaving in order to prepare the government's response to the statement from the development partners – an assumption that was confirmed later, although they never got the chance to deliver it.

The final one and a half hours of the session are supposed to be devoted to general discussions. The chair, however, gives primacy to the LC5 chairmen and representatives in asking questions, in order for them to address and scrutinize the government's proposed budget – in line with the Bank's intent with PER. The drawback is that there is no substantial discussion between government and the development partners, and the government – perhaps strategically and deliberately – never gets the opportunity to take up the donors' points of criticism. Instead, this Q&A section ends up akin to the previous discussion section. The LC5 chairmen demonstrate disdain of the national government and what they see as centralized politics and budget allocations. The district representatives' discontent with the government centres on the perceived lack of priority and allocation of government resources. One LC5 chairman asserts that it is difficult to collect taxes, and argues that the incremental tax rate makes it even harder: 'People in my district pay taxes but never experience development. When they travel to Kampala they witness your prosperity, roads and health clinics'. Of the thirty-odd questions posed by district chairmen, only three relate directly to or address the development partners.[21] As government is required to respond to these enquiries, in line with the formal reasoning for PER, no time is left for taking up the concerns of the development partners.

After the Q&A session and the subsequent concluding remarks – during which people start to leave the workshop – the remaining participants are invited for cocktails, finger-food and informal talks on the lawn by the swimming pool outside the meeting room. Most of the LC5 representatives and senior officials from both government and donors have already gone, leaving the social interaction to donor and government 'foot soldiers'. To them everything now seems very cordial; the donor–government controversy does not make its mark on the situation. Instead, they chat about the PER as a charade and a formalistic event which usually has little practical effect on government–donor relations, although, as one government representative remarks, 'it would have been interesting to see them [high officials of government and donors] engage each other in public'. Intrigued by the presumed 'charade' of PER, I ask donor and government representatives what they see as the practical implication of this meeting. 'Nothing', 'I don't know' and 'It remains to be seen' are the answers.

## Responding to Political Transition and the Formation of UJAS

While the Public Expenditure Review illustrates a specific attempt by development partners to harmonize around a joint statement to the government, there have been more overarching structural attempts at donor harmonization in Uganda. This section deals with the formation of the Ugandan Joint Assistance Strategy (UJAS) as the result of the interface of development partners – not its actual content.[22] The various development-partner narratives of UJAS reveal both the general knowledge battlefield among donors when harmonizing, and the specific problem of whether and the extent to which 'political language should be included in the document', which a bilateral representative described being the main issue of contention. 'Political language' is seen as paramount in responding to the wider context of Uganda's political transition. This caused critical tension among the development partners and affected the formation of UJAS, in content as well as process. Several donor representatives opined that the UJAS process and the final document would probably have been very different if the government had tackled the political transition differently, or if the UJAS process had taken place prior to the political turmoil. Although encompassing a challenging process, UJAS became increasingly celebrated as the apotheosis of harmonization in Uganda, and thus the main footprint of the new aid architecture among development partners.

## UJAS – Format and Scope

'UJAS is', according to a Bank staff member, 'our CAS. It is fully fledged a CAS – a strategic document', indicating both its function and the Bank's claimed ownership of it. The difference between a CAS – as the Bank's conventional policy response to government's PRSP, in Uganda called the PEAP – and UJAS is that the latter includes other development partners in the Bank's original structures and aid architecture. UJAS is celebrated for its newness, apparently being the first time that the Bank has harmonized comprehensively with other donors on budget support issues. Also here, Uganda is a pilot country, as it was with regard to the PRSP mechanism: 'What's going on here is more like a test to us, before we consider embarking on similar joint ventures in other countries', a bilateral representative holds.

There are diverging myths of origin and opinions internal to and amongst donors and government as to how the UJAS idea emerged. While the donor community holds it was approached by the government with a call to harmonize its efforts, government representatives say they were contacted by development partners who insisted that the government should make such a call: 'They came to us with the Rome and Paris stuff and asked whether we would like them to harmonize. To us it doesn't matter. We own the PEAP, and the Bank owns the CAS. It's up to the Bank if they like to include others in their strategy. If they like to do it we say go ahead'.

Several donors say that UJAS emerged as a result of the processes in Paris and Rome, which 'not only we have committed to. They [recipient governments] have also ratified the documents'. The formal representation of UJAS – the ratified document – does not state where the initiative came from. It is portrayed as something inevitable that emerged from various recognitions:

> Recognising the high transaction costs, [the] government promoted donor coordination and alignment throughout the 1990s ... The government laid out its intent for its relationship with donors in volume 3 of the 2000 PEAP, called 'Building Partnership to Implement the PEAP' ... [UJAS] is a natural next step to further enhance donor harmonization ... The idea of preparing a joint assistance strategy, first discussed in the fall of 2003, was quickly endorsed by several key donors ... In March 2004 the government circulated a first comprehensive draft of the revised PEAP. In July 2004, UJAS partners in a two-day workshop discussed the key risks to PEAP implementation ... In November 2004 the government issued the final PEAP. UJAS partners issued the first comprehensive draft of the UJAS shortly thereafter. (UJAS 2006: v–vii)

As mentioned, it was not until 17 January 2006 that UJAS was accepted by the Bank's board and thus formalized and made operational, although its timeframe started in fiscal year 2005 (i.e. from 1 June). The UJAS process started in 2003 and was finalized in early 2006. This period saw critical debates among donors, the most critical phase being 2005 when the Ugandan political transition came to a head. The final and rather polished UJAS document describes this as a drafting process that 'presented opportunities and challenges. UJAS partners have learned important lessons, in particular about the need for in-depth preparation to agree on joint approaches and expectations' (UJAS 2006:

vii). Challenges and delays to donor harmonization were exacerbated by the turmoil relating to the political transition, which also gave time for more countries to join the process.

> Originally there are eight UJAS partners. These are the Bank, DFID, the Netherlands, Norway, Sweden, the African Development Bank, Germany and Austria. Austria was not [a partner] from the outset. They just signed, but as they joined before ratification they are considered among the original UJAS partners. Now Denmark is on the verge of joining – and the EC and Ireland are considering it. They have not come earlier because they have to end their own development cycle and commitments before joining another one.

UJAS partners have to conform to the same development cycle and process, as this statement by a Bank staff member underlines. UJAS involves a radical change in signatories' policies and routines. Its formal aim is to streamline donor support to Uganda and align it with the government's own strategy, as spelled out in the PEAP. According to one Bank employee: 'The main benefit of UJAS is to reduce donors' transaction costs, save money and resources for the government, and cut the transaction costs the government are subject to. It is about improving effectiveness and efficiency, and getting more poverty reduction out of each dollar'.

Rationalization seems to be the main momentum and raison d'être of harmonization in general and UJAS in particular. However, the challenge, or perhaps result, was that the very process of harmonization itself became highly challenging and time-consuming, and involved an increase in transaction costs and resource use for all involved parties.

## Notions and Processes of Harmonization

How do the various partners perceive the UJAS process in retrospect? Whereas the brief presentation above has shown the integrative aspects of harmonization, this section looks into the differences and contestations among UJAS partners regarding the overall idea and process. As narrated by a representative of a bilateral UJAS partner:

> The UJAS process has been like a rollercoaster. It's been very much up and down, back and forth – a lot of struggles between donors. As you know, it took a long time to devise the UJAS. It was based on the Bank's initiative and we embraced this new idea. The response from the government was also positive, I remember. They said, 'Ok, you go ahead with this' … they bought into the UJAS … Surely the UJAS relates to Rome and

> Paris, but I think it was more the result of how donors worked, or how they intend to work, more than actually responding to Paris.

When the UJAS was initiated in 2003 it rapidly triggered enthusiasm among donors who had long struggled to harmonize and formalize the sector working groups where the thematic donor experts meet. According to a Bank official, there are two groups in which development partners meet at the top level: the local development partners group, chaired by the Bank,[23] and the Partners for Democracy and Governance,[24] co-chaired by the Netherlands and UK. The Bank has not participated in the latter group due to its apolitical mandate. 'The one that the Bank chairs is an economic forum where we discuss budget support, policy priorities, and other economic issues. The other is more a political tool where the bilaterals engage politics', a Bank official explained. The two groups have a joint harmonization sub-group, 'which illustrates that we [development partners] have been harmonizing for a long time, and that is where the UJAS enters the picture as it formalizes the dialogue between these two groups and connects them to the other sector working groups'.

Several bilaterals were intrigued at being invited to participate in the Bank's CAS model – a process the Bank 'has always kept to itself. It has been extremely reluctant to open it to others'. Bilaterals have regularly sought to get the Bank to open the CAS process, to increase transparency and make the Bank cooperate with others. Bilaterals are further satisfied that UJAS is to draw on the two top-level coordination groups although the Bank stays away from the governance and democracy group. It was nevertheless welcomed by bilateral actors and interpreted as signalling stronger political involvement by the Bank. This, however, eventually ended up being one of the main reasons for dispute among UJAS members, alongside how to configure the 'silent partnership' as an implied UJAS necessity.[25] Smaller, bilateral donors felt squeezed by this, as one of them explained:

> The Bank took the lead from the very start, and DFID became increasingly involved in the process, and we – the smaller donors – were sidelined and often felt very squeezed. In April 2005 there was a major upheaval. We didn't feel sufficiently included in the process so we threatened to withdraw. It was mainly Germany and Sweden that fronted this concern. We didn't have the impression that it was about harmonization anymore, but rather that we should align with the Bank and DFID. They seemed to agree with themselves, but did not welcome our involvement. We were under the impression that they only wanted to have us along as signatories to the final document – not as equal partners. We were never made relevant, and for a long time the UJAS was – at least for us – about making a strategy to cope with the major donors.

Representatives from Germany, Sweden, Norway and the Netherlands all stated that at some point in the process they considered withdrawing. Danish and Irish informants also raised this concern as the reason for their reluctant and late inclusion in the process. The various donors related differently to UJAS, as outlined by a representative for the bilaterals:

> There have been various contributions from different UJAS partners. For a long time Sweden was not too committed although they are among the original UJAS partners, due to their lack of capacity and because they have invested resources in devising new partnership principles with the government. Norway and the Dutch signalled strong commitment from the start but demanded greater attention to non-economic issues. The Bank and some other donors focus only on economic development, but Norway and the Netherlands placed emphasis on seeing economic and social development as interrelated and mutually reinforcing ... Germany had another UJAS position as they traditionally conduct a lot of smaller projects, which they managed alongside the UJAS process ... The Africa Bank was mostly concerned with the overall harmonization agenda and process, as it, as the Bank, has an apolitical mandate restricting it from the most controversial discussions ... The EC is strong financially, but has not done much on the political level – it rather saw UJAS as an important tool in bringing the various donors together. By and large it is DFID and the Bank that have driven the process. They have worked together from the very beginning.

The World Bank at one point withdrew from its own UJAS process. This was because the Kampala team saw it as too challenging to orchestrate the various donors while being pressed to include political issues. Moreover, the process had lost resonance and momentum among board members at headquarters level, who 'had difficulties in thinking newly about harmonization'. At this stage, according to a Bank staff member, 'DFID stood up and assumed responsibility to drive the process, before the Bank rejoined'.

The arrangement of silent partnership – or aid selectivity, or division of labour among development partners – caused problems for harmonization, as it meant that donors would have to surrender some of their preferred policies and focus to other agencies. Prior to UJAS, several donors had been involved in the same sectors, resulting in duplication of efforts among donors, and numerous and overlapping reporting systems to the government. As one smaller donor representative said, 'I acknowledge we cannot all do health and education,' which apparently are the most popular sectors,[26] 'but since we wanted to secure political and human rights language in the UJAS document, we had to sacrifice health'. This statement underscores that the most contentious issue of donor harmonization relates to politics and that donors may be willing to abandon their core competencies in exchange for more political language.

## UJAS and the Challenge of Politics

The issue of politics and political conditionality emerged as a central obstacle to the UJAS process, causing friction between the bilateral donors and the Bank, with ramification for the overall harmonization agenda. Due to its apolitical mandate, the Bank found it difficult to accommodate the bilaterals' request that political measures should be included in the UJAS, not least since the UJAS builds on the Bank's system, the CAS, around which it aims to harmonize the development partners. The Bank's apparent political neutrality and the overall harmonization agenda became increasingly challenged as the bilateral donors gradually intensified their demands for including political language, thus further delaying the UJAS process. As summarized by one donor representative:

> What delayed the process from our [the donors'] side was that we disagreed with the Bank's situational analysis of Uganda, which constituted the backdrop for UJAS and the overall donor harmonization. We were determined to include governance issues, human rights and the conflict in the North in the situation analysis. The problem is that the Bank still sees Uganda as a success story, while we are more sceptical.

The 'situation analysis' referred to here is a crucial tool for diagnosing and determining which policies and instruments are to be applied. Harmonization problems were due largely to the inability of the development partners to agree upon the situation analysis. Hence, the Bank commissioned an external team to write a report to aid the analysis, provide recommendations and help to facilitate the UJAS process. The report, 'The Political Economy of Uganda' (Barkan et al. 2004), was to assist in the Bank's situation analysis. However, as described in the previous chapter, it was condemned and disowned by the Bank even before publication, as it was seen to be too critical on political issues – as indicated by the subtitle, 'The Art of Managing a Donor-Financed Neo-patrimonial State' – while also recommending aid cuts unacceptable to the Bank.

The Barkan Report assesses the level of risk that the political economy poses for the Bank's lending programme in Uganda, and explicitly recommends that the Bank should cut its aid to Uganda. It lists numerous allegations of corruption, mismanagement of donor funds, critical aspects and prospects for good governance, and nepotism among central government officials. It became totally unacceptable for the Bank to put its signature to the report and release it, as this would mean that the Bank approved the content and recommendations. However, precisely because the report had been officially condemned, people became interested in its content. One of the two leading newspapers in Uganda, the *Daily Monitor,* reproduced extensive parts of the report, and an editorial in the same paper noted: 'Finally, the World Bank's "confidential" report ... has leaked to the press. While a lot of what the report says is common knowledge in Uganda, it is the institutional source of these views that makes it a potent political issue in the country'.[27] The confidential and condemned report that I had been told not to put too much into was now on everybody's lips. The Bank's country manager had to make a public denunciation of the report's findings, and its conclusion and recommendation of cutting aid, and instead reiterate its commitment to working with Uganda.[28] In conclusion, the report reads, with reference to the formation of UJAS:

> Extreme prudence is therefore required. First, the Bank should plan for the possibility of a 'low case' lending program in Uganda during the period of the forthcoming CAS [i.e. UJAS]. Second, the Bank and other donors must rethink the appropriateness of continued budget support, and especially the appropriateness of increasing budget support. Since the Bank cannot weigh in explicitly on Uganda's political process, this is the only mechanism at its disposal to signal its concern. Conversely, the continued provision of high levels of budget support, especially when such support can be diverted into classified budgets and used for political purposes, indirectly involves the Bank in the political process. This is itself beyond the Bank's mandate. Moreover, to continue budgetary support at present levels risks embarrassment to the Bank, especially after it has been warned – not only by this report, but in what is common knowledge and discourse among leading members of the diplomatic community in Kampala ... As noted at the outset of this report, a country's political process forms the broad context within which Bank programs to build state capacity and reduce poverty take place. That context sets the rough possibilities what any donor can and cannot achieve, and the strategy that is most appropriate for achieving its objectives. We regret that we cannot be more positive about the present political situation in Uganda, especially given the country's admirable record through the late 1990s. We strongly suggest, however, that the final design of the CAS [UJAS] reflect the findings presented in this study. (Barkan et al. 2004: 55–56)

It is an understatement to say that the Bank disliked the report and its content, and not least it being leaked to the press. Bilateral donors generally found the report 'interesting reading' and although they concurred with much of its content, conclusion and recommended actions, they also understood that it was difficult for the Bank to give its signature to it. 'I know many in my office share its views', an employee at the Bank's Kampala office admitted. Consequently, the report did not lead to any imminent changes on the part of the Bank, which rather effectively renounced and downplayed it – although the narrative of the report reveals the Bank's troublesome relation to politics in formulating UJAS. Many bilateral donors, however, embraced the report. Not only did the content overlap with the political concerns raised by some bilateral donors, it also provided momentum for pressing for greater inclusion of political language in the joint UJAS document. As one bilateral donor representative put it:

> There is some Norwegian and Dutch language in the document. [Two bilateral representatives] worked extremely hard to achieve this. It was a tug of war moving out of proportions. Particularly the Bank and DFID have financial muscles the rest of us only dream of. And you know the Bank's mandate… As such, it was a great achievement to get [our] language of governance, human rights and the North into the [UJAS] document.

The dilemma of whether and to what extent political language should be included in the final document was highly challenging to UJAS partners, potentially undermining the overall harmonization process. The debate over 'political language' served to split the signatories' harmony somewhat: 'As you will see from the document, it quite frequently reads that "for some UJAS partners" this or that is important', one informant explained to me. The phrase 'some UJAS partners' is found seven times, and the word 'some' occurs thirty-five times, of which seventeen imply reservations made on behalf of a partner – although it never says exactly who – as illustrated by: 'for some UJAS partners, issues concerning the political transition and human rights are also important' (UJAS 2006: xiii, 34). Reservations concern not only policy, but also the structural level.[29] Although UJAS partners read the reservations as implying a lack of harmony, the reservations were necessary to get any notion of politics included, and in order to get all partners to sign the document.

UJAS is binding on those ratifying it. That, as one informant from a small bilateral agency asserted, 'has enabled us to influence the Bank. Now we can go to the Bank's board and say: "Look here, you have signed onto it". That's why it was so crucial to get the political and human rights language into the UJAS'. Bank staff counter this argument by asserting that the political aspects are context-dependent and apply only to some (unspecified) donors, and that they were perfectly aware what they signed up to, knowing the potential use of political language to other donors in putting pressure on the Bank. To return to the representative of the smaller bilateral donor, she replied to this argument:

> There *was* a potential for UJAS to alter practice. It still remains to be seen how much UJAS alters our [development partners] practice. I think many joined because of this potential. So far, the only change is that we talk to each other ... UJAS represents a platform for a next step. There is still a long way to go. When I was commenting on earlier drafts, it often read that 'UJAS is a major leap'. I always deleted 'major'.

She maintained that UJAS had thus far had more impact on inter-donor harmonization, in terms of aid selectivity and division of labour, than on development partner relations with government. 'The changes we wanted to see never really materialized as we hoped', she said, referring apologetically to the reduced and disharmonized notion of political conditionality, and describing the formation of UJAS as a process whereby 'the smaller donors won a few important battles, but in the end lost the war', as not all were equally interested in raising the political stakes. That the bilaterals lost the war, she maintained, did not mean that the Bank won it. Disagreements and contestations were concealed in ambiguous and amorphous policy language in order to agree on the UJAS.

To sum up, the narratives pertaining to UJAS formation and the debate over UJAS and politics reveal interesting features of donor harmonization. First, the process of harmonization has been a struggle over ideas. Second, some ideas are more influential than others. Third, their influence largely corresponds to their institutional affiliation and what the institutions have seen as their mandate, core competency and policy priority at the time. The Bank was steadfast in maintaining its apolitical mandate, which hampered the inclusion of political language in donors' joint strategy, while other donors had to renounce their policy priorities in order to infuse a non-committal political language into the final UJAS document. Fourth, although UJAS partners made certain reservations – itself a blow to the overall harmonization agenda – these reservations, which chiefly relate to politics, are still open to all signatories, as the final document does not identify who made the various reservations. Consequently the political language may be employed by anyone who deems it relevant, including the Bank. Fifth, although the reservations show disharmony among UJAS partners, the implementation and approach to government can be unpredictably congruent. Sixth, UJAS was a harmonization process among donors – the Ugandan government was not involved in the process of crafting this document that was so central to its relationship with twelve donors and their individual budget-support mechanisms.

The formation of UJAS seems to have bypassed several ideas integral to the new aid architecture, like participation, partnership and ownership. The government was, at most, consulted, but was not involved in the actual negotiations. The distinction between consultation and negotiation is important, as the latter would require the government's approval to make UJAS effective, something that is not required when only consulting, or listening to, the government. As UJAS was to be aligned with the government's PEAP it could be criticized for lacking local ownership and participation. A donor representative responded to this criticism, which also was voiced by other involved parties, by saying:

> It's a myth at home that UJAS is donor driven. First of all, harmonization was desired by the government. They said: 'Here you have the PEAP for you to harmonize and align'. So sure, it's donor driven. That's the whole point. You can't accuse anything for being donor driven when that's the whole point. Secondly, UJAS is a CAS, a World Bank document, so the Bank owns the process. It's the Bank's initiative. Or, we [bilateral development partners] pushed the Bank to open up its CAS process. It's wrong to say UJAS is donor driven, because UJAS is donors' response to government's PEAP.

In any case, the practical formation of UJAS seems to have curtailed the very ideological framework – the new aid architecture and its notions of partnership and participation – that initially gave rise to it. Harmonization involves an intended interface between development partners – that is, a process akin to a battlefield of knowledge where the actors involved promote and seek influence for their own, established policies. Harmonization processes reveal the balance of power between donors as well as the challenges to the bottom–up rhetoric integral to the new aid architecture. As different donors vie for influence they also lose sight of the government's strategy that they were supposed to align with. Practices that run counter to the concepts of government participation and ownership thus seem as an integral effect of the very idea of harmonization. The new aid architecture, of which UJAS is supposed to be an expression, pertains more to conditionality than the nominal aspiration of government participation in devising and orchestrating the overall national development portfolio.

## Independent Donors and Uncoordinated Aid

Just how coordinated were the development partners? Although they were connected with harmonization, the processes relating to UJAS and PER illustrate critical challenges and contestation among donors. Although official representations of UJAS and PER celebrate harmony, this chapter has demonstrated underlying practices that reveal a story of contestation, knowledge battles and general disharmony. This disharmony was to reveal itself publicly when various development partners finally recognized the need to respond to the 'political transition' in Uganda.

In late April 2005, Britain announced it would withhold £5 million in direct budget support due to concerns about Uganda's political transition and insufficient progress in establishing a fair basis for a multiparty system.[30] Later, Ireland reduced its support to the Ugandan government by €3 million, citing the government's lack of progress in introducing a viable multiparty system.[31] This spurred considerable media interest, in which donor representatives and foreign diplomats voiced their concerns about the political reforms – often accompanied by statements from prominent members of the political opposition. As a result, the government, with reference to its sovereignty and independence, requested donors and foreign diplomats accredited to Uganda to stop making public statements about the country's political process, and to relate to government officials rather than the opposition parties. As the minister of state explained: 'If you are a diplomat and have strong views on the political system, you don't run to the media. Rather you channel them through the Ministry of Foreign Affairs. This is international practice, it's just a reminder'.[32] On 14 July, Norway decided to cut one-third of its budget support – about $4 million – on grounds of growing awareness related to the negative development in the Ugandan government's handling of democracy, human rights and the fight against corruption.[33] These aid cuts came in the context of general donor discontent with Uganda's political transition, alleged bribes given to MPs to pass the bill lifting presidential term limit, the slow pace in opening up for a multiparty system, and dissatisfaction with the forthcoming referendum which almost everyone except the government saw as unnecessary and redundant. In the autumn of 2005, in the run-up to the presidential elections in February, the situation deteriorated further, with the main opposition candidate regularly imprisoned and taken to court in what donors saw as an attempt to stall his political campaign. More aid cuts were announced: on 30 November, the Netherlands reduced its aid by €6 million; on 19 December, Sweden cut $8.3 million; and on 20 December the U.K. made an additional cut of £15 million and withheld a further £5 million pending the February elections, on which disbursement was made contingent. This decision, which in sum reduced British budget support by £20 million from a planned £50 million, took effect immediately and came after an economic and governance assessment had raised concerns over 'the government's commitment to the independence of the judiciary, freedom of the press and freedom of association following the events surrounding the arrest and trial of the leader of the Forum for Democratic Change, Kizza Besigye; delays in the government's own road map for the political transition; the continuation of state financing for the ruling party in a new era of multiparty politics; and a significant overrun on public administration expenditure'.[34]

On 17 January 2006 the Bank also cut aid to Uganda. But whereas the bilaterals were explicit as to the political reasoning for their actions, the Bank stated that its directors had 'approved a 10 per cent reduction of the PRSC5 amount to US$ 135 million to reflect their concerns about expenditure overruns in the public administration budget'.[35] Although the Bank's board 'expressed concern about aspects of political governance',[36] its rationale for reducing financial support was nominally detached from the Ugandan political context. As shown in the previous chapter with regard to government–Bank negotiations around the PRSC, disagreement on the attainment of the 'prior action' relating to public sector reform caused concern among the PRSC team. Then, more than half a year later when the PRSC was finally brought to the table for the board's consideration, this was reverted to and employed in order to bring about aid cuts.

Although the bilaterals cut aid with explicit reference to what they saw as a deteriorated political context, the Bank sought to maintain its political neutrality by cutting aid over technical and managerial concerns. As such, the Bank has sought to maintain distance to the nexus of development and politics propagating among bilateral actors. As has been shown throughout this chapter, bilateral representatives have advocated the inclusion of political language in both the development partners' joint PER statement and in UJAS. The concept of and relation to politics was also the reason why it took so long to agree on UJAS and the PRSC, and then to present them jointly to the Bank's board for approval as the Bank's official policy strategy and lending mechanism.

The PRSC, as the Bank's financial commitment to implement UJAS, was originally planned to be submitted to the Bank's Board of Executive Directors on 6 September 2005. Disagreement between the Bank and the government regarding the fulfilment of existing and defining future PRSC prior actions delayed the board's review several times. The Bank's Uganda team could not submit the UJAS to the board as long as there were still several unresolved issues. With the UJAS process dragged on, it became natural for the board to discuss both UJAS and PRSC at the same meeting. This was first planned for December 2006, but all the challenges underpinning and deriving from the Ugandan political transition and the bilateral donors' response of aid cuts meant that the board meeting was again postponed, this time until January 2007. There were concerns that the aid cuts undertaken by UJAS partners should be read as negative to the implementation of UJAS and that consequently it would be rejected by the board, where the UJAS partners are also represented. People within the Bank feared that the bilaterals' harsh criticism of the Ugandan government's mismanaged political transition would be restated by their representatives to the board, thus demoting both UJAS and PRSC. As a donor informant explained, concerning the situation and the Bank's dilemma:

> All this led to the board meeting on UJAS being postponed yet another month. It was supposed to be presented [to] the board in December, but due to the political situation and the imprisonment of Besigye it was delayed. Since we managed to include political language in UJAS, it would be impossible for the board to approve it when the main opposition candidate was behind bars. That's why they postponed taking UJAS to the board. It might have killed the whole harmonization process ... They were afraid to make the decision in the tough political context, so they waited until 17 January when the situation had calmed. Then the board cut 10 per cent of the PRSC due to what they said was dissatisfaction with public sector reform, but we all knew the reason ... If they had discussed UJAS and PRSC in December they would probably have cut even more. Then the Bank would have been perceived as too political – something it did not want. So they in fact suggested delaying the board meeting ... The problem was not UJAS as such, as we finally agreed on the language and sound of it. But to the Bank, UJAS is a CAS and a CAS is tied to PRSC and funding. Moneywise it would have been a problem if UJAS was discussed earlier, and more cuts would not only undermine UJAS but also be interpreted as an increased involvement in politics by the Bank.

This statement demonstrates the balancing act involved in juggling political concerns, harmonization and upholding momentum to processes integral to the aid architecture in Uganda. Throughout the donor community there were growing fears that UJAS would be trashed by the Bank's board – and that would mean not only a dismissal of 'two years of putting our heads together for the sake of harmonization', but also that development partners would have to devise new, independent strategies, and embark on new consultations and negotiations with the Ugandan government. Thus it became important to all involved UJAS partners to have UJAS and PRSC passed at the board level, which in turn made it crucial to stall the board's treatment of them.

Without making a counterfactual claim, it seems probable that the board would have cut by more than 10 per cent if UJAS and PRSC had been presented to them when the deteriorating political transition was at its worst. A more substantial cut in PRSC would not only have undermined implementation of UJAS but would also have heightened the 'political' character of the Bank. To prevent undermining the overall harmonization agenda, demoting the Bank's PRSC and prior actions instruments, and becoming too closely associated with politics, the already-delayed December board meeting was further postponed until 17 January. This was unprecedentedly late when compared to previous (and later) PRSC discussions, as the end of PRSC missions aim to align to the fiscal year of both the Bank and its clients, which begins on 1 July and ends on 30 June the following year – which in turn provides a good indication of the challenges of agreeing upon a joint approach to the government of Uganda.

The timing and rationale of the various development partners in cutting aid show little coherence. Although UJAS sought to promote harmonization, the various actors acted independently in cutting aid. Five of the original eight UJAS partners and one of the four latecomers cut aid, which signals that donor policy preferences and politics prevail not only over joint approaches but also over the rhetorical ambitions of government ownership and participation. Also, in aligning their budget support to the Bank's structure integral to UJAS, which was shielded from political reprimands as its presentation to the Bank's board was deliberately postponed, the bilateral development partners assented to the Bank's portrayal of UJAS as apolitical, thereby not only undermining their previous political statements but also rendering difficult any future political dialogue and debate between UJAS partners and client government.

## Harmonization and Developmentality

Harmonization became a troublesome endeavour to the development partners. Nevertheless, most donor representatives have upheld – both prior to and after completing the UJAS – the importance of harmonization, maintaining that they in fact are in harmony, which they see UJAS as illustrating. From the empirical material presented above, however, we can see the great discrepancy between donors' official rhetoric and statements, and the informal practices underpinning and preceding them. The two cases of the Public Expenditure Review (PER) and UJAS reveal ways in which official policy is crafted, established and maintained on the micro- and macro-level respectively, and how the 'formal scheme [is] parasitic on informal processes' (Scott 1998: 6). There are other donor interests and dynamics that not only bring to bear but also undermine the overarching harmonization agenda. The idea of harmonization may have been noble, but in practice it proved difficult to bring together the donors' various perspectives, ideas, policies and approaches. Yet the donors managed to devise a strategy which, despite its many caveats and reservations opening for uncoordinated independent action, made the donors appear to be in harmony – at least formally. The harmonization agenda did change donor behaviour but not to the extent intended. Instead, it served to warrant and give legitimacy to existing practices and diverging donor perspectives, as per Mosse's (2005b) argument on the inversion of the policy–practice relationship.

Bridging donors' multiple policies and procedures was both the objective and the challenge of harmonization. The challenges of agreeing on a joint strategy, as well as the inverted policy–practice relation, bear semblance to Neumann's analysis of diplomatic speech-writing in a Norwegian ministry (Neumann 2007) and the problems of instigated change from within the discursive frames. Both the speech-writing and harmonization cases demonstrate how the social dynamics involved in merging different perspectives in a joint statement rather end up reproducing the existing, leading to a growing ignorance and limited scope of new perspectives. In the context of harmonization we can consider development partners as one unit facing the same problem as the ministry's many divisions involved in establishing internal coherence for the sake of one, congruent external voice. As with harmonization, diplomatic speech-writing involves consolidating the views of all involved actors, the challenge being that those involved tend to merely restate their previous and institutionalized positions, without making concessions to the benefit of the larger whole or the objective of one congruent voice. Those involved in such practices seem to follow the logic, Neumann asserts, that policies and positions need to be repeated, otherwise they will be weakened (Neumann 2005). Riles makes a similar point with reference to an international UN conference at which the delegates tried to reach consensus on an international treaty, observing that norms and intentions 'are not hidden but excessively explicit and located on the surface, insistently posed and restated at every turn' (Riles 1998: 378; see also Riles 2006).

Change, then, cannot come from within but needs to be brought about by a higher order that outranks bureaucrats and diplomats – and the 'foot soldiers' of both the Bank and bilateral donors. As diplomats, the development foot soldiers act on instructions and guidelines from their respective headquarters level, or as Douglas puts it, 'the individual tends to leave the important decisions to his institutions while busying himself with tactics and details' (Douglas 1986: 111). The effect of this resembles Ferguson's reproduction thesis (Ferguson 1994). But whereas Ferguson claims that such reproduction is due to the totalizing power of discourses leading unknowing individuals to reproduce the discourses of which they are part, the cases of harmonization outlined above show how involved actors are in fact aware of what they are doing, and the limitations of what they try to achieve.

In the cases of the donor joint PER statement and the larger UJAS formation, informants seem to have acted and negotiated in terms of their institution's respective mandate and core competency, and not according to what they saw as most pragmatic for achieving the overall objective of harmonization. Most of my informants were quite explicit on this, referring to themselves as foot soldiers and implementers of headquarters guidelines. At the same time, they asserted that their home office's detachment from the local context – both the country context and the context of harmonization – were obstacles to the general harmonization agenda, which some saw as more driven by the concerns of their home offices. These respondents also recognized the need for themselves and other donors to step down on some of their core competencies for the sake of harmonization. 'If we are to harmonize, everyone can't be doing health and education', as one informant stated, before going on to say that he could understand how politicians at home needed support from their constituencies in order to be re-elected, and that it would be impossible to say in public that 'we don't do anything on health in Uganda anymore'. Hence, profound changes in aid relations and policy content are not promulgated by the foot soldiers. Instead, they claim that such change needs to be instigated by politicians, at the level of donor capitals and headquarters, although recognizing their limitations.

Despite the many challenges, the actors involved did manage to achieve a joint donor PER statement and the UJAS – so harmonization was achieved, at least nominally. The ambiguous, amorphous language and the reservations made on the part of the various stakeholders in order to merge different realms and get everyone behind the same statement and strategy served largely to dilute the texts and the prospects for harmonization. As donor representatives acknowledged, UJAS did not become as robust as they had wished. Instead, it opened for and legitimized non-harmonized and unconcerted action – as shown by the various donors' uncoordinated cutting of aid for different rationales.

A few observations from the harmonization cases show that developmentality is also integral to development partners and not only a feature in donor–recipient relationships. First, the harmonization efforts illustrate how bilateral development partners are gradually inscribed into the Bank's realm – its structures, aid modality and policies. The UJAS, seen among donors as the apotheosis of harmonization in Uganda, is an expanded version of the Bank's Country Assistance Strategy (CAS), which is an integral part of its general PRSP model. Second, although crafting UJAS was a challenging process with many donor discrepancies, the final outcome and official representation portray the donors as being in harmony. In policy-making processes, differences and contestations are downplayed for the sake of harmony. Harmonization creates a rather monolithic knowledge system that produces and is produced by ignoring the possible alternatives. This not only points to a growing neglect of deviant knowledge (see Hobart 1993a), but also to the formation of an *empire*-like (Hardt and Negri 2000) discourse disseminated and backed by a seemingly coherent donor apparatus. This interrelates with the third aspect that pertains to the conditionality–participation nexus. The donors' harmonization agenda challenges the possibility of government participation, not only because harmonization is a process internal and limited to the donor community, but also because the result is, at best, a donor-driven selection of the government's own policies – if not the sole product of the donors' own preferences, regardless of the client's PRSP strategy. As such, and fourth, developmentality is not a feature found only at the macro-structural policy level. It also impinges on the everyday practices of development actors.

Harmonization involves developmentality as a form of productive power pertaining to the 'conduct of conduct' of those involved in international, institutional development, on both the donor and recipient side. However, it should not be seen as a totalizing power. There are contestations within institutional development, as illustrated by challenges to harmonization and the aid cuts which demonstrate that donors were not fully successful in conducting the recipient's conduct. This demonstrates discontinuities between the formal order and its various representations in official policies and documents on the one side, and the informal processes and procedures on the other. Developmentality, however, enables the construction of a coherent official discourse to produce and sustain the formal order by – as illustrated here with harmonization – turning heterogeneity into homogeneity.

## Notes

1. The high-level forums led to the Rome Declaration on Harmonization (2003) and the Paris Declaration on Aid Effectiveness: Ownership, Harmonization, Alignment, Results and Mutual Accountability (2005).

2. The Commission for Africa was initiated in the spring of 2004 by the British government to examine and provide impetus for development in Africa. The report was later seen as a blueprint for action by the G8 Summit at Gleneagles the same year, with a doubling of aid and significant multilateral debt relief.
3. Excerpt of the speech is available at http://www.afrika.no/Detailed/8703.html (accessed 27 April 2015).
4. The U.K. does not have term limits. On 5 April, Blair announced 5 May as the general election day in U.K.
5. See www.mail-archive.com/ugandanet@kym.net/msg18659.html (accessed 27 April 2015).
6. Regarding the pro-Museveni stand, there were reports – both in the Geldof case and in later public rallies in support of the incumbent – that students and people from rural areas had been allured with small gifts and had been brought in to join the public rallies. In favour of the other side, rumour had it that the political opposition regularly met with the donor community to get moral and financial support. I could not confirm these stories, but in any case, the rumours and allegations of each party aimed at diminishing their opponents were important in organizing both sides.
7. Electoral Commission of Uganda, www.ec.or.ug/ (accessed 27 April 2015).
8. The final draft of the UJAS was circulated in late 2005, but was not presented to or accepted by the Bank's Board of Executive Directors until 17 January 2006, despite being in effect from the start of fiscal year 2005/06 (i.e. 1 July 2005). Different rationales behind the delay are important for understanding the wider processes and challenges to the overall harmonization agenda – as will be shown later in this chapter.
9. The USA is the third biggest donor to Uganda, after the World Bank and the U.K. Although not perceived as being interested in harmonizing with other development agencies, USAID – drawing on the explicit expression of security and humanitarian interests as operational motifs – has chaired the sector working groups that address the conflict in northern Uganda, the Parliament, democratic processes and private sector donor group (see USAID 2005).
10. I do not claim to understand the budget or the economics terms used by donors. What I find intriguing is that the majority of budget-support donors should meet to discuss the Ugandan government's national budget and lending portfolios, without a government representative being present.
11. I did not know what they were talking about, as I did not have a copy of the budget they were discussing.
12. The performance-based allocation (PBA) system is a Bank mechanism used to aid and determine the distribution of funding to eligible countries, and involves an assessment tool known as the Country Policy and Institutional Assessment (CPIA). Although this system is an important instrument for the Bank and builds on a rather narrow understanding of development – which illustrates the lack of bottom–up approaches and Bank trusteeship – this incident was the only time I heard my informants refer to this allocation system. That might be because the CPIA is largely internal

to the Bank; it is a highly technical exercise involving only a few experts; the system might have only marginal relevance in Uganda; and it is highly disputed in general (see Van Waeyenberge 2009). The CPIA consists of a set of criteria for the various policy and institutional dimensions the Bank deems important for an effective poverty-reduction and growth strategy. It is intended to guide the allocation of IDA lending resources; for each criterion, countries are rated on a scale of 1 (very weak performance) to 6 (very strong), from which a total, aggregate score is calculated. The CPIA measures countries' overall governance environment, policies and institutional arrangements, and rates their performance on a total of sixteen indicators against a standard for good policies and institutions. It covers only those aspects that are under the country's control, and focuses on actions and policies, not plans or results. The CPIA is not negotiated with the government – it is undertaken solely by Bank staff, and neither its benchmarks nor the detailed analysis are shared with the government. The government is merely 'consulted'. It does not hold any formal role within the CPIA process and thus cannot dispute the method, data, analysis or any other part of the assessment. This performance rating is used to allocate funds so that, *ceteris paribus,* strong performers receive larger allocations than weak performers. The CPIA and PBA system have been widely criticized for being subjective, for lacking transparency and for following a Bank-devised blueprint of development. This affects not only the allocation of funds to client states: the CPIA is also a central tool in the Bank's ongoing policy dialogue with its counterparts, and its incentive mechanisms represent a productive power akin to governmentality (Sending and Neumann 2007). Among its spillover effects is the gatekeeping role CPIA has for other donors (Sending and Lie 2009; 2015).

13. http://go.worldbank.org/K37K361EG0 (accessed 26 April 2015).
14. Uganda is divided into five administrative layers, called the local council (LC) system, 'being a hierarchical structure of councils and committees that stretches from the village (LC1) up to the district (LC5)' (Tukahebwa 1998: 15). Currently (autumn 2010) there are eighty districts, but at the time of fieldwork in 2005 there were fifty-six districts (LC5), subdivided into counties (LC4), sub-counties (LC3), parishes (LC2) and villages (LC1). LC3 and LC5 are the most important levels in being elected local government councils. 'Districts formulate their own development plans. However, district development plans have to take into account national planning objectives and priorities' (ibid.: 23), which is an important reason why LC5 chairmen are invited to the PER. LC5s are democratically elected, this being a bottom–up system. They are, however, under the constant scrutiny of the Resident District Commissioners (RDCs), who are administrative personnel at the LC5 level appointed by the central government to ensure that government interests are implemented at the local level (Makara 1998). The LC system thus involves the two-sided dynamics of bottom–up and top–down approaches. In theory, issues emerging from the local level are relayed up through the various layers until reaching an LC with sufficient authority, mandate or power, while centrally planned government

directives are conveyed downwards until they are implemented at the local level. At the district level, it is thus hard to determine the relative status and responsibility of the LC5 chairman and the RDC. Although they are supposed to work in concert, in practice they may conflict and infringe on each other. The number of districts is regularly expanded by the central government under the guise of 'decentralization' and 'good governance'. Donors, however, interpret the increase in districts as an attempt by the government to maintain control, via the RDC, in challenging districts. In criticizing the government, however, donors apply the language of public sector reform, to reduce public expenditures and transaction costs, and fiscal discipline.

15. The Commonwealth Heads of Government Meeting (CHOGM) is a biennial summit meeting of the heads of government of the Commonwealth nations. The selection of Uganda as host to CHOGM rapidly became the focus of public debate. Supporters read it as recognition of Uganda's leadership, its political system, an indication of progress, and that Uganda was no longer a developing country. Opponents saw it as legitimizing a derailed political system, a flawed political transition and a repressive regime. Hosting CHOGM would also necessitate vast government rechanneling of resources into infrastructure improvement and urban development at the expense of other pressing development needs. Only a few donors, however, subscribed to this criticism, as many of them are Commonwealth members.
16. Taken from the manuscript, 'Keynote Address by Professor Apolo Nsebambi, Rt Hon Prime Minister of the Republic of Uganda, on Public Expenditure Review Workshop at Speke Resort, Munyonyo, Kampala, on Tuesday 10 May 2005 at 9.15 AM'.
17. Ugandan shilling (also abbreviated UGX). The amount is equivalent to about 16.5 million USD.
18. This and the remaining quotations from the joint donor statement are taken from the 'Statement by Development Partners' manuscript, read aloud verbatim by the Bank's country manager.
19. The annual PER focuses on the government's annual Budget Framework Paper.
20. Medium Term Expenditure Framework (MTEF) is a government document evolving from a policy planning and budget formulation process that sets fiscal targets and allocates resources to strategic priorities within these targets.
21. Six concern the poor quality and lack of roads at district level. Five questions deal with the size of government and parliament, with discontent at the ever-expanding state sector at the central level. Interlinked to this, seven district representatives comment on the discrepancy between the government's rhetoric of economic decentralization and the central economic planning, as illustrated by the PER itself. Three district chairmen comment on the security situation in the North and the perceived inability of the government to deal with this, while two others note the weak national budget management. Additionally, a few comments criticize the government concerning the choice of venue, which made it difficult for

district representatives to visit and stay with friends and family in Kampala in order to save money. The three comments concerning the donor community are all pleas to the donor community to give more money and to press the government to deliver better services in the districts.

22. A Bank employee at the Kampala office sighed in relief when I explained this as the objective of a UJAS-focused interview: 'It is good we're not to talk about policy because it is too sensitive in many ways. I then probably wouldn't have been of much use as I need to clear all policy statements with the country manager'. Regarding UJAS this was a regular Bank staff response, rather contrary to my experiences with bilateral UJAS partners who stress the political aspect as the important contribution of the document.
23. This group is a top-level umbrella forum that comprises the different sector working groups, of which the PRSC/macroeconomic sector group described above is understood as the most important and influential.
24. Previously called the Donor Democracy and Governance Group (DDGG).
25. 'Silent partnership' here means the sharing of main responsibility of various sectors, akin to aid selectivity, among development partners. Although UJAS involves a joint approach, various different partners are to take the lead on policy sectors seen as being within their core competency.
26. The reason for their popularity is arguably that they are embraced by both recipient government and donor home constituencies, they appear to be non-controversial, as well as being technical and capacity issues, and not political.
27. *Daily Monitor,* 22 May 2005: 'Has Museveni outfoxed the donor community?' The report was first referred to in *The New Vision,* 17 May 2005: www.newvision.co.ug/D/8/12/435022 (accessed 27 April 2015).
28. This was done during the PRSC mission's wrap-up meeting, as described in the previous chapter.
29. For example: 'Although some UJAS partners expect to deliver an increasing proportion of their support through direct budget support, all will continue to provide some assistance as project support' (UJAS 2006: 31); and 'Some UJAS partners will provide joint support to Uganda Aids Commission Partnership Fund. Recognizing the role of UN system, especially UNAIDS, the partners will work to ensure that their assistance is complementary to that delivered by the UN agencies' (ibid.: 27).
30. 'Britain blocks aid to Uganda', *Daily Monitor,* 29 April 2005. See http://allafrica.com/stories/200504280794.html (accessed 27 April 2015).
31. 'Ireland cuts aid over third term', *Daily Monitor,* 13 May 2005.
32. 'Uganda warns diplomats over political statements', *Daily Monitor,* 17 May 2005.
33. 'Norway cuts aid over kisanja', *Daily Monitor,* 19 July 2005.
34. DFID Press Release, 'UK cuts direct budget support to Uganda by £15 million, withholds further £5 million', 20 December 2005. Available at http://reliefweb.int/report/uganda/uk-cuts-direct-budget-aid-uganda-%C2%A315-million-withholds-further-%C2%A35-million (accessed 29 April 2009).

35. World Bank News Release No. 2006/239/AFR: 'Uganda: Joint Assistance Strategy and World Bank Approval of US$ 135 Million for Fifth Poverty Reduction Support Operations'. http://www.worldbank.org/en/news/press-release/2006/01/17/uganda-joint-assistance-strategy-and-world-bank-approval-of-us135-million-for-fifth-poverty-reduction-support-operation (accessed 27 April 2015).
36. Ibid.

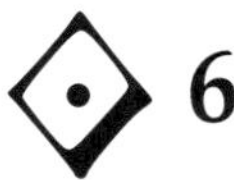 6

# A Metamorphosis of Power Relations?

## The New Aid Architecture, Partnership and the State

With the new aid architecture we see the introduction of a new order of development seeking to direct and manage the content, structure and practice of development. However, and as indicated throughout the previous empirical chapters, the practice of development has not followed accordingly. Disjuncture – here understood as the discrepancy between the formal order and practices – has characterized implementation of the new aid architecture. That is not to say that the new aid architecture is irrelevant to practice. Indeed, it has profoundly altered how donor and recipient institutions, in this case the Bank and its Ugandan counterpart, relate to each other and how policies are devised and implemented, as demonstrated with the new formative idea of partnership and the underpinnings of the developmentality concept. What has not changed, I argue, is the asymmetrical power relation between Bank and client institutions – which was among the main motives and rationales (at least on the rhetorical level) for the Bank to adopt the ideas of the new aid architecture. This chapter revisits and analyses the empirical findings, and puts them into the context of state formation processes and sovereignty.

The very institution of the post-colonial developmental state is increasingly being challenged by external development actors operating with and through state institutions, arguably with the host state's consent. The role of external donor agencies for state formation signals that the instituted orders and structures of the state are changing and questioned – even by actors purporting to state building, like the World Bank with its role in Uganda. The state, it seems, is relinquishing its once supreme regulatory hold over domestic politics as an effect of forces external to the state that gain momentum by operating in the name of development. The aid recipient state appears weakened as it seems to be losing – or (forced to) outsource – its former monopoly over domestic politics, power and policy-making processes. This comes as an effect of development donors' intent to revamp structures and practices upholding paternalistic and asymmetrical aid relations, i.e. the new aid architecture. The 'new' aid architecture is not that novel anymore, but as it is now commonplace to most aid-receiving states and manifests itself particularly in their partnership with the World Bank, we are better equipped to observe and analyse its effects. The effects involve the emergence of new, subtle and tacit governance mechanisms – or developmentality – that not only have been enabled by the new aid architecture but also curtail its girding ideas of partnership, participation and ownership while dismantling the internal–external divide between the client state and the Bank. Hence, and against the official rhetoric, the lopsided structures and practices of development are being reproduced with profound effects, not only for the new aid architecture itself but also and more substantially for state formation and, in turn, sovereignty.

## Disjunctures of the New Aid Apparatus

The new aid architecture aims at revamping 'development'. This involves focusing more on policy reform than on investment projects, a move away from donor-driven conditionalities to more inclusive participatory approaches, an enhanced focus on poverty reduction and not solely economic growth, and, thus, the emergence of a reform agenda that goes beyond mere economic and financial management to a focus on good governance policies. This restructuring of aid itself reveals an apparent contradiction that requires us to see participation and conditionality in nexus and as a continuum where practice is found somewhere in-between – and not as mutually exclusive concepts that describe practice, define the formal order or direct action. The first point for identifying the contradiction is in the formal order itself, as the emphasis of the Bank – and donors in general – on certain policy realms, reforms and modalities of aid relations has acted to counter their aspirations for reducing conditionality, promoting participatory approaches and transferring to the client decisive authority in order to engender ownership and local commitment to externally funded projects and processes.

## PRSP – An Inconsistent Model of and for Partnership?

The ideas of partnership and participation are the most prominent features of the new aid architecture, representing a fundamental shift in international aid whereby donors retreat from direct operational engagement and running their own projects to a more withdrawn role, primarily as funders of the activities of client institutions. Partnership requires recipient participation, and implies a joint commitment to long-term interaction, shared responsibility for achievements and failures, reciprocal obligations, equality, mutuality and balance of power. Although an equal relationship is seen as a value in itself, the ideas of partnership and participation emerged against the backdrop of increased critique of donors' policy enforcement and paternalism drawing on and reproducing a lopsided donor–recipient relationship. Mitigating these concerns was thus seen to enhance the legitimacy of both institutional development and the donor community.

To the Bank, the ideas inherent in partnership and participation became articulated through the Strategic Compact's Comprehensive Development Framework (Wolfensohn 1999; Weaver and Leiteritz 2005) and operationalized with the Poverty Reduction Strategy Paper model, which marked a critical break with the preceding era of structural adjustment. The PRSP is now central to clients' partnership with the Bank, the aim being a 'long-term, holistic and strategic approach' (Wolfensohn 1999: 30) based on the recipient's own priorities and preferences. The PRSP is to be produced by the borrowing government and thus signifies a decentralization of authority from the Bank to the recipient, client state. The model itself, however, is devised by the Bank, and although it aims to be context-sensitive in being 'produced' by the client government, it represents a global template that makes this particular form of partnership itself a condition for how the Bank engages clients who seek access to soft development loans and credits. The set-up of the PRSP model, moreover, frames not only the freedom of partnership but also the type of knowledge and policies to be included in it.

There is a challenge with the formal order of PRSP itself, which serves to undercut ambitions of holistic and long-term participatory planning. The formal order expects the client government to produce its own strategy to guide all national development initiatives. However, to become effective and qualify as a lending document, and thus serve as the foundation for partnership, the PRSP needs Bank approval on procedural and structural matters – meaning that Bank staff assess whether the strategy follows the intended format and has been devised in a participatory and consultative manner involving non-state, civil society actors. This approval – itself calling into question the idea of ownership and implying indirect governance, since the client needs to abide by the Bank's criteria as to what constitutes an acceptable strategy – does not mean that the Bank will support the whole strategy. Instead and in response, the Bank devises a Country Assistance Strategy (CAS) in which it picks and chooses from among the client's PRSP policies, thus effectively undermining the holistic ambition of PRSP. Although the CAS follows the same timeframe as the PRSP – usually a medium-term perspective with a three- to five-year framework – it does not come with any financial pledges. The Bank's aid disbursements draw on the Poverty Reduction Support Credit (PRSC), which involves an annual policy dialogue between the Bank and client government regarding assessment of performance, the prioritizing of policies and activities outlined in CAS, and negotiating the financial aspects of the partnership. This annual ritual, itself instigated by the PRSP model, challenges the idea of long-term planning.

## Partnership and Participation at the Bank

The PRSP model represents the formal order and official discourse of the Bank, and is held to have ramifications for the Bank's internal and external practices, its partnership model and the overall policy-making process. However, as illustrated by the ethnography from within the Bank, the basic tenets of this new order are not widely shared by or implemented throughout the Bank's various networks and operational departments. Chapter 3 showed how those seen to champion the ideas of the new aid architecture face friction in their encounters with other thematic networks and the regional, operational units. The interface between various thematic networks and the operational side of the Bank is an effect of the Bank's internal matrix organization where thematic networks compete for influence over the operational units that, as the Bank's external representatives responsible for negotiating lending arrangements with clients, have a decisive say as to which networks' ideas will be included or not in practical work. To the networks, having operational influence means they are more likely to maintain their funding and activities. There is thus internal competition for influence and resources, with effects for the Bank's external representation and lending arrangements. This is most evident with the Social Development (SD) unit, which, in championing the ideas of participation and bottom–up approaches to development with a focus on poverty reduction, is seen as propagating the ideas of the new aid architecture within the Bank. These approaches and mindsets produce information and knowledge fundamentally different from what is required by the operational side, to which the Poverty Reduction and Economic Management (PREM) network is more aligned. PREM's focus on economic growth facilitates a type of quantitative knowledge that enables measurable and legible units – the antithesis of the more qualitative, complex knowledge conveyed by the SD focus on participatory and bottom–up approaches to poverty reduction.

The organization of difference comes as a result of the internal matrix organization, which makes the internal working of the Bank akin to a battlefield of knowledge. This battlefield is produced and reproduced by the matrix organization, which not only compartmentalizes different thematic units but also instigates their interface as a competition for resources and operational influence. The operational side requires a particular type of knowledge that facilitates legibility through the active production of representations rendering the social terrain comprehensible and amendable at the abstract level of planning. The battlefield is thus not an equal one but is biased towards those networks better suited to serve the operational requirements of legibility, which is a kind of knowledge fundamentally different from that involved in the new aid architecture's promotion of participation. This is recognized by those within the Bank who support the ideas of the new aid architecture. They face the challenge of managing a balancing act: following a hard line and not compromising on the basic tenets of participation, while also being more pragmatic and modifying ideas and approaches in order to gain operational influence and relevance outside their own network. Either way, such participatory, bottom–up approaches are on weak terms, either rejected for their operational irrelevance or compromised in order to gain relevance.

This we saw in the two cases presented in chapter 3. The first was the LICUS meeting, where an operational officer had been invited to comment on the SD approach and strategy: it saw a tension between the SD pragmatists, who were willing to modify their stance in order to gain operational influence, and the SD hardliners, who were unwilling to make such compromises. Second, the wider outline of the core course on Public Sector Governance provided an even clearer illustration of the operational thinking and demands within the Bank and how different thematic networks, here exemplified and contrasted by the SD group and PREM, compete for operational influence. From that case we saw how that the unit most attuned to the girding ideas of the new aid architecture faces the greatest challenges in providing operational input and achieving relevance. This is in contrast to the PREM network, which embodies the Bank's more conventional approach and scope, with a focus on 'hard', measurable and legible issues like economic growth rates and other quantifiable measures.

A similar account is provided by my rendering of the making of the World Development Report (WDR) 2000/2001 'Attacking Poverty' (World Bank 2000; see chapter 2 above). The WDR is the Bank's flagship publication, setting out its future focus, scope and policies. The 2000/2001 report was to be based on the insights provided by the participatory, bottom–up ideas of the new aid architecture. Although these ideas were new at the time and perhaps not yet sufficiently institutionalized, they nevertheless enjoyed great momentum, being high on the agenda. Yet, as we saw, the case demonstrated the problems of applying the bottom–up perspective. The ambition of listening to the 'Voices of the Poor' (Narayan 2000) was soon abandoned, as what that conveyed was not a uniform voice but a heterogeneous and complex picture of the concerns of the poor, too intricate for the planners' need for tidy oversight and legible units. Such bottom–up and participatory approaches, in attending to the complex empiricism, were seen to engender perspectives that made planning and knowledge production difficult: the more voices that were listened to, the more difficult if became to codify them into a few, standardized categories without being reductionist to their multitude. Instead of furthering the 'civil society' perspective – associated with the new aid architecture and the Social Development group – the 'finance' perspective, more akin to the ideas of PREM, largely prevailed (see Kanbur 2001; Wade 2002b; Fox 2003).

Giving priority to certain knowledge-serving operational demands seems to be a function of the internal workings of bureaucracies (cf. Herzfeld 1992) and how large-scale planning necessarily depends on a particular view to promote legibility (see Scott 1998). As a general characteristic of the Bank's internal practices this has implications for the reception and application of the kind of knowledge conveyed by participatory approaches and the involvement of partners in policy-making processes. Moreover, it illustrates how the Bank still has a decisive say over policy formulation and choice, even though the PRSP model gives clients the responsibility for making and implementing their own strategy.

Knowledge battles within the Bank take place along two axes. The horizontal axis involves the encounter between, for instance, SD and PREM and their struggle for operational influence. As noted, the operational side favour the more legible and less complex kind of knowledge, as provided by PREM. The vertical axis refers to the relation between the knowledge produced on the ground and among the Bank's 'foot soldiers' on the one side, and their knowledge to higher, executive levels of the Bank on the other. The requirement of straight lines and legibility increases as knowledge 'moves upwards' within the Bank's bureaucratic organization and to levels where executive decisions are made. Moving upwards in a conical spiral with centrifugal effects, the empirical fuzz becomes progressively disregarded. By the time a staff report reaches the board level it will generally have been reduced to a two-page note. Influence is contingent on being able to condense complex arguments in a particular form to address decision-makers' concerns on their own terms, since the board, when it is to make decisions, needs clear and legible knowledge and alternatives that can demonstrate established links between input and output. Integral to bureaucratic organizational work is thus indifference to any complex knowledge that deviates from existing models and rationalities (Herzfeld 1992; Hobart 1993a). Those who can deliver knowledge of the kind demanded are bound to benefit.

The internal knowledge battles point to contestation and disjuncture of the formal order of the PRSP model within the Bank. Various departments and staff have different renderings of and uses for the PRSP model's central idea of a partnership based on recipient participation. This is not only – if ever – the result of sly intentions or lack of will to alter deeply embedded institutional structures and discourses, but rather an effect of the Bank's internal matrix organization, which, in aspiring to promote professional excellence, compartmentalizes departments and thus segregates various networks and knowledge systems. However, the matrix organization not only separates them but also institutionalizes their interface, which takes the form of a struggle over operational relevance and influence. The significance of this is not limited to our understanding of the Bank's internal practices and knowledge formation. Since the struggle is articulated in the Bank's operational units with its staff as arbitrators, it also has implications for the Bank's external representation and the interface with its counterparts.

## Partnership and Participation in Operations

The partnership relation between the Bank and Uganda is constructed around the PRSP model and its girding ideas of partnership and recipient participation. While practitioners on both sides largely reproduce the formal order in describing the new aid architecture, their practices and the interface between representations of the Bank and its Ugandan counterpart reveal disjuncture. The PRSP model is not irrelevant to their interface, even if its nominal version is not reflected in practice. It grants the Ugandan government certain freedoms and responsibilities under the guise of the liberal ideas of the new aid architecture. This does not, however, mean that the government has gained full control over the PRSP process, since the conditions for the formation of partnership and the scope of participation are framed by the Bank and its standardized model. The question, then, is not whether the government participates or not, but on whose terms.

In examining the historical trajectories and current formation of PRSP, or PEAP as it is called in Uganda, chapter 4 demonstrated how the Ugandan development strategy has increasingly come to resemble the Bank's PRSP model and how various mechanisms integral to the partnership formation enable the Bank to pursue its template and retain control by orchestrating the wider assemblage of Bank–client relations. Against the PRSP model's medium-term timeframe, the model involves annual PRSC missions. These serve to facilitate close negotiations between the Bank and the government, where the assessment and formulation of prior actions, or conditionalities, is done. Also known as 'budget-support operations', these missions involve discussions of financial issues and lending terms. The function of the PRSC underscores how the government's PRSP is disengaged from the financial side of the partnership. Moreover, the PRSC constitutes a mechanism that enables the Bank to retain control over the policy dimension of the partnership. Although the client (here, Uganda) produces its national development strategy, the PRSC enables the Bank to fine-tune and monitor its chosen selection of policies and their implementation, in a process resembling conditionality more than participation.

The annual PRSC exercises can be seen as a ritualized practice with generative effect for the formation and articulation of partnership, as well as for our understanding of it. PRSC missions are not mere routines of practice: they instigate, articulate and shape the interface between the Bank and its client, and thus represent a good vantage point for approaching the formation of partnership, the idea of participation and other features of the new aid architecture found in the Bank–client interface. Moreover, they are a central mechanism that enables the Bank to retain control over its broader lending portfolio, including the selection of policies, even if the client has been formally accorded this responsibility. Hence, the PRSC mechanism, itself part and parcel of the PRSP model, enables us to understand the historical formation of the Ugandan PEAP and how it gradually came to replicate the Bank's model, as well as representing the practical interface of the Bank and its counterpart, thereby reflecting the practical instigation and formation of partnership.

The PRSC mechanism plays an important role by enabling the Bank to retain some of the control it lost with the new partnership model. It has also brought the Bank closer to the heart of its clients' internal processes. As a budget-support instrument, the PRSC makes possible close dialogue between the Bank and central government bodies on issues that the Bank could not previously deal with, such as the client's budgetary and economic priorities, and not only on how the loan portfolio should be put to use. The Public Expenditure Review (PER), as outlined in chapter 5, is one such instrument and annual practice instigated by the PRSC mechanism. The PER serves as a forum where the Bank can officially comment on the client's national budget, and government spending and priorities. The PER also compels the government to open up the process to not only sub-governmental bodies but also non-state actors such as civil society organizations and foreign development actors.

A more profound way of exercising influence, however, is the negotiations over 'prior actions'. As a practice integral to the PRSC mechanism, the negotiation over prior actions – or 'conditionalities', in the sense of measures that must be undertaken before aid disbursement can take place – enables the Bank to assess the client's performance against certain stipulated policies. It also involves the stipulation of new ones, the achievement of which will be assessed by the next PRSC mission. Although the assessment of old and stipulation of future prior actions must be agreed upon by both the Bank and its government counterpart, these negotiations are not a neutral dialogue: they involve and illustrate a lopsided relationship. Here we may recall the Bank's mission team leader who refused to negotiate the financial disbursement plan before agreement on prior actions had been reached with representatives of the Ugandan government. The practical negotiations over prior actions thus not only demonstrate the asymmetrical interface between the two, but also how the Bank is still able to wield considerable influence as to which policies will be implemented and how. The responsibility for failure, however, must be borne by the client government, as the prior actions are seen to be the operationalization of and deducted from the government's own strategy – thus demonstrating how the Ugandan government is held accountable to the Bank for the implementation of its own policies.

While the formal and structural order, or the official representation, of partnership reflect the PRSP model's liberal scope of bottom–up partnership, the practices of this architecture draw attention to conditionality and the same paternalistic top–down approach that the new aid architecture set out to replace. The PRSC mission reveals practices that challenge the ideas of partnership and participation. In fact, the conditions under which such challenges emerge are produced and instigated by the formal order of partnership itself, as it is the PRSP model that has provided the partnership with the PRSC mechanism that enables the Bank's continuous control. This, I argue, points to the participation–

conditionality nexus and to developmentality as an integral feature of the new aid architecture. The partnership model gives the recipient certain freedoms, but these are limited by the Bank's formative framework and its ability to employ other mechanisms in order to retain control and exercise influence.

Another aspect that challenges the formal order of partnership and limits the frames for participation comes from the donors' harmonization agenda. With the harmonization of development partners we see the intentional establishment of a congruent and uniform knowledge system. Despite internal differences within the group, to the government development partners appear as a homogeneous entity. There are two features emerging from the idea of harmonization that have implications for the practical sides of partnership and for client participation. One concerns the construction of a homogeneous and seemingly hegemonic joint donor discourse. To those on the receiving end, this appears as a take-it-or-leave-it policy package that curbs possibilities for the government to go donor shopping. In effect, harmonization limits the client's room to manoeuvre and to search for alternative funding sources. The other feature concerns practices within the donor community, as harmonization instigates the interface of different donors, aimed at inscribing them in a congruent realm. Harmonization involves not only knowledge battles; it also limits difference and reduces diversity among development partners.

The processes and politics of harmonization demonstrate how various bilateral donors are gradually inscribed into the Bank's structural realm and become part of its practices. In Uganda, the harmonization of development partners is epitomized in the Ugandan Joint Assistance Strategy (UJAS), which builds on the Bank's traditional CAS framework. It took development partners two years to agree upon the UJAS, in a process reminiscent of a knowledge battlefield where development partners saw critical challenges in agreeing upon a joint framework. Most crucial were debates over aid selectivity: who was to take control of the various policy fields, how to respond to Uganda's political transition, and the extent to which political conditions should be included. The two latter points were a challenge to the Bank, since they could compromise its apolitical mandate and jeopardize its established relations with the government. Similar tensions developed when the development partners were to give a joint response to the government's national budget, since most donors – apart from the Bank – wanted to take up their concerns regarding Uganda's ongoing political transition. Even though UJAS draws on the Bank's structures and the Bank is the single largest donor, the Bank could not dictate to its development partners because it depended on their cooperation in establishing a harmonized approach. In order to reach harmony and agree on the UJAS, contentious issues were wrapped in ambiguous language that allowed the development partners to express reservations, thus diluting the objective of harmonization. The ambiguous language, however, served more to integrate donors by downplaying disagreement than to provide leeway for the recipient Ugandan government. As the government was not part of the internal donor processes, its point of reference for donor harmonization has been UJAS, which appears as a monolithic knowledge system that effectively limits the scope for alternatives that might evolve from government participation. Hence, in affecting both the donor community and the donor–recipient relationship, harmonization influences the formation of partnership.

## Partnership as Developmentality

Following the renderings of partnership at different levels and contexts of the Bank–Uganda relationship, we observe challenges to its formal representation as originally intended by the new aid architecture and as outlined by the Bank's PRSP model. From the ambiguity inherent in the formal order itself, to practices within the Bank, and to the interface between the Bank and its Ugandan counterpart, as well as the effects of the development partners' harmonization agenda – all reveal practices of and contestation of the formal order of partnership. This trajectory and its various renderings of partnership draw attention to the participation–conditionality nexus and the formation of developmentality. Whereas the order of development points to participation, its practice indicates that conditionality remains a prominent feature of the Bank's operations. It demonstrates how the liberal promises of the new aid architecture and its ambition to alter old lopsided development relationships have been paralleled and met by mechanisms and practices that not only reproduce the asymmetrical relations but also produce disjunctures towards the formal order. The formal order of partnership, I argue, opens for developmentality, as the instigation of partnership comes with the requirements of other mechanisms that, in sum, enable the Bank's continued control.

The concept of developmentality grasps how the Bank has come to employ new mechanisms of governance to retain control while simultaneously granting the client greater responsibility. This is premised on the Bank's ability to govern at a distance and to orchestrate the 'conduct of conduct' by framing the context for partnership. Partnership, as outlined with the PRSP model, provides a framework of possibilities for installing new kinds of mechanisms through which the Bank becomes able to exercise influence and involve itself in contexts and negotiations previously deemed beyond its remit. For instance, and as instigated by the PRSC mechanism, Bank representatives now sit around the table with central officials of the Ugandan government, negotiating on whether the government is achieving its 'own' policies and what their new policies should be (cf. 'prior actions'). This enables the Bank to influence its client from within and to make its own policies those of the recipient. Although this may involve some backstage arm-twisting, the official version holds that the policies are both produced and owned by the government. Nevertheless, the client government remains accountable to the Bank for implementing these ('its own') policies. The Bank retains control through orchestration partnership and its policy content – the partner's participation is largely on the Bank's terms. Developmentality thus signifies a means of governance that is indirect and more profound than direct coercion and policy imposition. The Bank's own representation and rendering of partnership refers to 'putting the country in the driver's seat'. Against this objective of client participation – and still following the Bank's metaphor – the practice of partnership shows how the Bank is involved in deciding the destination, producing the map and constructing the roads.

With the new formation of partnership the Bank's means for governance no longer depends on its ability to withhold funds or dictate policies alone. Instead, and more profoundly, it is premised on the Bank's ability to frame the context and content of partnership. Developmentality draws attention to the practices of partnership and how the liberal concepts of the new aid apparatus represent a form of productive power that both produces and depends on the production of a limited range of policies and structures available to the client. The Bank defines the frames within which choices can be made and freedom exercised. As such, developmentality signifies a form of governance that can be just as compelling as the more direct coercion associated with the era that preceded the new aid architecture. Developmentality also shows that the inertia experienced in trying to change structures deeply embedded in institutional development is not only caused by discursive reproduction but is very much associated with the practical sides and tasks of development. The formation of aid relations, the formal order of development and its disjunctures, and the discrepancy between the liberal rhetoric and coercive practices of partnership, reveal developmentality as a mechanism for governance that reproduces the asymmetrical donor–recipient relationship, but in a more subtle version. Developmentality and the current formation of partnership are thus premised on the liberal rhetoric of self-governance and the granting of restricted freedom.

One of these restricted freedoms concerns the formulation of national development policy, now formally a designated task of the client country. However, to the Ugandan government it seems impossible to get around the Bank's policy priorities. This is shown by the attention to good governance issues, which involves a focus on how public institutions conduct their affairs and manage public resources. In itself, this policy realm draws attention to developmentality through the way it seeks to alter structures, practices and mentalities of the government's internal affairs. Good governance policies have been instrumental in the formation of the new aid architecture, gaining momentum by the PRSP model and its ideas of partnership. First, this combination enabled the Bank to bypass its restrictive apolitical mandate and to engage in the political reform of the client's internal affairs. Second, while the PRSP model reinstated the state at the structural level of partnership, the state has become a paramount objective of Bank operations following the rise of good governance. This indicates how developmentality concerns the partnership relation itself but also has wider ramifications for state formation and the conditions under which the Bank, as an external actor, involves itself in processes internal to its client.

## The Bank and State Formation – Challenging the State?

The new aid architecture as set up and articulated by the Bank involves a kind of new thinking around the state, with a transition from less to more state as both active partner in and objective for development. Earlier thinking around the Bank's policy conditionality as a part of the structural adjustment programmes largely bypassed the state as a partner while also making explicit attempts to dismantle state structures. With the PRSP model, the practical formation of partnership and the focus on good governance policies, the Bank has effectively reinstated the state as both means and objective of development. Now the state is back on the agenda of international development discourse, and the provision for it, the new aid architecture, has brought a set of thinking and practices that not only reinstate the state but also instigate various practices whereby the Bank can produce effects generally associated with the state. The materialization of this draws on the Bank's internal bureaucratic culture pertaining to planning and its need for legible units, which, in effect, impinge on the partnership relation and make the Bank, intentionally or not, produce state-like effects and assume a greater role and influence over processes otherwise thought of as beyond the scope of the Bank and indeed as the supreme responsibility of the sovereign, client state. How, then, did the Bank manage to overcome its restrictive apolitical mandate?

## Bypassing the Apolitical Mandate to Engage the State

The PRSP model and its ideas of partnership reinstated the state as an actor at the structural level. The resurgence of the state at the policy level came against the backdrop of a greater and novel focus on aid effectiveness and the belief that aid works best in conducive policy environments (see Burnside and Dollar 1997). This view was propelled by and paved the way for good governance policies, and soon attained authoritative status within the Bank. It stimulated the idea that the Bank would have to engage more closely with its counterparts and also deal with the troublesome concept of politics in order to improve the policy environment. One consequence was that the Bank started to take seriously the problem of rent seeking, which it, even at the presidential level, branded as outright corruption and thus became explicit about its concerns with its counterparts' internal side, including issues of politics and in-house practices. This produced a demand for good governance and the Bank's political and institutional reform packages, justified by the Bank as a matter of increasing aid efficiency and the argument that it would not lend money to countries whose institutional structures, politics or policies were seen as counterproductive to the work of the Bank. However, dealing with mismanaged governance systems and producing conducive policy environments also meant greater involvement in and of the recipient state – and this was made possible by the PRSP model, with its ideas of partnership and the growing focus on good governance issues. Prevented by its apolitical mandate but realizing the importance of taking up political issues among recipients, the Bank put greater emphasis on state formation. Moreover, improving the client's governance system was crucial to the Bank's partnership model: if the Bank was to retreat from direct operational activities and the client to assume greater responsibility for Bank-funded activities, the Bank saw the promotion of good governance issues as a means to ensure effective and conducive partners. Through the partnership model the Bank could now install its good governance policies on the recipient side, all the while asserting that the client was responsible for their implementation, since their inclusion in the PRSP meant, to the Bank, that these policies were to be seen as part of the government's own development strategy.

The historical formation of the Ugandan PEAP demonstrates how the Bank gradually managed to realign the government's strategy with the Bank's PRSP template in order to enable it to attend to governance issues. Through the interface offered by the new partnership arrangement and the instruments integral to the PRSP model, the Bank was able to influence the government to remould its strategy. Most crucial for the governance agenda was Bank pressure to get the government to disentangle security and governance issues, making them separate pillars. Security concerns are still considered to be beyond the scope of the Bank and the wider donor community, and the secrecy surrounding the sector makes the government hesitant to open it to external scrutiny. By disentangling security issues from governance, the Bank was able to take up issues pertaining to the government's internal structures, practices and policies.

The Bank has assumed a greater role for practices internal to the client through the combination of the formation of partnership and the focus on good governance policies. In this respect partnership becomes relevant through the effects it produces, as seen in its practical formation and disjunctures to the formal order. Good governance is germane by intention and the explicit ambition it reveals for the Bank to make itself relevant to client's internal processes. The combination of these has provided synergetic momentum to the Bank's aspirations for good governance, as the formation of partnership and the instruments integral to the PRSP model facilitate processes that make the Bank's policies those of the recipient. In so doing, the policies are framed as owned and produced by the government, thereby making it responsible for the implementation of governance policies while remaining accountable to the Bank for their attainment. This demonstrates – against the Bank's apolitical mandate and the liberal ideas underpinning the new aid architecture – how the Bank becomes involved in its counterpart's internal–political dimension without coming into formal conflict with its own mandate. With the PRSP model, the Bank operates through existing state structures and with the consent of the host government – both factors crucial for mitigating concerns and allegations of external imposition. This is premised on the policies being understood as produced and owned by the client, as demonstrated by their inclusion in the client's national development strategy, or PRSP. It is, however, not only the enactment of certain policies that draws attention to the state and state formation. In the following, we will see how the PRSP model and practices of planning facilitate a particular kind of knowledge, and thereby produce representations and effects associated with the state.

## Planning and Legibility

To escape fetishizing and reifying the state while also opening it to empirical studies, Trouillot (2001, 2003) ascertains that the state has no institutional fixity and that its effects obtain not only in governmental institutions and national sites (cf. Abrams 1988; Krohn-Hansen and Nustad 2005). Thus, in associating the state with practices and effects, he removes the state's empirical boundaries and opens for the possibility that other non-state actors can produce similar effects. Trouillot identifies at least four state effects: an *isolation* effect that produces atomized, individualized subjects to be moulded and modelled for governance; an *identification* effect that realigns the atomized subject along collective lines and categories; a *legibility* effect that draws on concepts to classify and regulate the collectives; and a *spatialization* effect that delimits and decontextualizes the social sphere from external factors that might preclude legibility.

These effects are identified in the five core principles of the PRSP model (Wolfensohn 1999). First, the Bank's insistence that the national development strategy should be country-driven pertains to both the isolation and the spatialization effects. The emphasis on ownership not only produces territorial and juridical boundaries (spatialization) but in doing so also produces atomized aid recipients that become detached from external factors. The PRSP is to be the sovereign product of client government, tailored to the specific circumstances, thus reflecting the liberal individualization of clients. Second, the PRSP is to be result-oriented, with a focus on outcomes. This entails establishing causal relations between input and output to validate development programmes and to get maximum aid effectiveness out of every dollar. This favours a particular form of knowledge and produces a language for governance, similar to the legibility effect as an inherent feature of development planning efforts. Third, the Bank's requirement that the PRSP must be comprehensive parallels Trouillot's identification effect, where atomized subjectivities are realigned along collective lines. In being comprehensive, the PRSP should provide a unison version of the multidimensional nature of poverty at all levels of society and in all sectors,[1] while also being based on the actors representing these – that being the fourth, partnership-oriented principle of PRSP. The fifth principle, as a long-term perspective, does not directly achieve any of Trouillot's state effects, but nevertheless pertains to the internal workings of government and the demand for institutional reforms to enhance good governance, anti-corruption measures and accountability in all forms.

The structural set-up of the PRSP model facilitates the production of state effects. This might, perhaps, not be too surprising, given that including the state as both means and objective of development are among the intentions of the PRSP model and good governance policies. The model is, however, constructed at and by the Bank; and although the PRSP is to be produced and owned by the client government, any effects that government produces in the process of making its national development strategy can thus be seen as instigated and framed by the Bank's PRSP model. This underscores Trouillot's point of departure (2001): that the state has no institutional fixity and that state effects do not necessarily obtain or originate in government sites alone. Hence, to understand the Ugandan state and state formation efforts we cannot disregard external actors like the Bank.

The Bank's production of state-like effects is not only contingent upon its PRSP model as a template for its clients' national development strategies. It also relates to internal practices of social engineering and planning, which depend on the production of representations (Rottenburg 2009) and legible units (Scott 1998). The internal practices of the Bank and the battlefield of knowledge facilitated by its matrix organization reveal how the interface of various networks and their quest for operational influence privilege a particular knowledge. In chapter 4, and as recapitulated above, I demonstrate such knowledge battles with reference to the interface between the Social Development (SD) and PREM networks. The former draws on bottom–up perspectives to poverty reduction and thus, in following the ideas and approaches of the new aid architecture, represents and produces qualitative, complex and contextual knowledge. PREM, with its focus on economic growth, provides a more quantitative knowledge that, in facilitating legible units, is better attuned to operational demands. Whilst the thematic networks produce development knowledge, the regional and operational side is the implementing part and as such controls and distributes finance. Hence, networks' operational influence converts into financial pledges from the regions – and those networks that are more attuned to the regions' operational thinking and demands are more likely to receive funding. This is no secret to the SD group, which, recognizing that social engineering and planning require straight lines and legible units, modifies its stance in order to boost its relevance to the operational side – although it seems to have been only modestly successful.

The production and facilitation of legibility, one of Trouillot's state effects, is thus a feature not only of the PRSP model but also of the Bank's internal practices of planning operational activities. Trouillot's work on legibility draws inspiration from Scott's work (1998) on statecraft and how social engineering and planning are contingent on a particular view. Planning necessitates a view from above that favours straight lines and legibility, enabling planners to 'see' their field in a particular way that validates intervention. Hence, the challenges that the SD unit faced in achieving operational influence can be explained by its inability to serve planners' requirements for reducing the complexity of the field in order to advance simplified knowledge that can fit neatly into standardized, predefined categories. The Bank's internal practices and production of legibility are akin to the processes that characterize the state, thus making the Bank a state-like institution. Through practices of partnership, this state-like institution gradually assumes a larger role towards the state system of its clients.

Practices and discursive knowledge battles within the Bank seem to privilege a particular way of seeing the world, akin to Scott's assumption concerning how a state needs to 'see' for the sake of planning and intervention. According to Scott, the legibility of a society is what provides the capacity for large-scale social engineering. This involves, in effect, a reductionist view of society and the production of representations. In practice, planning – by the Bank or the state – entails the production of utilitarian simplifications that can be acted upon, and is similar in character to maps, in being 'designed to summarize precisely those aspects of a complex world that are of immediate interest to the map-maker and to ignore the rest' (Scott 1998: 87). Practices of planning operational activities within the Bank, then, show Scott's general characteristics of the state's large-scale social engineering.[2] First, the internal practices of the Bank reflect Scott's notion of state simplifications and the administrative ordering of nature and society. Second, they reflect what Scott calls a high-modernist ideology: a strong and self-confident belief in scientific and technical progress. This, I argue, is a general feature of the Bank that is especially conspicuous in its operational thinking, which provides the foundation for the Bank's external representation. Scott's third and fourth elements are more readily identified in the Bank's practical operational work and in its interface with its Ugandan counterpart.

## The Bank – Becoming the State in Uganda?

Scott's third and fourth elements concern an authoritarian state capable of using its coercive power, and a prostrate civil society lacking the capacity to resist the imposed plans (1998: 5). These points are not directly applicable to the Bank–Uganda encounter without some reconceptualization. As Scott himself notes, his elements are characteristics of state interventions but they are not limited to them. Scott's latter two elements point to the conventional patron–client, or principal–agent relation of state theory – the relationship between the state and its citizens. This relationship has its parallel in the Bank–client relationship, so here we may speak of the potential for an authoritarian Bank and a prostrate client government. This is nonetheless to be determined empirically, although we are alerted to this already. For instance, the historical formation of the Ugandan PEAP demonstrates how the Ugandan version of the PRSP gradually came to resemble, and in the end largely replicate, the Bank's PRSP template, even though the first Ugandan PEAP had been produced before the PRSP model came about. This indicates an asymmetric relation between the two as regards developmentality, in which the Bank inscribes its realm onto recipients. As argued above, the pillars of the Bank's PRSP model have the capacity to produce state-like effects in the Trouillotian sense by stipulating how the client state ought to make the PRSP and by framing its content. Although the Ugandan government itself is expected to produce and have ownership of its national development strategy, the formation of it and the effects it might produce draw on the Bank's seminal PRSP template.

The more comprehensive outline (see chapter 5) of the Bank's PRSC mission and the team's encounter with the Ugandan government provides a more minute and detailed outline of the wider PEAP formation and, as such, the relationship between a potentially authoritarian Bank and a prostrate client state. The PRSC mission involves the assessment of old and the formulation of new 'prior actions' – or policy measures that the government needs to undertake before the wider lending arrangements can be concluded – and reveals the complexity of the participation–conditionality nexus, where rhetoric attends to the former and practice to the latter. The overall story of the PRSC mission demonstrates the prevalence of conditionality, although the rhetoric coming with the new aid architecture suggest otherwise. The corollary is that it points to an authoritarian Bank using its coercive power to influence the recipient side, and the greater the dissonance is between the views of these two, the more friction is created and the more imbalanced and asymmetrical this relation becomes. This is true, however, only up to a given point. The fact that the Bank, as well as other bilateral donors, cut their aid to Uganda can be read as indicating the government's reluctance to comply with all the conditions put forward by a seemingly harmonized donor community. Regardless of whether the Bank cut aid due to concerns with a mismanaged public sector reform, which was its formal reasoning, or because of the problems with the political transition, which was the Bank's unofficial version and the bilaterals' explicit reason, the Ugandan government did not comply with the demands. Thus we see that the Bank does not hold total coercive power, nor is the client government fully incapacitated.

There are parallels between the empirical material and Scott's third and fourth elements, but the lack of analogy makes the result not as detrimental and the analysis not as conclusive as Scott's framework does. Here it should be noted that Scott's focus is on how 'well-intended schemes to improve the human condition have gone so tragically awry' (Scott 1998: 4). Scott is not concerned with fiascos, which he finds 'too lighthearted a word for the disasters' (ibid.: 3) from which the four characteristic elements emerge. The present book deals with the new aid architecture in the Bank–Uganda relationship, and although there is a great discrepancy between the formal order and rhetoric on the one side and the informal practices on the other, this is not as severe as 'tragically awry', which was the basis for identifying all four of Scott's elements. There is also a disconnect between Scott's work and mine with regard to the concept of power. Scott is more concerned with the direct and dominant modality of power and not the indirect governance based on seemingly mutual complicity, as captured by the concept of developmentality.

To return to Trouillot's state effects (2003), these are, I argue, observable as part of developmentality and how the Bank engages its Ugandan counterpart with respect to the PRSC mission and its component regarding 'prior actions'. The government's overall development strategy as articulated in the PEAP is, by the Bank, disintegrated into tangible and legible objectives, thus creating the effects of both isolation and legibility. The national strategy is broken down into isolated, atomized sectors and objectives as a means to monitor and control, or govern, their implementation without recourse to the larger context. This governance regime is contingent on and (re)produces a particular language and knowledge in which the complex is abridged into neat, legible units and representations to facilitate classification and regulation. In responding to the PEAP in 2005, the Bank defined eleven prior actions it saw as important for the wider PEAP implementation. The Bank makes its own assessment in comparing the prior actions against actual performance, and as a matter of enhancing legibility and creating concepts to act upon, the prior actions are hierarchically classified in a range from 'off track' to 'completed'. In assessing two prior actions as 'at risk' and another as 'off track', this created categories for action, and framed the Bank–government negotiations. Achieving and implementing the prior actions are important because, as part of the

Bank's internal bureaucracy, the mission team cannot move on in its PRSC project cycle before implementation of these policy measures has been accounted for. It is also necessary to finalize and have the PRSC approved in order to formalize the financial aspects of the lending agreement and to disburse funds. An identification effect is evident in how the PRSC realigns the atomized knowledge emerging from its isolation and legibility effects. Although the government has produced its PEAP, the Bank nevertheless reproduces parts of this in selecting the policies it deems important and relevant for its support. These are then are compiled in the Bank's PRSC approach, without necessarily taking the whole spectrum of PEAP measures into account.

Similar effects can be seen with regard to development partners' harmonization agenda and the Ugandan Joint Assistance Strategy (UJAS). Making the UJAS involved processes whereby donors made a selection from the government's PEAP policies, thus contributing to both atomize and isolate these for the sake governance and to gain oversight, while also disentangling them from their original context (PEAP), before realigning and identifying them as part of something new – UJAS. Moreover, the development partners' UJAS product – that is, the text and document that donors eventually managed to agree upon – is, like the PEAP and PRSC documents, characterized by bullet-point knowledge of the context with an unambiguous description of problems and how to solve them, usually organized in a matrix with clear lines and causality between input and output – all to facilitate a language and knowledge that enable governance, thereby producing the legibility effect.

Trouillot's fourth state effect relates to the production of internal and external boundaries of territories and jurisdiction, which he terms the spatialization effect (2003). Although there is no complete analogy between this effect and my empirical material, there are still some points to be made. The boundaries between what is conventionally thought of as internal or external to the state system are being redrawn. On the one hand this relates to the shared physical presence and involvement of external actors in a foreign state system, operating both at the margins and the centre of the state (cf. Das and Poole 2004). This is prompted by the resurrection of the state as both means and objective for development. (The next section is devoted this point.) On the other hand, the redrawing of borders emerges from other state effects produced by the Bank. As established above, many of the Bank's activities – its internal practices, including planning and the production of legibility, and its interface with clients and the formation of partnership – produce the same effects as those associated with the state. Might we then argue that the Bank *has become* the state? Within the development literature such a perspective is not new – but the premises here are somewhat novel. In its older version, donors were criticized for bypassing the state and setting up their own systems parallel to those of the state, thereby not only duplicating but also undermining the state (Morss 1984; Moss, Pettersson and van de Walle 2006). Come the new aid architecture and the Bank's retreat from operational activities, there is no more duplication of effort or establishment of parallel structures. Instead, the Bank has become part of and involved in the existing structures and practices of its clients. According to the formal order the Bank has retreated from running its own projects to a role primarily as a partner funding the activities of its client states. Project planning and implementation have become the responsibility of the recipient – operating on contracts where the Bank, in outsourcing project management, plays a more remote and self-appointed role as quality assurer, evaluator and funder. The practices of partnership, however, reveal another story, in which the Bank is engaged in an intense, close interface with its counterpart that entails not only indirect governance influencing the state's internal processes, but also the Bank's actual participation in these processes.

New managerial mechanisms emerging from the restructuring of aid relations around new principles of partnership have enabled the Bank to retain control in a more subtle and indirect way, by orchestrating the 'conduct of conduct' and govern from a distance, as captured by the developmentality concept. The conduct of conduct is illustrated by the Bank's ability to frame the conditions for actions. Making the government's use of the PRSP model a condition for partnership signals a transgression of the boundaries between the domestic and the external. There is, however, a more profound transgression pertaining to developmentality: although it is the government that nominally produces the PRSP, its structural set-up and the content permitted are outlined by the Bank's template, which then conveys to the government a particular way of framing and seeing the world. This facilitates the government's production of state effects – but the frames for doing this have come from the Bank.

If we were to follow Trouillot (2003), the above would mean that, through the production of state effects, the Bank in Uganda has become a state-like institution; and, if we return to Abrams (1988), it has become part of the state system. The Bank not only produces state-like effects, it also progressively instigates this productive capacity onto the client state, thus demonstrating Hansen and Stepputat's argument on how 'international aid agencies have emerged as major transmitters of new administrative technologies in the field of development' (Hansen and

Stepputat 2001: 7). Consequently, the Bank becomes state-like as a result of the effect it produces and the processes, knowledge and systems with which it infuses its client state. However, to argue that the Bank *is* or *has become* the state seems a bit tendentious. I would, however, hold that we cannot understand the Ugandan state and its formation without considering the role of the Bank and other donor agencies. The above presentation points to such new forms of state formation processes, the workings of new governance technologies and the productive power of developmentality that, in sum, direct attention to a reconfiguration of the social forces and how these command practice of and in the name of the state. This blurs the distinction between what is considered inside and outside the state, and thus shows how 'the idea of development is tied to that of state sovereignty' (Cowen and Shenton 1996: 8).

The next section deals with the internal–external dimension of sovereignty, which the literature (see Krasner 2004) has seen as the defining character of the state. This defining character is increasingly challenged by developmentality and partnership practices, yet both the Bank and the Ugandan government, as well as their partnership, depend on reproducing the internal–external divide. To the government it is crucial to flag its sovereignty, as the converse would mean acknowledging having fallen prey to the influence of the Bank and other external actors, thus undermining its own mandate and legitimacy. Likewise, the Bank is dependent on portraying the client as sovereign in order to have a legal signatory and an accountable counterpart to its lending agreements. As the partnership arrangements instigated by such lending arrangements actually seem to undermine sovereignty, I claim that we need to bypass conventional and static definitions of sovereignty and instead advance a perspective that focuses on the practical interface between the external and the internal actors: the Bank and its client.

## Partnership: Transgressing the Internal–External Divide of Sovereignty

As outlined in the introduction, conventional ideas of sovereignty relate to an external or an internal dimension (Krasner 1999). The external dimension refers to factors exogenous to the state, like the need for reciprocal recognition as sovereign and the principle of non-intervention allowing the state to exclude external actors from interference in its domestic realm. Being considered sovereign by other states enables the state to join international treaties and international organizations, such as the Bank. The internal dimension concerns the state's institutional form – that is, the relationship between the state and its citizens and the internal organization and practices of the state apparatus. However, these two dimensions should not be seen as distinct. The internal dimension is considered to be under the supreme authority of the state's government, and is protected by the external dimension's principle of non-intervention.

Different aspects of the Bank–Uganda relationship and the Bank's inclination to state formation inform and are informed by issues pertaining to the two dimensions of sovereignty. First – and illustrating the external dimension – Uganda is a member of the World Bank, which is not only seen as reaffirming its sovereignty but also as constitutive for the partnership. Second, there is Uganda's ratification of, inter alia, the Rome (2003) and Paris (2005) declarations on aid harmonization and effectiveness, conventions that not only alter aid practice but also involve a voluntary erosion of the sovereignty principle. Third, although Uganda is not categorized as a 'failed' or 'fragile' state by the donor community, several donors have called it 'weak', and raised concerns over its institutional form in referring to the problems of the political transition, concerns over good governance issues and weak public sector management. Fourth, in raising concerns about Uganda's institutional form and deeming it dysfunctional, donors not only mingle with the internal side and institutional form of their counterpart but indeed – and fifthly – produce the momentum and rationale for transgressing the sovereignty principle of non-intervention. This is further illustrated by and exacerbated by a sixth point: namely the practice and effect of the PRSC mechanism – the budget support modality integrated with the PRSP model, which enables close policy dialogue between the Bank and Ugandan government and allows the Bank to stipulate 'prior actions' on policies and processes usually seen as the government's own realm. This sixth point transgresses the external dimension's principle of non-intervention and the internal dimension concerning the authority and control of own institutional forms. The final point concerns the policy conditions attached to the PRSC mechanism, according to which the Bank's financial assistance – in itself largely the motivation for partnership – will not be disbursed unless the borrower is willing to accept changes to its domestic structures and institutional form. This latter element clearly demonstrates the interrelatedness of the internal and external dimensions of sovereignty.

With the new aid architecture and the formation of partnership, the external principle and internal institutional form of sovereignty should not be seen as distinct. Rather, by focusing on practice and the interface between the Bank and its Ugandan client we are drawn to what constitutes and challenges these internal and external dimensions and how they interrelate.

The formation of the new aid architecture within the Bank and the evolvement of the PRSP model as the main vehicle for partnership involve a more subtle relationship to sovereignty and the borders between what is considered internal and external to the state. With the earlier structural adjustment programmes (SAP), this relationship was less ambiguous. Although highly criticized, SAP involved a straightforward transgression of borders, in being explicit on the external imposition of ready-made policies. With the new aid architecture what we see instead is the co-optation of national policy-making processes by external actors (Whitfield 2005), blurring the borders between inside and outside. In theory, the PRSP model to a greater extent than SAP accommodates the external dimension of sovereignty, in that the Bank rolls back its direct policy imposition and gives priority to national self-determination over how funds lent by the Bank should be spent by the borrowing part. The emphasis on ownership and participation could thus be seen as a means for strengthening the external principles of sovereignty and manifesting the government's authority over its own institutional form.

The Bank's retreat from operational activities to a more remote role as funder of its counterpart's activities represents a fundamental shift with implications for sovereignty. At the formal level, this shift can be seen to revere the principle of non-intervention. There are, however, some issues that reveal an ambiguity to this that blurs the borders between the internal and external. The PRSP model as it evolved as PEAP in Uganda has an external origin, and although it is produced by the government, Bank staff assess whether it fulfils the intended requirements before the PEAP becomes active and qualifies as a national development strategy. While this signifies a transgression, or blurring at best, of the internal–external divide, it is nonetheless interesting to note that all involved parties stress the government's ownership to the PEAP and its status as the government's sovereign product. Government denial of ownership would mean renouncing its sovereignty over processes pertaining to its domestic, institutional form. It is likewise important for the Bank to assert government ownership of and sovereignty over the PEAP, as this enables the Bank to hold government responsible for any mismanagement and deviations, while instilling Bank policies and procedures within the government that enable the Bank, via developmentality, to govern at a distance. Eriksen sums up this basic tension embedded in the new aid architecture:

> According to the principle of 'national self-determination', donors are not supposed to interfere in a state's own priorities. Aid must be based on voluntary agreements between donors and individual states, and activities funded by donors are defined as the state's activities. Donors therefore always emphasize the principle of national ownership, even as their policies undermine it. This has the advantage (for the donors) of enabling them to place the responsibility for failure on governments, rather than taking the blame themselves in the event that aid programmes do not succeed. However, by receiving tied aid, national governments appear both as objects to be shaped by donor policies and as subjects with whom agreements are made. (Eriksen 2010: 43)

This transgression and merger of the internal and external, of national self-determination and donors' demands, bring us to the wider participation–conditionality nexus and developmentality. Developmentality challenges sovereign state boundaries and blurs the inside–outside distinction. Conditionality, also in the indirect form of developmentality, implies that the state is being put under external supervision, and that instead of acting on behalf of and being accountable to its citizens, the state becomes accountable first and foremost to donors (Doornbos 1995; see also Eriksen 2010). There is another dimension to this: that donors themselves legitimize the use of conditionality and the breaches of sovereign borders with reference to these representing the people, claiming that their responsibility is the individual's well-being, and if the state's internal, institutional form cannot guarantee this, then this becomes the responsibility of the donors.[3]

The dismantling of borders also points to a more profound concern pertaining to the crisis of the state (Kapferer and Bertelsen 2009b). As Manger (2011) asserts, the crisis of the state is related to the problem of legitimacy and sovereignty, on the one hand, and the problem of state effectiveness on the other. While the former problem draws attention to the external dimension and the principle of non-intervention, the latter concerns the internal, institutional form and the extent to which the state system is capable of delivering on its promises. From the perspective of the citizenry, these are not necessarily contradictory 'in the sense that people might not question the legitimacy of the state itself but they do react to the inability of the state to run things' (ibid.: 2). From the donor perspective these are interrelated, and donors undermine both dimensions in relating to – or trespassing – them. This dual dilemma has evolved with the new aid architecture and the resurrection of the state as both means and objective for development. Instilling the state with agency and seeing it as an active subject in development cooperation on equal footing with the donor brings tension when the state itself is seen to be in need of being developed and thus becomes the object of development partnership. While the state's sovereignty and position as an autonomous actor with rights and responsibilities is affirmed by the principle of national ownership, its incapacity to fulfil these responsibilities is met by donor calls for state formation and programmes of good governance, capacity building and public sector reforms. Hence, 'in paying lip service to the principle of national ownership, donors, through the use of conditionalities, contribute to undermining the state even as they reassert their commitment to the state idea' (Eriksen 2010: 44). For donors, overcoming the internal–external is thus closely connected to the formation of partnership and practices identified in the participation–conditionality nexus that pertain to the various indirect governance instruments of developmentality.

On the one hand, both sides of the donor–recipient dyad insist on recipient participation and ownership of policy processes and strategies, while on the other hand the donor seeks to instil its policies in the recipient. The new modality of aid and its pivotal claim of government ownership of structures and policies heavily influenced, if not dictated, by outside actors enables the Bank to pursue certain conditionalities and involve itself in processes at the heart of the state's realm – and that has 'transformative impact on the character of post-colonial states and their political domain' (Gould 2005b: 136). Gould goes on to say:

> the rhetoric of 'local ownership' notwithstanding, PRS[P] processes perpetuate and, indeed, deepen the external patronage of state reform. External agencies, above all the BWIs, define and assess the criteria and benchmarks of 'good government' or, to put it another way, the substance and direction of state formation. (ibid.: 141)

The practice of partnership along the participation–conditionality axis thus also involves the practice of negotiating sovereignty and the distinction between its internal and external dimensions. The partnership relation between the Bank and Ugandan authorities cannot be characterized as being one of pure participation or one of sheer conditionality, with rhetoric indicating the former and practice indicating the latter. The new aid architecture and developmentality propel the demotion of borders and alter the ways in which external actors engage with structures and practices internal to the state. Recognizing the lack of clearly delineated borders between the external and internal, we should avoid operating with a static concept of sovereignty and state formation (see Nordstrom 2000; Ong 2006). Instead, we need to see sovereignty as a set of processes and 'as a concept that has been worked and re-worked in different periods, and in which various understandings of what the concept entails have been at base for political conflicts and the definition of the political field itself' (Manger 2011: 2). The following section on fluid borders draws on the debate on sovereignty. However, it also has ramifications for the wider role of the state in donor–recipient relationships and the conditions under which the Bank as an external actor can impose its realm on its recipients. In consequence, the section serves to contextualize the final part, on developmentality and the articulation of the new aid architecture.

## The Threshold of Sovereignty – Frontier or Border?

Development partnerships trigger the consideration of internal–external relations. Where partnerships involve the recipient state – as means or objective, or both – it becomes increasingly relevant to consider partnership together with sovereignty issues. Neither the internal–external dimension of sovereignty nor the formation of partnership between donor and recipient should be understood as clearly demarcated 'either/or' categories, but rather as a political field where different meanings and understandings of sovereignty and partnership are negotiated and framed. The considerations above give rise to 'the important question of whether the notion of sovereignty is suitable to analyse Bank interventions in African states and societies' (Harrison 2004: 24). Harrison argues, as I do above, that the conventional concept of sovereignty is too closely linked to a juridical understanding, and not an empirical one. Referring to Jackson (1990), Harrison holds that states are 'dependent on the international system for their recognition and affirmation; domestic sovereignty may well be a different matter' (Harrison 2004: 24), from which he embarks on a rethinking of sovereignty by asserting that 'one cannot start with a concept of sovereignty and then put it to work on the Bank–state encounter in Africa: it is empirically too provisional and theoretically contested' (ibid.: 24–25). This is in line with my argument above, where I show the lack of resonance between my empirical material and conventional notions of sovereignty (cf. Krasner 1999). On the general level, one consequence has been that sovereignty issues have been disproportionately absent from literature on Africa. This is, however, due in part to the incommensurability of the peculiarities of the post-colonial state (see Hansen and Stepputat 2005) and the literature's bias towards the European experience (Manger 2011). Nevertheless,

> the concept of sovereignty necessarily posits a state of self-containment or inviolateness that exists before intervention which … is not relevant to the Bank's 50 years of lending, technical assistance, policy advice, conditionality and general politicking. Sovereignty readily appears to be en-

> cumbered rather than strengthened by the caveats that have accreted to it. (Harrison 2004: 25)

The dominant role of donors in Africa and their focus on a particular state formation imbued with a European conception of sovereignty do not mean that the concept is irrelevant for understanding African state formation. Not only is the notion of sovereignty crucial to the establishment and formation of development partnership with the Bank, but its apparently constitutive features also underpin the Bank's good governance policy realm. We should not abandon the concept, but rather, I propose, think anew about sovereignty. Sovereignty should not be understood as a dichotomized either/or category – as something a state is or has, or not. Instead we can see it as an anomaly, a phenomenon that does not fit with established categories – here sovereign/non-sovereign – but retains features that can be mutually exclusive or complementary to the categories it falls in-between (see Douglas 1966).[4] We should attend to the ontological notion of sovereignty and escape pre-empirical definitions, instead treating it as constituting a frontier, not a boundary (Harrison 2004: 25). Harrison borrows the frontier–boundary distinction from Palan, who writes that 'geographers distinguish between the concept of boundary and frontier: boundaries are lines, frontiers are zones' (Palan 2000: 1).[5] To make explicit the relevance to my material, this means we should not treat sovereignty as a clearly delineated concept drawing on a state's juridico-constitutional grounds (cf. Agamben 2005) but rather as a field, or zone, of politics and practice where this conceptual delineation is constantly worked and reworked through negotiations and the interface between the Bank and its Ugandan counterpart. Although Harrison is somewhat concerned with the territoriality of sovereignty,[6] his main focus here is on conceptual issues. In his view, sovereignty conceived of as a border clearly demarcating the inside from the outside resonates badly with the post-colonial African context – and with my empirical material. Seeing sovereignty as a zone, or frontier, can enable us to establish and analyse 'a *space* within which different actors can work to define sovereignty in different ways, and it produces a less severe delimitation of one territory from another. In other words, a sovereign frontier is formed by the interaction of forces therein, rather than by the delimitation between one space and another' (Harrison 2004: 25–26). Whereas the notion of border is inner-oriented, the concept of frontier is outer-oriented and points to how different ideational surfaces interact and are defined in their temporal, spatial and social context. This is also akin to, inter alia, Foucault's concept of power as relational (Foucault 1991), the study of interface and knowledge encounters (Long and Long 1992), the study of how ethnic groups are constituted towards others (Barth 1969), as well as the anthropological literature on politics – all of which highlights the relational aspects. In the Introduction to *Beyond the Frontier*, Paul Bohannan (1967) writes:]

> The new frontier is no longer distinguished by space alone. The people on it no longer merely face one another in a struggle for a common culture for their interactions. Rather, the frontier is marked by the cultural selectivity of peoples and interest groups in a world in which variety is rapidly swelling, not ebbing. The frontier is all around us. (Bohannan, quoted in Donnan and Wilson 1999: 19)

The notion of 'frontier' enables us to disengage concepts that otherwise require categorization and distort the analysis. With regard to sovereignty and the Bank–Uganda relation, the idea of a sovereign frontier provides distance to the limiting concerns that often insulate studies of the encounter between African states and external agencies, such as external imposition, national independence and self-determination. Harrison further notes that seeing sovereignty as a frontier means that

> we do not have to 'solve' the apparent contradiction that the Bank both undermines sovereignty (as a boundary) through conditionality and strengthens it through its lending to states. Instead, we can understand the Bank as working within the sovereign frontier to constitute a specific role for governance states as mediators of African societies' interactions with global forces. (Harrison 2004: 26)

It is within this frontier that sovereignty, and thus the partnership relation between internal and external actors, is negotiated, thus shaping developmentality. This enables borrowing states to 'evoke national sovereignty as a discourse to support their actions against the Bank' (ibid.).

There is another important dimension to the frontier approach that is not captured by Harrison. As noted above, the Bank can refer to the client's internal dimension of sovereignty, or institutional form, as a means to enforce policies and alter the aid relation, including its policy content, where the Bank – at least formally – is merely the funder of the government's own strategies and priorities. The Bank makes its client responsible for any deviations from planned practice or objectives by insisting on government sovereignty and ownership of the Bank-funded development strategy, making the government responsible for the whole planning-to-implementation process. Hence, when the Bank affirms the sovereignty of its client, the client also becomes responsible for any actions or policy choices it makes – including failure – regardless of whether the policies and strategies were initially informed, or dictated, by the Bank itself. This expression of developmentality impinges on the formation of partnership, which leans more towards conditionality than participation. In the case of Uganda, the Bank faced increasing concerns with the institutional form of its client government. That meant stricter conditions, or 'prior actions', which eventually led the Bank to undertake a 10 per cent cut in its budget support to the government strategy that it had already pledged to support. This was, however, not a feature of the Bank only, but involved the wider donor community operating under the auspices of the new aid architecture and harmonization. With reference to the internal dimension of sovereignty and the institutional form of the Ugandan state system, development partners violated the external dimension of sovereignty and the principle of non-intervention by involving themselves in the internal affairs of the counterpart, through their many cuts in development assistance. In consequence, this placed great challenges on the Ugandan government's ability to implement its overall development strategy (PEAP) and also undermined the improvement of its own institutional form, as the strategy involved a prominent focus on good governance policies.

The conceptual transition from seeing sovereignty as implying a conceptual border to seeing it as a frontier or zone enables us to 'consider the "content" of sovereignty – its construction, discourse, the interplay between actors – more fully than would be possible of we were merely concerned with the extent to which an imagined boundary has been defended or violated' (Harrison 2004: 26). Whether and how sovereignty evolves as central to the analysis is contextual, just as the articulation of the various actors' interface within the sovereignty frontier, or zone, would be.

## Developmentality and Frontiers

Regardless of the empirical realities of how the concept of sovereignty itself is shaped by and shapes the relationship between the Bank and Uganda, the fact remains that the formal, juridical concept of sovereignty is important as a constitutive premise to the formation of partnership. The discussion above concerns especially the practical encounter between the Bank and the Ugandan authorities after the nominal partnership had been set up. What enables the transgression of the formal border and makes it possible for the Bank and other international development agencies to operate within the sovereign frontier, or zone, is, I argue, what is captured by the idea of developmentality as a derivative of the transmutation involved with the new aid architecture and the formation of partnership. Where such transmutations could otherwise propel forms of resistance against external agencies' challenges to state power, the productive power of developmentality serves to curb such forms of resistance.

Developmentality, as an indirect form of governance operating in the nexus of conditionality and participation, produces and depends on the production of mutual complicity and the assimilation of the recipient's realm to the donor's. This makes it possible to move beyond the border of sovereignty and into its frontier where the Bank, through various bureaucratic practices and mechanisms of control instigated by the PRSP model, is able to influence the conduct of government and to govern at a distance. The new aid architecture, the idea of partnership framed in the conditionality–participation nexus, and developmentality all point to instances bypassing sovereignty as a border and to encounters where sovereignty is negotiated and articulated in the practical encounters of donor and recipient institutions.

In this respect, developmentality parallels Harrison's notion of post-conditionality, which he employs to make sense of the dynamics of external agency involvement in African states, referring to how some states, among them Uganda, 'embody a politic of donor-intervention which cannot adequately be encapsulated by the general notion of conditionality' (Harrison 2001a: 658). Harrison's post-conditionality, as developmentality, is conditioned on the way in which the aid recipients have internalized the donors' way of thinking and the extent to which there is a conducive political environment receptive to donor politics. As noted in the Introduction, developmentality departs from post-conditionality as developmentality also involves the production of such conducive policy environments.

This is relevant to our approach to sovereignty and its internal and external dimension, and the opening of strict conceptual borders to the advance of frontiers, as within 'post-conditionality regimes, it becomes far less insightful to make distinctions between external and internal interest' (Harrison 2001a: 660). The perspectives of developmentality and post-conditionality thus come together in seeing client–donor, internal–external and national–international relations and boundaries as somewhat empirically redundant. With the new aid architecture and the formation of partnership, the boundaries implied by these conceptual pairs have not collapsed but become 'more porous by a historically embedded "mutual assimilation" of donor and state power and ideas' (ibid.: 661), or by the creation of mutual complicity based on the asymmetrical relation between donor and recipient institutions.

With the evolvement of the new aid architecture and the resurrection of the state as development's means for transitive action and an intransitive end of action, ideas of the state, state formation and sovereignty have gained in importance. However, the state finds itself increasingly challenged as a result of how the new aid architecture is manifested and the recasting of aid relations into partnerships that, through their inherently asymmetrical relations, seek to instil the donor's realm into the recipient side.

This may provide a base for challenges to state authority, drawing on at least two prominent and interrelated features that have evolved from the new aid architecture and the construction of partnership. The first concerns the state-like effects produced by development actors external to the state; the second relates to the transgression of the sovereign border separating external actors from the internal and domestic realm of the client state. Not only does the Bank produce effects akin to those normally associated with the state, thereby assuming the role of a state-like institution; it also transmits a particular model onto its counterpart (here, the Uganda government), making the government produce its own state effects under the auspices of this model, and framed by it.

What is additionally transmitted to the government is a specific way of seeing the world, as the Bank's requirements for planning are based on a particular optic and require knowledge that involves the production of representations that fit the imposed model. This gives rise to concerns over sovereignty. The new aid apparatus, and its formation of partnership, enables the Bank to transgress the borders that have otherwise delineated and epitomized the sovereign state. This has opened up a frontier, or zone, breaching the sovereignty principle of non-intervention. However, this breach concerns the internal dimension and how the Bank assesses the Ugandan state's institutional form as measured against the Bank's own standards of good governance. When client's domestic realm is assessed to be in conflict with the Bank's policies and benchmarks, this, to the Bank, warrants a stronger push for conditionalities, or 'prior actions'.

True, the formal order of development designates the policy-making role to the recipient. However, the formation and actual practices of partnership evident in the interface between the Bank and Uganda demonstrate disjuncture to this order, with the Bank exercising influence through mechanisms that make possible indirect governance – or 'developmentality'.

## Notes

1. The levels of society include grassroots, private sector, civil society and government institutions. The sectors include structural, economic, social and human aspects of development.

2. These four elements comprise an administrative ordering of society based on legible units and standardized units in order to gain overview, a high-modernist ideology revealing strong self-confidence and belief in managerialism and technocracy, an authoritarian state able and willing to use its coercive power, and finally an impotent civil society unable or unwilling to defy these plans.
3. In 1999 the Bank president stated: 'My colleagues and I decided that in order to map our own course for the future, we needed to know about *our clients as individuals*' (Narayan 2000; emphasis added).
4. Douglas refers to Sartre's analysis in *Being and Nothingness* to the experience of viscosity, an intermediate state between liquid and solid, as an example of anomaly. For purposes of categorization, Douglas denotes such anomalies as dirt, being 'matter out of place' and thus impossible to categorize, somewhat akin to Turner's concept of liminality (1967) – i.e. betwixt and between, or the transitional state between two phases.
5. It should be noted that Palan writes about disciplinary boundaries in the study of global political economy, and not about sovereignty as such.
6. Harrison challenges the conventional wisdom that modern sovereign states are intrinsically territorial and cartographically defined prior to gaining their social and political content with the idea of African borders, which result from the Treaty of Berlin (1884/85) – as 'handshake over new African boundaries at European conference tables' (Harrison 2004: 25). Nevertheless, 'many African societies related to these delimitations far more effectively than Western academe, crossing them, using them to their advantage, and respecting them provisionally when the state succeeds in compelling them to' (Harrison 2004: 25). Although African borders might be porous – only 25 per cent of Africa's borders are physically delineated (Okumu 2010) – and allow for uncontrolled transnational movement of humans and materials, they are nevertheless respected by international actors in bilateral agreements with the state and usually by the states themselves, even in times of conflict – as illustrated, for example, by cross-border refugee flows and the establishment of camps in the border area (see Borchgrevink and Lie 2009).

# Conclusion

## Revisiting Developmentality

Institutional, international development assistance has passed through various discursive phases ever since its establishment in the aftermath of the Second World War. This book has focused on the most recent and profound shift, as represented by the new aid architecture, which – at least nominally – has involved a fundamental revamping of the structures and policies of institutional development. In general terms, this has meant the intentional and donor-driven transition from a paternalistic top–down approach to a more inclusive and comprehensive bottom–up approach, pivoting around ideas of partnership and recipient participation. While previously it was clear who called the shots, as donors were explicit in what they wanted to achieve and how, responsibility for the overall policy-making and implementation process has now been consigned to the recipient who, from being passive, is now vested with an active role and agency by being included at the structural and policy levels of development.

This revamping of aid relations has not only had transformative effects for the practitioners' engagement in the development sector, it has also reconfigured the modality of power inherent in aid relations. Rather than being coercive and restraining, this new modality of power is productive in working through, not over, the presumably subaltern recipients. This enables the donor institution to retain control and influence over the formulation and implementation of the policies it finances. That in turn is premised on the liberal character of the new aid architecture and how freedom becomes a mechanism and formula for rules that conceal the asymmetrical power relations between donor and recipient institutions.

I call this form of power 'developmentality', which we have here observed and analysed in the interface between the World Bank and Uganda (Lie 2015). Developmentality is an indirect modality of power emerging from the nexus of new practices, ideas and structures pertaining to the new aid architecture and its formation of partnership. Hence, developmentality pertains not only to the Bank's formal order and policy objectives but also to processes and practices instigated by this order and articulated in the partnership arrangement and interface between the Bank and its counterpart – here, the Ugandan government.

## Interfacing Discourse and Agency, Order and Practice

In order to reveal and analyse developmentality it is necessary to move away from development actors' self-representation, and their renderings of the formal order of development, to an approach that takes account of the interface between agency and this formal order, so as to grasp practices and the spatial and temporal contextualization of this order. The empiricism above shows that we should not accept the formal order prima facia as the only and authoritative version of what is going on. This does not mean that the formal order is irrelevant to the formation of developmentality – as I argue, the first point of identifying developmentality is within the formal order itself – the Bank's structural set-up of the PRSP model and the seeming paradox of the participation–conditionality nexus. No, what we must do is to combine various approaches to different levels of development.

We need perspectives that open towards interface and agency, enabling us to see more clearly how the actions of real people, and what goes on in actual situations, are important starting points for understanding how the structural frameworks actually 'work'. To do so, I argue for combining an actor-oriented approach with a discursive approach to different levels of development and, through the concept of interface, seeing how these levels interrelate and impinge on each other, both empirically and analytically.

A focus on *agency* allows us to get past seeing structures and official discourses as static, formative entities. It facilitates a more open-ended approach that takes account of the dynamicity and change of social relations and transformation, without instilling development discourses with pre-empirical formative power. Such an agency focus addresses how actors through their practices not only enact but also challenge aspects pertaining to the discursive realm, showing that the outcomes of such interfaces need to be decided upon empirically. A focus on agency combined with discourse allows us to deal with the social dimension of development and how different levels affect each other through the study of interfaces between otherwise dichotomized realms like structure/actor, donor/recipient and order/practice.

Such dichotomies – largely innate to the development sector and conventional analysis of it – give rise to opposition and distort the analysis (see Kapferer 2004a). The concept of interface enables us to escape such dichotomization and look into their social dimension – that is, how they interrelate and impinge on each other. Interface and the focus on agency can help us to avoid not only compartmentalizing different realms and lifeworlds but also, by facilitating an ethnography of development and aid partnerships, subsuming to a pre-empirical notion of donor power and discursive formation that override agency and practice. The focus on agency and interface allows us to grasp how structures work and are reworked by actors' practices, as well enabling us to examine how such practices might contest or reproduce the formal structural order.

In this book I have employed perspectives informed by post-development for understanding the discursive formation of the formal order of development, and combined this with an actor-orientation that takes account of agency and how various discourses and the formal order are enacted and contested in practice. The formal order not only aims to guide the practices of development actors but also represents the 'ideal world' that aid practitioners seek to realize through their policy making and project design (Lewis and Mosse 2006a). Bringing about this ideal world is, however, not simply a matter of mechanically implementing predefined programmes. It involves ongoing and permanent processes of translation and negotiation by and between actors spanning the donor–recipient divide who often represent very different interests, strategies, discourses and lifeworlds. These processes, which reveal deviations from the formal order, represent disjunctures emerging from 'the gap between the ideal worlds and the social reality they have to relate to' (ibid.: 2). While aid practitioners see disjunctures as a gap between intention and outcome, to be mitigated through better policies and implementation, to the researcher disjunctures represent prototypes of social and cultural interface and therefore indicate privileged places for anthropological observation and analysis (see Bierschenk and Le Meur 1996). Disjunctures reveal friction with the formal order: thus they have generative analytical consequences in telling us something about the interface of official development discourse and practices pertaining to and evolving from it, as well as how these two levels, or arenas of development, interrelate.

To identify and make sense of disjunctures, I have combined a post-development discursive approach to the formal order with an actor-oriented approach that attends to the individual and collective agency and how this relates to and enacts discourses of development. This enables us to make use of post-development without adhering to its rigid notion of discursive power and how this approach envisions the recipient side of partnership, the subaltern and indigenous social movements, as blindfolded vehicles for benefactors' politics and development order (Watts 2003). On the other side, it provides an empirically grounded approach not only to local contestation but also to how the formal order might influence practices, the formation of partnership and the overall implementation of the new aid architecture. Hence, combining two approaches allows us to see the interface between the levels of discourse and agency, and the way they affect each other (Lie 2008a) – which is important for grasping the formation of developmentality.

The interface between discourse and agency, or order and practice, is akin to the relationship between formal and informal. As Scott notes with reference to planned, social engineering, the '[f]ormal order … is always and to some considerable degree parasitic on informal processes, which the formal scheme does not recognize, without which it could not exist, and which it alone cannot create or maintain' (Scott 1998: 310). This has its parallel to the Bank's imposition of its PRSP model – itself drawing attention to the relationship between policy and practice, which, in the present work, are better characterized in terms of disjuncture than blueprint. Hence, disjuncture represents a kind of informality, as practices that emerge against the intentions of the formal order. These are also conducive for upholding and disseminating the formal order. The informal practices identified in the encounter between Bank staff and government representatives not only show the need for an actor-oriented approach to the formal order, but also demonstrate their importance in upholding the formal order and representation of the PRSP model. Interestingly – and underscoring Scott's point – these informal practices have been instigated by the formal order.

In the introduction I made a note to Mosse (2005b) regarding his inversion of the relationship between policy and practice. Nominally and as the raison d'être of policy makers' policy making, policy is supposed to direct practice, which is also one reason why aid practitioners put so much effort into this social drill. Mosse holds that such processes are the product of practitioners' social relations; therefore, in inverting the relationship between policy and practice, he asks whether policies and the making of formal order serve to conceal and legitimize existing practices instead of altering them. This provides an interesting approach to the PRSP model and the lack of analogy between its formal order and what actually goes on in the interface between the Bank and Uganda: the practices and mechanisms that the PRSP model instigates seem more to reproduce than dismantle the lopsided donor–recipient relationship that the model it aimed to dethrone, with its girding ideas of partnership, participation and ownership. That is not to say that the

PRSP model and formal order are irrelevant – they have a role in anchoring practises pertaining to the structures and content of development partnerships. The PRSP model is important, because its liberal rhetoric and promises of freedom enable the instigation and concealment of the indirect governance mechanisms – *developmentality.*

## Developmentality

The notion of developmentality draws on an apparent paradox in development aid: the contradiction between conditionality and participatory approaches. This contradiction becomes evident when we compare the formal order of development with practice. Disjuncture with the formal order reveals an intention on the part of the donor to make indirect use of force as a means of retaining its control of and governance over the content and practices of development. Through the formation of partnership, donors attempt to install their own concepts, practices and policies in recipients so that 'the people' can take control of and become responsible for their own development. This entails a process aimed at making the donor's conditionalities those of the recipient, to facilitate self-governance. Altering the personal and collective mentalities of aid practitioners is thus integral to institutional development. This evokes power/knowledge formations as a means for indirect governance, as illuminated by Foucault in his concept of governmentality as the 'conduct of conduct' (Foucault 1991).

My developmentality concept builds on Foucault's work but also denotes the particularities of governmentality within the development sector. Foucault saw governmentality as a new type of power technology emerging as an effect of modern, European state formation and in response to the challenges arising with the establishment of a civil society (Neumann and Sending 2010). Developmentality draws not only on the effects emerging with the new aid architecture and the formation of partnership, but also on explicit intentions by the donor community seeking to change client states in terms of a particular standard. This standard relates to the policy objective of good governance and other forms of intended state formation activities pursued by donors that aim to produce recipients able to develop and govern themselves. The notion and promise of self-governance are liberal in character, yet it is limited as the execution of freedom is framed by donors' objectives and standards. Although developmentality emerged as an effect of the new aid architecture, it should be noted that donors' interpretations and appropriations of its girding ideas have been highly intentional, drawing momentum from the need for greater aid effectiveness and the legitimacy of external ideas to internal processes. This has a particular bearing within the Bank, with the PRSP model and its implication for the formation of aid structures and polices, which allowed developmentality to emerge as a combination of the interface between emerging effects and explicit intent.

This book has involved an investigation of developmentality as an indirect modality of power emerging from new practices, ideas and structures instigated by the new aid architecture and as interpreted by the Bank in its PRSP model. Developmentality has permeated the development sector and the relationship between the Bank and its Ugandan counterpart. We have traced developmentality in various contexts and at different levels of institutional development as articulated in this partnership. All the book's chapters have looked into the construction and working of the donor–recipient relationship, arguing for developmentality as a phenomenon emerging with the new aid architecture and epitomized in the practices of partnership implied by this new order. Developmentality evolved from the new aid architecture's underpinning ideas of partnership, participation and ownership (chapters 1 and 2). It has been identified as part of the Bank's structure, official discourse and model for partnership (PRSP) (chapter 3), with implications for and gaining momentum from the Bank's internal organization and practices that facilitate the encounter of various internal knowledge regimes forming its external representation around legible knowledge (chapter 4); it has a predominant role in ordering Bank–Uganda relations under the auspices of partnership (chapter 5); it contributes not only to orchestrate – or harmonize – the relation between the Bank and other development partners but also to inscribe them into the Bank's realm (chapter 6). Finally, we have seen that developmentality has implications for state formation and how the Bank increasingly assumes a state-like role that enables it to transmit its realm to its client and thereby transgress what are otherwise seen as the sovereign borders of the state (chapter 7).

Thus, we have seen how developmentality has contributed to reproducing the lopsided relationship between the Bank and Uganda – even though the grand ambitions of the new aid architecture, which itself provides the conditions for indirect governance, were to emancipate and empower the receiving end, to engender ownership and greater commitment so as to increase aid efficiency, and to thereby counter allegations of donor-paternalism. Instead, Uganda has become accountable to the Bank for implementing its 'own' strategy and policies, which are in fact framed by the Bank.

The concept of developmentality, I argue, enables us to make sense of how the Bank manages to retain control over how the loans and credits it disburses are used, although overall responsibility for policy making and implementation are now – as a result of the Bank's interpretation of the new aid architecture as converted into its PRSP model – tasks designated to the client (Lie 2010). Contrary to its promises of freedom, the way the PRSP model is enacted and its ramifications for client participation represent the instantiation of mechanisms that enable the Bank to frame the conditions under which the client can exercise freedom – akin to Foucault's view of governmentality as the 'conduct of conduct' (Foucault 1991). The formation of partnership and its liberal rhetoric translate into a formula for rule (Abrahamsen 2004a), as the curtailed freedom granted to the Ugandan counterpart not only frames the government's room for manoeuvre and self-governance but also involves other governance mechanisms that enable the Bank to govern at a distance (Rose and Miller 1992).

The Bank's PRSP model is based on a liberal rhetoric of empowerment and emancipation to promote self-governance, but the practices and mechanisms it instigates as part of the partnership formation reveal the desire to retain control – but in a more subtle and indirect manner. While the PRSP model gives rise to certain structures and practices, the prominence of the good governance realm shows how the Bank, at the policy level, seeks to make its clients internalize a particular governance discourse. Developmentality points to governance mechanisms that seek to get the client to conform to the donor's good governance agenda. It illustrates how the Bank moulds recipients around a particular standard, which, if achieved, would not only provide a more conducive policy environment for the Bank but also facilitate client self-governance and a frictionless partnership.

Moreover, with the move from *ex ante* to *ex post* conditionality based on client performance, the Bank 'awards grants to countries on the basis of their demonstrated quality of governance' (Booth 2011: 16), thus introducing a form of 'governance conditionality' (ibid.: 17). The policy realm of good governance directs attention to developmentality in expressing the intention to instil clients with a particular policy realm that pertains to its internal practices and governance system. The pursuit of good governance is thus linked to technologies of power and bureaucratic practices that aim to legitimize the enforcement of the PRSP model's structures and practices (see Anders 2005).

Developmentality enables the Bank to get its clients to acquire the capacities and attributes of responsibility and freedom through calculated practices to implement and enforce techniques of (self-)discipline, (self-)management, and (self-)governance (Ilcan and Phillips 2010). Developmentality recasts governance and the relationship between ruler and governed, or donor and recipient. As an indirect technology of power, developmentality can be just as compelling as the direct rule of policy imposition and enforcement associated with the structural adjustment era that preceded the PRSP model. Indeed, developmentality is not merely compelling but can be more intrusive and profound, in operating not over the governed but through them. Such a productive power makes possible ways to influence the actions of others who are made responsible for governing and developing themselves, while remaining accountable to the Bank for their self-governance and the implementation of their own development strategy. Although responsibilized, the Bank's clients are not free to make whatever choices they themselves deem relevant or preferable. Their choices are tied to the assumption that the Bank's structures, practices and policy preferences are the most appropriate; hence developmentality also relates to the Bank's internal processes of defining the objects and objectives of development, and how to attain them.

Developmentality concerns both the production and dissemination of development discourse as a particular system of knowledge. Just as Foucault's 'governmentality' term, a merger of government and mentality, signifies that subjects' self-governance is contingent on their internalization of the particular mentality of the governor, so 'developmentality' denotes how aid recipients' self-governance and self-development are premised on their accepting the mentality of the donor. Hence, developmentality privileges a particular conception of knowledge and expertise as forces for social transformation. Developmentality carries with it a particular discourse which, in contrast to the new aid architecture's notions of bottom–up approaches and participation, is produced by the donor and disseminated through technologies of rule. The policy realm of good governance represents one such discourse that is produced on the donor side of the aid chain, and, embedded in the donors' development programmes, is transmitted to the receiving end, with the aim of altering governance structures and directing social transformation.

Developmentality relates to the structures, practices and policies of the new aid architecture, and is evident in the interface between the Bank and its Ugandan counterpart as disjuctures with the formal order and the grand ambitions of revamping aid relations. At the structural level, the configuration of the PRSP model indicates how the Bank has altered the way it engages its clients. There has been a shift towards greater recipient participation and involvement in processes previously confined to the Bank, but the client's participation is still framed by and must be on terms with the Bank. In the alteration of aid relations, the PRSP model has also given rise to various practices and policies that together undermine the seminal idea of the new aid architecture and, consequently, facilitate developmentality. At the level of practice, the formation of partnership now involves close policy dialogue between the Bank and its client, which enables the Bank to install its policies within the government while the government becomes accountable to the Bank for their implementation. At the policy level, the Bank's good governance agenda – transmitted through the arrangement of partnership – reveals the explicit intention to alter its client's internal structures and practices.

In sum, then, incongruence and challenges to a verbatim implementation of the new aid architecture at the levels of structure (PRSP), practice (partnership) and policy (good governance) reveal the disjuncture with the formal order. Their interrelatedness provides greater momentum to developmentality and synergetic effects for how the Bank manages to retain control over its lending arrangements, even though its official discourse and representation of partnership proclaim the opposite.

Developmentality has intrusive effects on the formal order of development. However, while arguing for the coercive and compelling effects developmentality has in ordering the structural and policy dimension of donor–recipient relationship, I hold that should not construct developmentality as a hegemonic power in order to avoid committing the same fallacy as post-development did when constructing a totalizing development discourse that lost sight of agency, practice and the possibility for contestation. Friction in the Bank–Uganda relationship – as illustrated, inter alia, by the disagreement over 'prior actions' and the budget cuts decided by the Bank and other donors – indicates contestation and the failure of the Bank to thoroughly install its policies among its counterpart, which would be the implication of a frictionless partnership.

Had I proposed a static notion of an authoritarian developmentality regime, such contestation would have falsified the concept. Rather, I see developmentality as an indirect governance technology specific to the development sector and emerging from the relational interface and the analysis of the contextual practices pertaining to donor–recipient relationships. Hence, developmentality is different from a rigid notion of governmentality, which in being 'chided for its panoptical sense of closure and overwhelming aura of domination [is conceived of as a] well-oiled machine of disciplinary and biopower' (Watts 2003: 26). Such a view 'hardly admits disjuncture' (Lewis and Mosse 2006a: 3). Developmentality, I hold, not only opens for but also involves disjuncture, since it is not a pre-empirical concept but is grounded in an empirical approach to development and aid partnerships.

Frictions in the partnership relation between the Bank and Uganda indicate disjuncture and that developmentality is not a totalizing power. However, friction does not only indicate contestation. It also reveals the presence of other modalities of power employed by the Bank in its attempts to enforce policies. Foucault (1991) conceived of power as having three different modalities: dominance, discipline and governmentality. 'What was key for Foucault was not the displacement of one form of power by another, nor the historical substitution of feudal by modern governmentality, but the complex triangulation involved in sustaining many forms of power put to the purpose of security and regulation' (Watts 2003: 14).

The frictions in the Bank–Uganda partnership show how the Bank employs other modalities of power to enforce its policies. In the conflict over prior actions, the Bank employed sanctions and threats to withhold aid as direct, coercive means of imposing its policies. Although the power modality was direct, the effect proved conducive to the indirectness of developmentality, as the arm-twisting involved forced the government to adopt the prior actions as its own policies while remaining accountable to the Bank for their implementation. In this instance, the Ugandan government was 'forced to freedom' by being compelled to assume ownership and thus responsibility over the Bank's policies. In this we can see how various power modalities interrelate, and that direct coercion can be used as a means to enforce and pave the way for developmentality by forcing ownership and participation upon the recipient institution.

Disjuncture with the formal order and friction in the partnership represent privileged analytical points that are generative to developmentality and the general approach to practices and effects of institutional development. Identifying friction and disjuncture is contingent on combining the approaches of discourse and agency, which makes it possible to address the interface of otherwise separate analytical and empirical realms. The idea of interface enables us to connect and make sense of the relationship between, inter alia, discourse and agency, order and practice, the formal and informal, donor and recipient in general and the Bank and Uganda in particular. The attention to interface reminds us not to assume analogy or causality between these conceptual pairs. Nor should we take the official representation as the only authoritative rendering. Rather, we should examine, through the study of interface, how these dichotomies affect each other and become transformed in practice, as articulated by actors in their contextual setting.

This analysis of the new aid architecture and the partnership relation of the Bank and Uganda has been informed by and informed the concept of developmentality. The concept itself, I argue, is not contingent on this relationship alone.[1] Developmentality is a feature of the way in which international development discourse has intentionally been altered by donor institutions, evolving as an effect of the emergence of the new aid architecture and its girding ideas of partnership, ownership and participation – all of which are ideas embraced by the donor community in general. Since the concept draws on ideas widely shared by the international development community, developmentality is relevant for and provides a framework for analysing aid relations that draws on these ideas and how they might make possible new mechanisms of governance, in the face of their seemingly liberal appearance.

The relevance of developmentality to other development partnerships remains an empirical question to be further explored. The concept should not, however, be disregarded in studies involving the Bank, since its partnership model revolves around the PRSP which, in its formal order, implies developmentality. How and whether developmentality is enacted and affects the Bank's relationships with other PRSP-producing clients involves questions that must be determined through empirical study. Such analysis will necessitate a two-pronged approach that can account for the levels of structure and practice, as well as how they interface, in order for us to identify and understand the workings and effects of developmentality.

## Note

1. Recall that my first encounter and use of developmentality drew on the study of partnership between a Norwegian NGO and Ethiopian institutions, where I was drawn towards the Bank's PRSP model to understand the relevance of the Ethiopian government's development strategy for the small, remote project I was studying (Lie 2004).

# Bibliography


Abrahamsen, Rita. 2004a. 'The Power of Partnerships in Global Governance', *Third World Quarterly* 25(8): 1453–67.

———. 2004b. 'The World Bank's Good Governance Agenda: Narratives of Democracy and Power'. Occasional paper no. 24, in J. Gould and H.S. Marcussen, *Ethnographies of Aid: Exploring Development Texts and Encounters*. Roskilde: Roskilde University.

Abrams, Philip. 1988. 'Notes on the Difficulty of Studying the State (1977)', *Journal of Historical Sociology* 1(1): 58–89.

Agamben, Giorgio. 2005. *State of Exception*. Chicago, IL: University of Chicago Press.

Alonso, Ana M. 2005. 'Sovereignty, the Spatial Politics of Security, and Gender: Looking North and South from the US–Mexico Border', in Christian Krohn-Hansen and Knut G. Nustad (eds), *State Formation: Anthropological Perspectives*. London: Pluto Press, pp. 27–52.

Anders, Gerhard. 2005. 'Good Governance as Technology: Towards an Ethnography of the Bretton Woods Institutions', in David Mosse and David Lewis (eds), *The Aid Effect: Giving and Governing in International Development*. London: Pluto Press, pp. 37–60.

Andrews, David M. (ed.). 2008. *Orderly Change: International Monetary Relations since Bretton Woods*. Ithaca, NY: Cornell University Press.

Arce, Alberto, and Norman Long. 1992. 'The Dynamics of Knowledge: Interfaces between Bureaucrats and Peasants', in Norman Long and Ann Long (eds), *Battlefields of Knowledge: The Interlocking of Theory and Practice in Social Research and Development*. London: Routledge, pp. 211–46.

———. 1993. 'Bridging Two Worlds: An Ethnography of Bureaucrat–Peasant Relations in Western Mexico', in Mark Hobart (ed.), *An Anthropological Critique of Development*. London: Rountledge, pp. 179–208.

———. 2000a. 'Reconfiguring Modernity and Development from an Anthropological Perspective', in Alberto Arce and Norman Long (eds), *Anthropology, Development and the Post-modern Challenge*. London: Routledge, pp. 1–31.

——— (eds). 2000b. *Anthropology, Development and Modernities: Exploring Discourses, Counter-tendencies and Violence*. London: Routledge.

Atingi-Ego, Michael. 2005. 'Budget Support, Aid Dependency, and Dutch Disease: The Case of Uganda'. Paper presented at the Practitioners' Forum on Budget Support, 5–6 May, Cape Town, South Africa. Available at http://siteresources.worldbank.org/PROJECTS/Resources/40940-1114615847489/AidBudgetSupportandDutchDiseaserevised.pdf.

Baaz, Maria Eriksson. 2005. *The Paternalism of Partnership: A Postcolonial Reading of Identity in Development Aid.* New York: Zed Books.

Barkan, Joel, Saillie Simba Kayunga, Njunga Ng'ethe and Jack Titsworth. 2004. 'The Political Economy of Uganda: The Art of Managing a Donor-Financed Neo-patrimonial State'. Background paper commissioned by the World Bank in fulfilment of purchase order 7614472.

Bartelson, Jens. 1995. *A Genealogy of Sovereignty.* Cambridge: Cambridge University Press.

Barth, Fredrik (ed.). 1969. *Ethnic Groups and Boundaries: The Social Organization of Cultural Difference.* Oslo: Universitetsforlaget.

———. 1993. 'A General Framework for Analyzing the Meaning of Acts', in F. Barth, *Balinese Worlds.* Chicago, IL: University of Chicago Press.

Bayart, Jean-Francois. 1993. *The State in Africa: The Politics of the Belly.* London: Longman.

Bebbington, Anthony J., Scott Guggenheim and Michael Woolcock. 2006. 'The Ideas–Practice Nexus in International Development Organizations: Social Capital at the World Bank', in A. Bebbington, S. Guggenheim and M. Woolcock (eds), *The Search for Empowerment: Social Capital as Idea and Practice at the World Bank.* Bloomfield, CT: Kumarian Press, pp. 1–30.

Berg, Rob van den, and Philip Quarles van Ufford. 2005. 'Disjuncture and Marginality: Towards a New Approach to Develoment Practice', in David Mosse and David Lewis (eds), *The Aid Effect: Giving and Governing in International Development.* London: Pluto Press, pp. 196–212.

Bierschenk, Thomas, Jean-Pierre Chauveau and Jean-Pierre Olivier de Sardan. 2002. 'Local Development Brokers in Africa: The Rise of a New Social Category'. Working Paper No. 13. Mainz, Germany: Johannes Gutenberg University, Department of Anthropology and African Studies.

Bierschenk, Thomas, and Pierre-Yves Le Meur (eds). 1996. 'Negotiated Development: Brokers, Knowledge, Technologies'. Niamey, Niger: Euro-African Association for the Anthropology of Social Change and Development (APAD). APAD Bulletin No. 12. Also available from LIT Verlag (1999).

Bøås, Morten, and Jonas Vevatne. 2004. 'Sustainable development and the World Trade Organization', in Morten Bøås and Desmond McNeill (eds), *Multilateral Institutions and Development: Framing the World?* London: Routledge, pp. 95–107.

Bohannan, Paul. 1967. 'Introduction', in Paul Bohannan and Fred Plog (eds), *Beyond the Frontier: Social Process and Cultural Change.* New York: Natural History Press, pp. xi–xviii.

Booth, David. 2011. 'Aid, Institutions and Governance: What Have We Learned?', *Development Policy Review* 29(S1): 5–26.

Borchgrevink, Axel. 2008. 'Limits to Donor Influence: Ethiopia, Aid and Conditionality', *Forum for Development Studies* 35(2): 195–220.

Borchgrevink, Axel, and Jon Harald Sande Lie. 2009. 'Regional Conflicts and International Engagement on the Horn of Africa'. NUPI Report. Oslo: NUPI.

Brauer, Dieter. 2000. 'The Paternalistic Attitude of the North Must Change: Why Joseph Stiglitz Retired from the World Bank. Interview with Joseph Stiglitz', *Development and Cooperation* 2: 26–27.

Brigg, Morgan. 2002. 'Post-development, Foucault and the Colonialisation Metaphor', *Third World Quarterly* 23(3): 421–36.

Bull, Benedicte, Alf Morten Jerve and Erlend Sigvaldsen. 2006. 'The World Bank's and the IMF's Use of Conditionality to Encourage Privatization and Liberalization: Current Issues and Practices'. Report prepared for the Norwegian Ministry of Foreign Affairs as background for the Oslo Conditionality Conference, November 2006.

Bull, Benedicte, and Desmond McNeill. 2007. *Development Issues in Global Governance: Public–Private Partnerships and Market Multilateralism.* New York: Routledge.

Burchell, Graham, Colin Gordon and Peter Miller (eds). 1991. *The Foucault Effect: Studies in Governmentality. With two lectures by and an interview with Michel Foucault.* Chicago: University of Chicago Press.

Burnside, Craig, and David Dollar. 1997. 'Aid, Policies and Growth', *Working Paper 1777.* Washington, DC: World Bank.

———. 2000. 'Aid, Policies and Growth', *American Economic Review* 90(4): 847–68.

———. 2004. 'Aid, Policies and Growth: Revisiting the Evidence', *Working Paper 3251.* Washington, DC: World Bank.

Calderisi, Robert. 2006. *The Trouble with Africa: Why Foreign Aid isn't Working.* New York: Palgrave Macmillan.

Calhoun, Craig. 1995. *Critical Social Theory. Culture, History, and the Challenge of Difference.* Oxford: Blackwell.

Cargill, Tom. 2004. 'Uganda: Still the Donors' Darling', *The World Today* 60(2): 26–27.

Chambers, Robert. 1983. *Rural Development: Putting the Last First.* London: Longman.

———. 1995. 'Paradigm shifts and the practice of participatory research and development', in Nici Nelson and Susan Wright (eds), *Power and Participatory Development.* London: Intermediate Technology Publications, pp. 30–42.

Chapman, Jennifer, and Senorina Wendoh. 2007. 'Review of Norwegian CSO Partnerships with Organisations in Tanzania'. Oslo: Norwegian Development Network.

Chwieroth, J.M. 2008. 'Organizational Change "From Within": Exploring the World Bank's Early Lending Practices', *Review of International Political Economy* 15(4): 481–505.

Cleaver, Frances. 2001. 'Institutions, Agency and the Limitations of Participatory Approaches to Development', in Bill Cooke and Uma Kothari (eds), *Participation: The New Tyranny?* London: Zed Books, pp. 36–55.

Collier, Paul. 1997. 'The Failure of Conditionality', in Catherine Gwin and Joan M. Nelson (eds), *Perspectives on Aid and Development.* Washington, DC: Overseas Development Council, pp. 51–78.

Cooke, Bill, and Uma Kothari. 2001. 'The Case for Participation as Tyranny', in Bill Cooke and Uma Kothari (eds), *Participation: The new tyranny?* London: Zed Books, pp. 1–15.

Cornwall, Andrea, and Ian Scoones (eds.). 2011. *Putting the Last First: Reflections on the Work of Robert Chambers.* London: Earthscan.

Cowen, Michael P., and Robert W. Shenton. 1996. *Doctrines of Development.* London: Routledge.

Crewe, Emma, and Elizabeth Harrison. 1998). *Whose Development? An Ethnography of Aid.* London: Zed Books.

Cruikshank, Barbara. 1999. *The Will to Empower: Democratic Citizens and Other Subjects.* Ithaca, NY: Cornell University Press.

Crush, Jonathan (ed.). 1995. *Power of Development.* London: Routledge.

Da Costa, Dia. 2010. 'Introduction: Relocating Culture in Develompent and Development in Culture', *Third World Quarterly* 31(4): 501–22.

Das, Veena, and Deborah Poole (eds). 2004. *Anthropology in the Margins of the State.* Santa Fe, NM: School of American Research Press.

DDGG. 2002. 'Memorandum of Understanding. Donor Democracy and Governance Group'. Kampala. (Available at www.u4.no/document/showdoc .cfm?id=52).

Dean, Mitchell. 1999. *Governmentality: Power and Rule in Modern Society.* London: SAGE.

———. 2007. *Governing Societies: Political Perspectives on Domestic and International Rule.* Berkshire: Open University Press.

Dijkstra, A. Geska, and Jan Kees van Donge. 2001. 'What Does the "Show Case" Show? Evidence of and Lessons from Adjustment in Uganda', *World Development* 29(5): 841–63.

Donnan, Hastings, and Thomas M. Wilson. 1999. *Borders: Frontiers of Identity, Nation and State.* Oxford: Berg.

Doornbos, Martin. 1995. 'State Formation Processes under External Supervision: Reflections on Good Governance', in Olav Stokke (ed.), *Aid and Political Conditionality.* London: Frank Cass, pp. 377–91.

———. 2003. '"Good Governance": The Metamorphosis of a Policy Metaphor', *Journal of International Affairs* 57(1): 3–17.

Douglas, Mary. 1966. *Purity and Danger.* London: Routledge.

———. 1986. *How Institutions Think.* Syracuse, NY: Syracuse University Press.

Durkheim, Émile. (1893) 1997. *The Division of Labour in Society [1983],* trans. W.D. Halls. New York: Free Press.

Easterly, William. 2006. *The White Man's Burden: Why the West's Efforts to Aid the Rest have Done so Much Ill and so Little Good.* New York: Penguin Press.

Einhorn, Jessica .2001. 'The World Bank's Mission Creep', *Foreign Affairs* 80(5): 22–35.

———. 2006. 'Reforming the World Bank', *Foreign Affairs* 85(1): 17–22.

Eriksen, Stein Sundstøl. 2010. 'The Theory of Failure and the Failure of Theory: "State Failure", the Idea of the State and the Practice of State Building', *Comparative Social Research* 27: 27–50.

Eriksen, Thomas Hylland (ed.). 1989. *Hvor mange hvite elefanter? Kulturdimensjonen i bistandsarbeidet.* Oslo: Ad Notam Forlag AS.

Escobar, Arturo. 1984. 'Discourse and Power in Development: Michel Foucault and the Relevance of his Work to the Third World', *Alternatives* 10(3): 377–400.

———. 1995. *Encountering Development: The Making and Unmaking of the Third World.* Princeton, NJ: Princeton University Press.

———. 1997. 'Anthropology and Development', *International Social Science Journal* 154: 497–515.
———. 2007. '"Post-development" as Concept and Social Practice', in Aram Ziai (ed.), *Exploring Post-development: Theory and Practice, Problems and Perspectives*. London: Routledge, pp. 18–31.
Evens, T.M.S., and Don Handelman. 2005. 'Introduction. The Ethnographic Praxis of the theory of practice', *Social Analysis* 49(3): 1–11.
——— (eds). 2006. *The Manchester School: Practice and Ethnographic Praxis in Anthropology*. New York: Berghahn Books.
Falzon, Mark-Anthony (Ed.). 2009. *Multi-sited Ethnography*. Farnham: Ashgate.
Fardon, Richard (ed.). 1990. *Localising Strategies: Regional Traditions of Ethnographic Writing*. Edinburgh: Scottish Academic Press.
——— (ed.). 1995. *Counterworks: Managing the Diversity of Knowledge*. London: Routledge.
Fendler, L. 2001. 'Educating Flexible Souls: The Construction of Subjectivity through Developmentality and Interaction, in K. Hultqvist and G. Dahlberg, *Governing the Child in the New Millennium*. New York: Routledge, pp. 119–42.
Ferguson, James. 1994. *The Anti-politics Machine: 'Development', Depoliticization, and Bureaucratic Power in Lesotho*. Minneapolis: University of Minnesota Press.
———. 1997. 'Anthropology and its Evil Twin: Development in the Constitution of a Discipline', in Frederick Cooper and Randall Packard (eds), *International Development and the Social Sciences*. Berkeley: University of California Press, pp. 150–75.
———. 2006. *Global Shadows: Africa in the Neoliberal World Order*. Durham, NC: Duke University Press.
Ferguson, James, and Akhil Gupta. 2002. 'Spatializing States: Toward an Ethnography of Neoliberal Governmentality', *American Ethnologist* 29(4): 981–1002.
Fisher, J. 2014. 'When it Pays to be a "Fragile State": Uganda's Use and Abuse of a Dubious Concept', *Third World Quarterly* 35(2): 316–32.
Foucault, Michel. 1980. *Power/Knowledge*. Brighton: Harvester.
———. 1988. 'Technologies of the Self', in Luther H. Martin, Huck Gutman and Patrick H. Hutton (eds), *Technologies of the Self: A Seminar with Michel Foucault (at University of Vermont, October 1982)*. Amherst: University of Massachusetts Press, pp. 16–59.
———. (1978) 1991. 'Governmentality', in Graham Burchell, Colin Gordon and Peter Miller (eds), *The Foucault Effect: Studies in Governmentality*. Chicago, IL: University of Chicago Press, pp. 87–104.
———. 1993. 'About the Beginning of the Hermeneutics of the Self: Two Lectures at Dartmouth', *Political Theory* 21(2): 198–227.
———. 1994. 'L'éthique du souci de soi comme pratique de la libertè', *Dits et ècrits 1954–1988, binding IV 1980–1988*. Paris: Gallimard, pp. 708–29.
———. 2007. *Security, Territory, Population [1978]*. Basingstoke: Palgrave Macmillan.
——— (1979) 2010. *The Birth of Biopolitics: Lectures at the College de France, 1978–1979*. New York: Picador.

Fowler, Alan. 2000. 'Introduction – Beyond Partnership: Getting Real about NGO Relationships in the Aid System', *IDS Bulletin* 31(3): 1–13.

Fox, Jonathan. 2003. 'Advocacy Research and the World Bank: Propositions for Discussion', *Development in Practice* 13(5): 519–27.

Fraser, Nancy. 1989. *Unruly Practices: Power, Discourse and Gender in Contemporary Social Theory.* Cambridge: Polity Press.

Friedman, John. 2012. 'On text and Con-text: Toward an Anthropology in Development', in Soumhya Venketesan and Thomas Yarrow (eds), *Differentiating Development: Beyond an Anthropology of Critique.* New York: Berghahn Books, pp. 23–41.

Friedrich, Carl Joachim. 1946. *Constitutional Government and Democracy.* Boston: Ginn & Co.

Gardner, Katy, and David Lewis (eds). 1996. *Anthropology, Development and the Post-modern Challenge.* London: Pluto Press.

Gilbert, Christopher L., and David Vines. 2000. 'The World Bank: An Overview of Some Major Issues', in Christopher L. Gilbert and David Vines (eds), *The World Bank: Structure and Politics.* Cambridge: Cambridge University Press, pp. 10–38.

Gledhill, John. 2000. *Power and its Disguises: Anthropological Perspectives on Politics* (2nd edn). London: Pluto Press.

Gordon, Colin. 1991. 'Governmental Rationality: An Introduction', in Graham Burchell, Colin Gordon and Peter Miller (eds), *The Foucault Effect: Studies in Governmentality.* Chicago, IL: University of Chicago Press, pp. 1–51.

Gould, Jeremy. 2004. 'Introducing Aidnography', in Jeremy Gould and Henrik Secher Marcussen (eds), *Ethnographies of Aid: Exploring Development Texts and Encounters.* Roskilde, Denmark: Graduate School, International Development Studies, Roskilde University, pp. 1–12.

———. 2005a. 'Poverty, Politics and States of Partnership', in Jeremy Gould (ed.), *The New Conditionality: The Politics of Poverty Reduction Strategies.* London: Zed Books, pp. 1–16.

———. 2005b. 'Conclusion: The Politics of Consultation', in Jeremy Gould (ed.), *The New Conditionality: The Politics of Poverty Reduction Strategies.* London: Zed Books, pp. 135–51.

———. 2005c. 'Timing, Scale and Style: Capacity as Governmentality in Tanzania', in David Mosse and David Lewis (eds), *The Aid Effect: Giving and Governing in International Development.* London: Pluto Press, pp. 61–84.

GoU MoFPED. 1999. 'Vision 2025. A Strategic Framework for National Development'. Kampala: Government of Uganda, Ministry of Finance, Planning and Economic Development.

GoU OPM. 2006. 'The National Integrated Monitoring and Evaluation Strategy Framework. Final Document'. Kampala: Government of Uganda, Office of the Prime Minister.

Green, Maia. 2003. 'Globalizing Development in Tanzania: Policy Franchising through Participatory Project Management', *Critique of Anthropology* 23(2): 123–43.

———. 2012. 'Framing and Escaping. Contrasting Aspects of Knowledge Work in International Development and Anthropology', in Soumhya Venketesan and Thomas Yarrow (eds), *Differentiating Development: Beyond an Anthropology of Critique*. New York: Berghahn Books, pp. 42–57.

Grillo, Ralph, and Alan Rew. 1985. *Social Anthropology and Development Policy*. London: Tavistock.

Grønhaug, Reidar. 2001. 'Antropologi som arena for ny enhetsvitenskap', *Norsk Antropologisk Tidsskrift* 1–2: 60–67.

Gulrajani, Nilima. 2007. 'The Art of Fine Balances: The Challenge of Institutionalizing the Comprehensice Development Framework inside the World Bank', in Diane Stone and Christopher Wright (eds), *The World Bank and Governance: A Decade of Reform and Reaction*. London: Routledge, pp. 48–66.

Gusterson, Hugh. 1997. 'Studying Up Revisited', *POLAR – Political and Legal Anthropology Review* 1, 114–19.

Hansen, Thomas Blom, and Finn Stepputat. 2001. 'Introduction: States of Imagination', in Thomas Blom Hansen and Finn Stepputat (eds), *States of Imagination: Ethnographic Explorations of the Postcolonial State*. Durham, NC: Duke University Press, pp. 1–38.

———. 2005. 'Introduction', in Thomas Blom Hansen and Finn Stepputat (eds), *Sovereign Bodies: Citizens, Migrants and States in the Postcolonial World*. Princeton, NJ: Princeton University Press, pp. 1–36.

Hardt, Michael, and Antonio Negri. 2000. *Empire*. Cambridge, MA: Harvard University Press.

Harper, Richard. 2005. 'The Social Organization of the IMF's Mission Work', in Marc Edelman and Angelique Haugerud (eds), *The Anthropology of Development and Globalization: From Classical Political Economy to Contemporary Neoliberalism*. Malden, MA: Blackwell, pp. 323–33.

Harrison, Graham. 2001a. 'Post-conditionality Politics and Administrative Reform: Reflections on the Cases of Uganda and Tanzania', *Develoment and Change* 32(4): 657–79.

———. 2001b. 'Administering Market Friendly Growth? Liberal Populism and the World Bank's Involvement in Administrative Reform in sub-Saharan Africa', *Review of International Political Economy* 8(3): 528–47.

———. 2004. *The World Bank and Africa*. London: Routledge.

———. 2006. 'Neo-liberalism and the Persistence of Clientelism in Africa', in Richard Robinson (ed.), *The Neo-liberal Revolution: Forging the Market State*. Basingstoke: Palgrave Macmillan, pp. 98–113.

Hatcher, Pascale. 2007. 'Partnership and the Reform of International Aid: Challeing Citizenship and Political Representation?', in Diane Stone and Christopher Wright (eds), *The World Bank and Governance: A Decade of Reform and Reaction*. London: Routledge.

Hendry, Joy, and C.W. Watson. 2001. 'Introduction', in Joy Hendry and C.W. Watson (eds), *An Anthropology of Indirect Communication*. London: Routledge, pp. 1–15.

Henkel, Heiko, and Roderick Stirrat. 2001. 'Participation as Spiritual Duty: Empowerment as Secular Subjection', in Bill Cooke and Uma Kothari (eds), *Participation: The New Tyranny?* London: Zed Books, pp. 168–84.

Herzfeld, Michael. 1992. *The Social Production of Indifference: Exploring the Symbolic Roots of Western Bureaucracy*. Chicago, IL: University of Chicago Press.

Hobart, Mark. 1993a. 'Introduction: The Growth of Ignorance?', in Mark Hobart (ed.), *An Anthropological Critique of Development: The Growth of Ignorance*. London: Routledge, pp. 1–30.

——— (ed.). 1993b. *An Anthropological Critique of Development: The Growth of Ignorance*. London: Routledge.

Hopkins, Raul, Andrew Powell, Amlan Roy and Christopher L. Gilbert. 2000. 'The World Bank, Conditionality and the Comprehensive Development Framework', in Christopher L. Gilbert and David Vines (eds), *The World Bank: Structure and Politics*. Cambridge: Cambridge University Press, pp. 282–98.

Howland, Douglas, and Luise White (eds). 2009. *The State of Sovereignty: Territories, Laws, Populations*. Bloomington, IN: Indiana University Press.

Hyden, Goran, Julius Court and Kenneth Mease (eds). 2004. *Making Sense of Governance: Empirical Evidence from Sixteen Developing Countries*. London: Lynne Rienner.

Ilcan, Suzan, and Lynne Phillips. 2006. 'Global Developmentalities', Keynote address delivered before the Technology@Development Conference, University of Wageningen, The Netherlands, 26–28 June (Available at http://www.ceres.wur.nl/old%20website/summerschool/papers/Global%20Developmentalities%20Keynote%20Address%202006.doc).

———. 2010. 'Developmentalities and Calculative Practices: The Millennium Development Goals', *Antipode* 42(4): 844–74.

IMF and IDA. 1999. *Poverty Reduction Strategy Papers – Operational Issues*. Available at http://www.imf.org/external/np/pdr/prsp/poverty1.htm (accessed 10 February 2006).

International Monetary Fund (IMF). 2005. *Poverty Reduction Strategy Papers (PRSP) – A Factsheet* (September 2005). Available at www.imf.org/external/np/exr/facts/prsp.htm.

Isooba, Moses. 2005. 'Civil Society Participation in Uganda's PRS Process: Opportunities and Dilemmas', in Alexandra Hughes and Nicholas Atampugre (eds), *Civil Society and Poverty Reduction* (Participatory Learning and Action no. 51: International Institute for Environment and Development), pp. 43–46.

Isooba, Moses, and Richard Ssewakiryanga. 2005. 'Setting the Scene: The Ugandan Poverty Eradication Action Plan', in Alexandra Hughes and Nicholas Atampugre (eds), *Civil Society and Poverty Reduction* (Participatory Learning and Action No. 51: International Institute for Environment and Development), pp. 39–42.

Jackson, Robert H. 1990. *Quasi States: Sovereignty, International Relations and the Third World*. Cambridge: Cambridge University Press.

Jensen, Carsten Bruun and Brit Ross Winthereik. 2012. 'Recursive Partnerships in Global Development Aid', in Soumhya Venketesan and Thomas Yarrow (eds), *Differentiating Development: Beyond an Anthropology of Critique*. New York: Berghahn Books, pp. 84–106.

Kanbur, Ravi. 2000. 'Ravi Kanbur's Response to Final Summary', PovertyNet Newsletter, 24 May. Washington, DC: World Bank (available at http://go.worldbank.org/BQSZ0KK3C0).

———. 2001. 'Economic Policy, Distribution and Poverty: The Nature of Disagreements', *World Development* 29(6): 1083–94.

Kapferer, Bruce. 2004a. 'Introduction. The Social Construction of Reductionist Thought and Practice', *Social Analysis* 48(3): 151–61.

———. 2004b. 'Introduction. Old Permutations, New Formations? War, State and Global Transgression', in Bruce Kapferer (ed.), *State, Sovereignty, War: Civil Violence in Emerging Global Realities.* New York: Berghahn Books.

———. 2004c. 'Democracy, Wild Sovereignties and the New Leviathan', *Bulletin of the Royal Institute for Inter-Faith Studies* 6(2): 23–38.

——— (ed.). 2005. *The Retreat of the Social: The Rise and Rise of Reductionism* (Critical Interventions 6). Oxford: Berghahn Books.

Kapferer, Bruce, and Bjørn Enge Bertelsen. 2009a. 'Introduction. The Crisis of Power and Reformations of the State in Globalizing Realities', in Bruce Kapferer and Bjørn Enge Bertelsen (eds), *Crisis of the State: War and Social Upheaval.* New York: Berghahn Books, pp. 1–26.

——— (eds). 2009b. *Crisis of the State: War and Social Upheaval.* New York: Berghahn Books.

Kaufmann, Daniel. 2006. 'Chapter 2.1 Myths and Realities of Governance and Corruption', in World Economic Forum (ed.), *The Global Competitiveness Report 2005–2006.* Basingstoke: Palgrave Macmillan, pp. 81–98.

Kaufmann, Daniel, and Aart Kraay. 2002. 'Governance Indicators, Aid Allocation, and the Millennium Challenge Account. Draft for Discussion'. Available at http://siteresources.worldbank.org/INTWBIGOVANTCOR/Resources/gov_indicators_aid.pdf (Washington, DC: World Bank).

Kelly, Ann. 2012. 'The Progress of the Project: Scientific Traction in The Gambia', in Soumhya Venketesan and Thomas Yarrow (eds), *Differentiating Development: Beyond an Anthropology of Critique.* New York: Berghahn Books, pp. 65–83.

Kiely, Ray. 1999. 'The Last Refuge of the Noble Savage? A Critical Assessment of Post-development Theory', *European Journal of Development Research* 11(1): 30–55.

Koeberle, Stefan, Harold Bedoya, Peter Silarszky and Gero Verheyen (eds). 2005. *Conditionality Revisited: Concepts, Experiences, and Lessons.* Washington, DC: World Bank.

Krasner, Stephen D. 1999. *Sovereignty: Organized Hypocrisy.* Princeton, NJ: Princeton University Press.

———. 2004. 'Sharing Sovereignty: New Institutions for Collapsed and Failing States', *International Security* 29(2): 85–120.

Krohn-Hansen, Christian, and Knut G. Nustad. 2005. 'Introduction', in Christian Krohn-Hansen and Knut G. Nustad (eds), *State Formation: Anthropological Perspectives.* London: Pluto Press, pp. 3–26.

Lawson, Andrew, David Booth, Alan Harding, David Hoole and Felix Naschold. 2003. 'General Budget Support Evaluability Study. Phase 1. Synthesis Report. Volume 1'. Oxford: Oxford Policy Management and Overseas Development Institute, p. 91.

Legg, Stephen. 2006. 'Post-colonial Developmentalities: From the Delhi Improvement Trust to the Delhi Development Authority', in Saraswati Raju, Satish Kumar and Stuart E. Corbridge (eds), *Colonial and Post-colonial Geographies of India.* New Delhi: SAGE, pp. 182–204.

Lemke, Thomas. 2000. 'Foucault, Governmentality and Critique', Paper presented at the Rethinking Marxism conference, University of Amherst, MA, 21–24 September. Avaliable at www.andosciasociology.net/resources/Foucault$2C+Governmentality$2C+and+Critique+IV-2.pdf.

———. 2001. '"The Birth of Bio-politics": Michel Foucault's Lecture at the Collège de France on Neo-liberal Governmentality', *Economy and Society* 30(2): 190–207.

Lewis, David, Anthony J. Bebbington, Simon P.J. Batterbury, Alpa Shah, Elizabeth Olson, M. Shameem Siddiqi and Sandra Duvall. 2003. 'Practice, Power and Meaning: Framework for Studying Organizational Culture in Multi-agency Rural Development Projects', *Journal of International Development* 15(5): 541–57.

Lewis, David, and David Mosse. 2006a. 'Encountering Order and Disjuncture: Contemporary Anthropological Perspectives on the Organization of Development', *Oxford Development Studies* 34(1): 1–13.

——— (eds). 2006b. *Development Brokers and Translators: The Ethnography of Aid and Agencies.* Bloomfield, CT: Kumarian Press.

Li, Tania Murray. 2007. *The Will to Improve: Governmentality, Development, and the Practice of Politics.* Durham, NC: Duke University Press.

Lie, Jon Harald Sande. 2004. 'Discursive Development Order and Local Informal Practices: A Development Project in Northern Ethiopia', Cand. Polit. Thesis. Oslo: University of Oslo.

———. 2006a. 'An Ethnography of "Participation" as Governance', *Forum for Development Studies* 33(2): 387–96.

———. 2006b. 'Developmentality: CDF and PRSP as Governance Mechanisms'. Paper for Workshop on the World Bank, National University of Singapore, 18 September. Arranged by Centre for Study of Globalisation and Regionalisation, University of Warwick. Available at: www2.warwick.ac.uk/fac/soc/csgr/events/workshops/2006ws/world_bank/papers/developmentality1._cdf_and_prsp_as_governance_mechanisms.pdf.

———. 2007. 'Post-development and the Discourse–Agency Interface', in Aram Ziai (ed.), *Exploring Post-development: Theory and Practice, Problems and Perspectives.* London: Routledge, pp. 47–62.

———. 2008a. 'Post-development Theory and the Discourse–Agency Conundrum', *Social Analysis* 52(3): 118–37.

———. 2008b. 'The World Bank and Conflicts: From Narrow Rules to Broader Principles'. Oslo: NUPI, Security in Practice No. 9.

———. 2009. *Discursive Development Order and Local Informal Practices: A Development Project in Northern Ethiopia.* VDM Verlag.

———. 2010. 'Developmentality and the World Bank in the New Aid Architecture', in John-Andrew McNeish and Jon Harald Sande Lie (eds), *Security and Development.* New York: Berghahn Books, pp. 36–51.

———. 2013. 'Challenging Anthropology: Anthropological Reflections on the Ethnographic Turn in International Relations', *Millennium* 41(2): 201–20.

———. 2015. 'Developmentality: Indirect Governance in the World Bank–Uganda Partnership', *Third World Quarterly* 36(4): 723–40.

Long, Norman. 1989. *Encounters at the Interface: A Perspective on Social Discontinuities in Rural Development.* Wageningen, The Netherlands: Agricultural University.

———. 1992a. 'From Paradigm Lost to Paradigm Regained: The Case of an Actor-oriented Sociology of Development', in Norman Long and Ann Long (eds), *Battlefields of Knowledge: The Interlocking of Theory and Practice in Social Research and Development.* London: Routledge, pp. 16–43.

———. 1992b. 'Conclusion', in in Norman Long and Ann Long (eds), *Battlefields of Knowledge: The Interlocking of Theory and Practice in Social Research and Development.* London: Routledge, pp. 268–277.

———. 2001. *Development Sociology: Actor Perspectives.* London: Routledge.

———. 2004. 'Contesting Policy Ideas from Below', in Morten Bøås and Desmond McNeill (eds), *Global Institutions and Development: Framing the World?* London and New York: Routledge, pp. 24–40.

Long, Norman, and Ann Long (eds). 1992. *Battlefields of Knowledge: The Interlocking of Theory and Practice in Social Research and Development.* London: Routledge.

Løngreen, Hanne. 2001. 'The Development Gaze. Visual Representation of Development in Information Material from Danida', in Mai Palmberg (ed.), *Encounter Images in the Meetings between Africa and Europe.* Uppsala, Sweden: The Nordic Africa Institute, pp. 221–232.

Makara, Sabiti. 1998. 'Political and Administrative Relations in Decentralisation', in Apolo Nsibambi (ed.), *Decentralisation and Civil Society in Uganda.* Kampala: Fountain Publishers, pp. 31–46.

Mallaby, Sebastian. 2004. *The World's Banker: A Story of Failed States, Financial Crises, and the Wealth and Poverty of Nations.* New York: Penguin Press.

———. 2005. 'Saving the World Bank', *Foreign Affairs* 84(3): 75–85.

Mamdani, Mahmood. 2002. 'African States, Citizenship and War. A Case Study'. *International Affairs* 78(3): 493–506.

Manger, Leif. 2011. 'Sovereignities in the Making: Reflections on State and Society in the Sudan'. Unpublished paper.

Manzo, Kate. 1991. 'Modernist Discourse and the Crisis of Development Theory', *Studies in Comparative International Development* 26(2): 3–36.

Marcus, George E. and Judith Okely. 2007. '"How Short Can Fieldwork be?"', *Social Anthropology* 15(3): 353–367.

Marshall, Katherine. 2008. *The World Bank: From Reconstruction to Development to Equity.* London: Routledge.

Mauss, Marcel. 1954. *The Gift: Forms and Functions of Exchange in Archaic Societies* (Glencoe, IL: Free Press).

Mawuko-Yevugah, Lord Cephas. 2010. *Governing through Developmentality: The Politics of International Aid Reform and the (Re)production of Power, Neoliberalism and Neocolonial Interventions in Ghana.* Edmonton: University of Alberta.

McGee, Rosemary. 2004. 'Unpacking Policy: Actors, Knowledge and Spaces', in Karen Brock, Rosmary McGee and John Gaventa (eds), *Unpacking Policy: Knowledge, Actors and Spaces in Poverty Reduction in Uganda and Nigeria.* Kampala, Uganda: Fountain Publishers.

Mitchell, Timothy. 1991. 'The Limits of the State: Beyond Statist Approaches and their Critics', *American Political Science Review* 85(1): 77–96.

Montgomery, John D. 2002. 'Sovereignty in Transition', in John D. Montgomery and Nathan Glazer (eds), *Sovereignty under Challenge: How Governments Respond.* New Brunswick, NJ: Transaction Publishers, pp. 3–30.

Moore, David. 2007. 'Introduction: The World Bank and its (Sheepish) Wolves', in David Moore (ed.), *The World Bank: Development, Poverty, Hegemony.* Scottsville, South Africa: University of KwaZulu-Natal Press, pp. 1–26.

Morss, Elliott, R. 1984. 'Institutional Destruction Resulting from Donor and Project Proliferation in Sub-Saharan African Countries', *World Development* 12(4): 465–70.

Mosley, Paul, Jane Harrigan and J.F.J. Toye. 1995. *Aid and Power: The World Bank and Policy-based Lending* (2nd edn). London: Routledge.

Mosley, Paul, John Hudson and Arjan Verschoor. 2004. 'Aid, Poverty Reduction and the "New Conditionality"', *The Economic Journal* 114: 217–43.

Moss, Todd, Gunilla Pettersson and Nicolas van de Walle. 2006. 'An Aid-Institutions Paradox? A Review Essay on Aid Dependency and State Building in Sub-Saharan Africa', Center for Global Development, Working paper No. 74: 28.

Mosse, David. 2004a. 'Is Good Policy Unimplementable? Reflections on the Ethnography of Aid Policy and Practice', *Development and Change* 35(4): 639–71.

———. 2004b. 'Social Analysis as Product Development', in Ananta Kumar Giri, Anton van Harskamp and Oscar Salemink (eds), *The Development of Religion, the Religion of Development.* Delft: Eburon, pp. 77–88.

———. 2005a. 'Global Governance and the Ethnography of International Aid', in David Mosse and David Lewis (eds), *The Aid Effect: Giving and Governing in International Development.* London: Pluto Press, pp. 1–36.

———. 2005b. *Cultivating Development: An Ethnography of Aid Policy and Practice.* London: Pluto Press.

———. 2006. 'Anti-social Anthropology? Objectivity, Objection, and the Ethnography of Public Policy and Professional Communities', *Journal of the Royal Anthropological Institute* 12(4): 935–56.

——— (ed.). 2011. *Adventures in Aidland: The Anthropology of Professionals in International Development.* New York: Berghahn Books.

———. 2013. 'The Anthropology of International Development', *Annual Review of Anthropology* 42: 227–246.

Mosse, David, and David Lewis (eds). 2005. *The Aid Effect: Giving and Governing in International Development.* London: Pluto Press.

———. 2006. 'Theoretical Approaches to Brokerage and Translation in Development', in David Lewis and David Mosse (eds), *Development Brokers and Translators: The Ethnography of Aid and Agencies.* Bloomfield, CT: Kumarian Press, pp. 1–26.

Mugambe, Kenneth. 2010. 'The Poverty Eradication Action Plan', in Florence Kuteesa, Emmanuel Tumusiime-Mutebile, Alan Whitworth and Tim Williamson (eds), *Uganda's Economic Reforms: Insider Accounts.* Oxford: Oxford University Press, pp. 157–71.

Museveni, Yoweri Kaguta. 1997. *Sowing the Mustard Seed: The Struggle for Freedom and Democracy in Uganda.* London: Macmillan Education.

Mwenda, A. 2010. 'Uganda's Politics of Foreign Aid and Violent Conflict: The Political Uses of the LRA Rebellion', in T. Allen and K. Vlassenroot, *The Lord's Resistance Army: Myth and Reality.* London: Zed Books, pp. 45–58.

Nader, Laura. 1972. 'Up the Anthropologist: Perspectives Gained from Studying Up', in Dell Hymes (ed.), *Reinventing Anthropology*. New York: Pantheon Books, pp. 284–311.

Narayan, Deepa (ed.). 2000. *Voices of the Poor. Volume 1: Can Anyone Hear Us?* Washington, DC: World Bank.

Narayan, Deepa, Robert Chambers, Meera Kaul Shah and Patti Petesch. 2000. *Voices of the Poor. Volume 2: Crying Out for Change*. Washington, DC: World Bank.

Narayan, Deepa, and Patti Petesch (eds). 2002. *Voices of the Poor. From Many Lands*. Washington, DC: World Bank.

Nelson, Nici, and Susan Wright. 1995. 'Participation and Power', in Nici Nelson and Susan Wright (eds), *Power and Participatory Development*. London: Intermediate Technology Publications, pp. 1–18.

Neumann, Iver B. 2005. 'A Speech that the Entire Ministry may Stand For', in Christian Krohn-Hansen and Knut G. Nustad (eds), *State Formation: Anthropological Perspectives*. London: Pluto Press, pp. 195–211.

———. 2007. '"A Speech that the Entire Ministry may Stand For", or: Why Diplomats Never Produce Anything New', *International Political Sociology* 1(2): 183–200.

Neumann, Iver B., and Ole Jacob Sending. 2010. *Governing the Global Polity: Practice, Mentality, Rationality*. Ann Arbor: University of Michigan Press.

Nielson, D.L., M.J. Tierney and C.E. Weaver. 2006. 'Bridging the Rationalist–Constructivist Divide: Re-engineering the Culture of the World Bank', *Journal of International Relations and Development* 9: 107–39.

Nordstrom, Carolyn. 2000. 'Shadows and Sovereigns', *Theory, Culture & Society* 17(4): 35–54.

Nustad, Knut G. 1998. 'Community Leadership and Development Administration in a Durban Squatter Settlement'. Ph.D. dissertation. Cambridge: University of Cambridge.

———. 2004. 'The Development Discourse in the Multilateral System', in Morten Bøås and Desmond McNeill (eds), *Global Institutions and Development: Framing the World?* London: Routledge, pp. 13–23.

OECD. 2006. 'Partnership General Budget Support – Overall Findings', in Steven Lister and Rebecca Carter (eds), *Joint Evaluation of General Budget Support 1994–2004*. Paris.

Oksala, Johanna. 2005. *Foucault on Freedom*. Cambridge: Cambridge University Press.

Okumu, Wafula. 2010. 'Resources and Border Disputes in Eastern Africa', *Journal of Eastern African Studies* 4(2): 279–97.

Olivier de Sardan, Jean-Pierre. 2005. *Anthropology and Development: Understanding Contemporary Social Change*. London: Zed Books.

Ong, Aihwa. 2002. 'Globalization and New Strategies of Ruling in Developing Countries', *Études Rurales* 163/164 (July–December): 233–48.

———. 2006. *Neoliberalism as Exception: Mutations in Citizenship and Sovereignty*. Durham, NC: Duke University Press.

Palan, Ronen. 2000. 'New Trends in Global Political Economy', in Ronen Palan (ed.), *Global Political Economy: Contemporary Theories*. London: Routledge, pp. 1–18.

Paris Declaration. 2005. 'Paris Declaration on Aid Effectiveness: Ownership, Harmonization, Alignment, Results and Mutual Accountability'. High Level Forum, 28 February – 2 March. Paris.

Peet, Richard. 1997. 'Social Theory, Postmodernism, and the Critique of Development', in George Benko and Ulf Strohmayer (eds), *Space and Social Theory: Interpreting Modernity and Postmodernity.* Oxford: Blackwell, pp. 72–87.

Pender, John. 2001. 'From "Structural Adjustment" to "Comprehensive Development Framework": Conditionality Transformed?', *Third World Quarterly* 22(3): 397–411.

Pieterse, Jan Nederveen. 2000. 'After Post-development', *Third World Quarterly* 21(2): 175–91.

Pincus, Jonathan R., and Jeffrey A. Winters. 2002. 'Reinventing the World Bank', in Jonathan R. Pincus and Jeffrey A. Winters (eds), *Reinventing the World Bank.* Ithaca, NY: Cornell University Press, pp. 1–25.

Pomerantz, Phyllis R. 2004. *Aid Effectiveness in Africa: Developing Trust between Donors and Government.* Lanham, MD: Lexington Books.

Porter, Douglas J. 1995. 'Scenes from Childhood: The Homesickness of Development Discourses', in Jonathan Crush (ed.), *Power of Development.* London: Routledge, pp. 63–86.

Pouligny, Béatrice. 2009. 'Local Ownership', in Vincent Chetail (ed.), *Post-conflict Peacebuilding: A Lexicon.* Oxford: Oxford University Press, pp. 174–87.

Rahnema, Majid. 1992. 'Participation', in Wolfgang Sachs (ed.), *The Development Dictionary: A Guide to Knowledge as Power.* London: Zed Books, pp. 116–31.

Rakner, Lise, and Vibeke Wang. 2007. 'Governance Assessments and the Paris Declaration'. A CMI Issues Paper. Prepared for the UNDP Bergen Seminar, September 2007. Bergen: CMI.

Randel, Judith, Tone German and Deborah Ewing. 2002. *The Reality of Aid, 2002: An Independent Review of Poverty Reduction and International Development Assistance.* Manila, The Philippines: IBON Books, IBON Foundation.

Rich, Bruce. 2002. 'The World Bank under James Wolfensohn', in Jonathan R. Pincus and Jeffrey A. Winters (eds), *Reinventing the World Bank.* Ithaca, NY: Cornell University Press, pp. 26–53.

Riles, Annelise. 1998. 'Infinity within the Brackets', *American Ethnologist* 25(3): 378–98.

——— (ed.). 2006. *Documents: Artifacts of Modern Knowledge.* Ann Arbor: University of Michigan Press.

Ritzen, Jozef. 2005. *A Chance for the World Bank.* London: Anthem Press.

Rome Declaration. 2003. 'Rome Declaration on Harmonization'. 25 February. Rome, Italy.

Rose, Nikolas. 1996. 'Governing "Advanced" Liberal Democracies', in Andrew Barry, Thomas Osborne and Nikolas Rose (eds), *Foucault and Political Reason: Liberalism, Neo-liberalism, and Rationalities of Government.* Chicago, IL: University of Chicago Press, pp. 37–64.

———. 1999. *Powers of Freedom: Reframing Political Thought.* Cambridge: Cambridge University Press.

Rose, Nikolas, and Peter Miller. 1992. 'Political Power beyond the State: Problematics of Government', *British Journal of Sociology* 43(2): 173–205.

Rossi, Benadetta. 2006. 'Aid Policies and Recipient Strategies in Niger: Why Donors and Recipients should not be Compartmentalized into Separate "Worlds of Knowledge"', in David Lewis and David Mosse (eds), *Development Brokers and Translators: The Ethnography of Aid and Agencies.* Bloomfield, CT: Kumarian Press, pp. 27–49.

Rostow, Walt. 1961. *The Stages of Economic Growth: A Non-Communist Manifesto.* Cambridge: Cambridge University Press.

Rottenburg, Richard. 2009. *Far-fetched Facts: A Parable of Development Aid.* Cambridge, MA: MIT Press.

Rubongoya, Joshua B. 2007. *Regime Hegemony in Museveni's Uganda.* New York: Palgrave Macmillan.

Sachs, Wolfgang (ed.) 1992. *The Development Dictionary: A Guide to Knowledge as Power.* London: Zed Books.

Sahlins, Marshall. 2004. *Apologies to Thucydides: Understanding History as Culture and Vice Versa.* Chicago, IL: University of Chicago Press.

SAPRIN. 2004. *Structural Adjustment: The SAPRI Report: The Policy Roots of Economic Crisis, Poverty, and Inequality.* London: Zed Books; US distribution: Palgrave Macmillan.

Schech, Susanne, and Sanjugta Vas Dev. 2007. 'Governing through Participation? The World Bank's New Approach to the Poor', in David Moore (ed.), *The World Bank: Development, Poverty, Hegemony.* Scottsville, South Africa: University of KwaZulu-Natal Press, pp. 171–201.

Schmitt, Carl. 2006. *Political Theology. Four Chapters on the Concept of Sovereignty (1922).* Chicago, IL: University of Chicago Press.

Schuurman, Frans J. 2000. 'Paradigms Lost, Paradigms Regained? Development Studies in the Twenty-first Century', *Third World Quarterly* 21(1): 7–20.

Scott, James C. 1985. *Weapons of the Weak: Everyday Forms of Peasant Resistance.* New Haven, CT: Yale University Press.

———. 1998. *Seeing Like a State: How Certain Schemes to Improve the Human Condition have Failed.* New Haven, CT: Yale University Press.

———. 2009. *The Art of not being Governed. An Anarchist History of Upland Southeast Asia.* New Haven, CT: Yale University Press.

Sending, Ole Jacob, and Jon Harald Sande Lie. 2009. 'The Role of CPIA and PBA at the Country Level. Case Studies of Ethiopia and Malawi'. NUPI report. Oslo: NUPI.

Sending, Ole Jacob, and Iver B. Neumann. 2007. 'Banking on Power: Practices in an International Organisation'. Paper presented at International Studies Association, Chicago, 28 February – 2 March.Ssewakiryanga, Richard. 2005. 'The Politics of Revising the PEAP/PRSP in Uganda'. PowerPoint Presentation at International Conference on Political Dimensions of Poverty Reduction, 9–11 March 2005 (Mulungushi International Conference Center, Lusaka, Zambia).

Stirrat, Roderick, and Heiko Henkel .1997. 'The Development Gift: The Problem of Reciprocity in the NGO World', *Annals, American Academy of Political and Social Science* 554: 66–80.

Stokke, Olav. 1995. 'Aid and Political Conditionality: Core Issues and State of the Art', in Olav Stokke (ed.), *Aid and Political Conditionality.* London: Frank Cass, pp. 1–87.

Stone, Diane, and Christopher Wright. 2007. 'Introduction. The Currency of Change: World Bank Lending and Learning in the Wolfensohn Era', in Diane Stone and Christopher Wright (eds), *The World Bank and Governance.* London: Routledge, pp. 1–25.

Stone, Randall W. 2008. 'The Scope of IMF Conditionality', *International Organization* 62(4): 589–620.

Strathern, Marilyn. 2000a. 'New Accountabilities: Anthropological Studies in Audit, Ethics and the Academy', in M. Strathern (ed.), *Audit Cultures: Anthropological Studies in Accountability, Ethics and Academy.* London: Routledge, pp. 1–18.

——— (ed.). 2000b. *Audit Cultures: Anthropological Studies of Accountability, Ethics and the Academy.* London: Routledge.

Swidler, Ann. 2001. 'What Anchors Cultural Practices', in Theodore R. Schatzki, Karin Knorr Cetina and Eike von Savigny (eds), *The Practice Turn in Contemporary Theory.* London: Routledge, pp. 74–92.

Tan, Celine. 2007. 'The Poverty of Amnesia: PRSPs in the Legacy of Structural Adjustment', in Diane Stone and Christopher Wright (eds), *The World Bank and Governance: A Decade of Reform and Reaction.* Warwick Studies in Globalisation. New York: Routledge.

Trouillot, Michel-Rolph. 2001. 'The Anthropology of the State in the Age of Globalisation', *Current Anthropology* 42: 125–38.

———. 2003. *Global Transformations: Anthropology and the Modern World.* New York: Palgrave Macmillan.

Tukahebwa, Geoffrey B. 1998. 'The Role of District Councils in Decentralisations', in Apolo Nsibambi (ed.), *Decentralisation and Civil Society in Uganda: The Quest for Good Governance.* Kampala: Fountain Publishers, pp. 12–30.

Turner, Victor W. 1967. 'Betwixt and Between: The Liminal Period in Rites de Passage [1964]', in Victor W. Turner (ed.), *The Forest of Symbols: Aspects of Ndembu Ritual.* Ithaca, NY: Cornell University Press.

UJAS. 2006. 'Joint Assistance Strategy for the Republic of Uganda (2005–2009)'. Available at http://siteresources.worldbank.org/INTUGANDA/Resources/UJAS.pdf.

UN. 1996. 'First United Nations Decade for the Eradication of Poverty'. UN General Assembly A/RES/51/178.

USAID. 2005. 'Uganda. Annual report FY 2005', 16 June.

Van Waeyenberge, Elisa. 2009. 'Selectivity at Work: Country Policy and Institutional Assessment at the World Bank', *European Journal of Development Research* 21(5): 792–810.

Venketesan, Soumhya, and Thomas Yarrow (eds). 2012. *Differentiating Development: Beyond an Anthropology of Critique.* New York: Berghahn Books.

Wade, Robert Hunter. 2001. 'Making the World Development Report 2000: Attacking Poverty', *World Development* 29(8): 1435–41.

———. 2002a. 'US Hegemony and the World Bank: The Fight over People and Ideas', *Review of International Political Economy* 9(2): 215–43.

———. 2002b. 'Showdown at the World Bank', *New Left Review* 7: 124–37.

———. 2004. 'The World Bank and the Environment', in Morten Bøås and Desmond McNeill (eds), *Global Institutions and Development: Framing the World?* London: Routledge, pp. 72–94.

Wallace, T., L. Bornstein and J. Chapman. 2006. *The Aid Chain: Coercion and Commitment in Development NGOs*. Bourton-on-Dunsmore: ITDG Publishing.

Watts, Michael. 2003. 'Development and Governmentality', *Singapore Journal of Tropical Geography* 24(1): 6–34.

Weaver, Catherine. 2008. *Hypocrisy Trap: The World Bank and the Poverty of Reform*. Princeton, NJ: Princeton University Press.

———. 2010. 'The Meaning of Development: Constructing the World Bank's Good Governance Agenda', in R. Abdelal, M. Blyth and C. Parsons, *Constructing the International Economy*. Ithaca, NY: Cornell University Press.

Weaver, C., and R.J. Leiteritz. 2005. '"Our Poverty Is a World Full of Dreams": Reforming the World Bank', *Global Governance* 11: 369–88.

Weber, Max. 1970. *From Max Weber: Essays in Sociology*. Edited by H.H. Gerth and C. Wright Mills. London: Oxford University Press.

Whitfield, Lindsay. 2005. 'Trustees of Development from Conditionality to Govenance: Poverty Reduction Strategy Papers in Ghana', *Journal of Modern African Studies* 43(4): 641–64.

——— (ed.). 2009. *The Politics of Aid: African Strategies for Dealing with Donors*. Oxford: Oxford University Press.

Williamson, John. 1990. 'What Washington Means by Policy Reform', in John Williamson (ed.), *Latin American Adjustment: How Much has Happened?* Washington, DC: Institute for International Economics.

———. 2000. 'What should the World Bank Think about the Washington Consensus?', *The World Bank Research Observer* 15(2): 251–64.

Wohlgemuth, Lennart. 2008. 'Can Africa Make Use of the New Aid Architecture?', *Africa Development* 33(4): 31–41.

Wolfensohn, James. 1999. 'A Proposal for a Comprehensive Development Framework' (A discussion draft to the board, management and staff of the World Bank Group: 21 January).

———. 2005a. '"People and Development". Address to the Board of Governors at the Annual Meeting of the World Bank and the International Monetary Fund. October 1, 1996', in James Wolfensohn and Andrew Kirchner (eds), *Voice for the Poor: Selected Speeches and Writings of World Bank President James D. Wolfensohn 1995–2005*. Washington, DC: World Bank Publications, pp. 45–54.

———. 2005b. '"Coalitions for Change". Address to the Board of Governors at the Annual Meeting of the World Bank and the International Monetary Fund, September 28 1999', in James Wolfensohn and Andrew Kirchner (eds), *Voice for the Poor. Selected Speeches and Writings of World Bank President James D. Wolfensohn 1995–2005*. Washington, DC: World Bank Publications, pp. 154–65.

———. 2005c. 'The Message of Kampala', in James Wolfensohn and Andrew Kirchner (eds), *Voice for the Poor: Selected Speeches and Writings of World Bank President James D. Wolfensohn 1995–2005*. Washington, DC: World Bank Publications, pp. 92–102.

———. 2005d. 'Creating Better Lives for Poor People: PRSPs. Remarks at a Townhall Meeting at World Bank Group Headquarters, January 14 2002', in James D. Wolfensohn and Andrew Kirchner (eds), *Voice for the Poor: Selected*

*Speeches and Writings of World Bank President James D. Wolfensohn 1995–2005.* Washington, DC: World Bank Publications, pp. 323–28.

Wood, Angela. 2005. 'World Bank's Poverty Reduction Support Credit: Continuity or Change?' Dublin: Debt and Development Coalition Ireland.

Woods, Ngaire. 2006. *The Globalizers: The IMF, the World Bank, and their Borrowers.* Ithaca, NY: Cornell University Press.

World Bank. 1992. 'Effective Implementation: Key to Development Impact' (The Wapenhans Report). Washington, DC.

———. 1997. 'The State in a Changing World. World Development Report 1997'. Oxford: Oxford University Press.

———. 1998. 'Assessing Aid: What Works, What Doesn't, and Why' (A World Bank Policy Research Report). Washington, DC: Oxford University Press.

———. 2000. 'Attacking Poverty', in Ravi Kanbur and Nora Lustig (eds), *World Develoment Report 2000/2001.* Washington, DC.

———. 2003a. *A Guide to The World Bank.* Washington, DC.

———. 2003b. *Toward Country-led Development: A Multi-partner Evaluation of the Comprehensive Development Framework.* Washington, DC.

———. 2004a. 'A History of the Social Development Network in the World Bank, 1973–2002' (Paper No. 56., March, by Gloria Davis). Washington, DC.

———. 2004b. 'Global Monitoring Report: Policies and Actions for Achieving the Millennium Development Goals and Related Outcomes'. Washington, DC.

———. 2004c. 'The Poverty Reduction Strategy Initiative: An Independent Evaluation of the World Bank Support through 2003'. Washington, DC.

———. 2005a. *Empowering People by Transforming Institutions: Social Development in World Bank Operations.* Washington, DC.

———. 2005b. 'Case Study: The Democratic Republic of Uttarstan: Improving Governance and Reducing Corruption' (Case Study for Public Sector Governance and WBIs course on Governance and Anti-corruption, 14–17 February 2005). Accessible at www1.worldbank.org/publicsector/anticorrupt/CoreCourseDec2003/UttarstanIIIAdventure.doc.

———. 2006. 'A Decade of Measuring the Quality of Governance' (Governance Matters 2006. Worldwide Governance Indicators). Accessible at www.govindicators.org.

———. 2007. 'Strengthening the World Bank Group Engagement on Governance and Corruption. 21 March, 2007'. Washington, DC.

Ziai, Aram. 2007. 'Development Discourse and its Critics: An Introduction to Post-development', in Aram Ziai (ed.), *Exploring Post-development: Theory and Practice, Problems and Perspectives.* London: Routledge, pp. 3–17.

Zizek, Slavoj. 1989. *The Sublime Object of Ideology.* London: Verso.

# Index

**Z**